WORKING PAPERS

Chapters 1 - 18

to accompany

ACCOUNTING PRINCIPLES

9TH Edition

Jerry J. Weygandt, Ph.D., C.P.A.
Arthur Andersen Alumni Professor of Accounting
University of Wisconsin - Madison
Madison, Wisconsin

Donald E. Kieso, Ph.D., C.P.A.
KPMG Peat Marwick Emeritus Professor of Accountancy
Northern Illinois University
DeKalb, Illinois

Paul D. Kimmel, Ph.D., C.P.A.
Associate Professor of Accounting
University of Wisconsin - Milwaukee
Milwaukee, Wisconsin

Prepared By
Dick D. Wasson, M.B.A., C.P.A.
Southwestern College
San Diego State University
University of Phoenix

John Wiley & Sons, Inc.

Cover Photo Credit: OJO Images/SuperStock

To order books or for customer service call 1-800-CALL-WILEY (225-5945).

ISBN-13 978-0-470-38669-9

Printed in the United States of America

10 9 8 7 6 5 4 3 2 1

Printed and bound by Courier Kendallville, Inc.
Covers printed at Courier Kendallville, Inc.

CONTENTS

Working Paper templates are provided for end-of-chapter brief exercises, Do It! exercises, exercises, problems, and broadening your perspective problems. Working Paper templates are not provided for solutions that are textual in nature.

Name

Section

Date

BE1-1	Assets	Liabilities	Owner's Equity
(a)	$ 90000	$ 50000	
(b)		40000	70000
(c)	94000		60000

BE1-2			
(a)		$ 120000	$ 232000
(b)	190000		80000
(c)	800000		

BE1-3

(a)

(b)

(c)

BE1-4

BE1-5 See next page

(a)		Accounts receivable	(d)		Office supplies
(b)		Salaries payable	(e)		Owner's investment
(c)		Equipment	(f)		Notes payable

BE1-6	Assets	Liabilities	Owner's Equity
(a)			
(b)			
(c)			

BE1-7	Assets	Liabilities	Owner's Equity
(a)			
(b)			
(c)			

BE1-8

(a)	(e)
(b)	(f)
(c)	(g)
(d)	

Name

Section

Date

Chapter 1 Brief Exercises

Expanded Accounting Equations

BE1-4

						Owner's Equity							
		Assets	=	Liabilities	+	Owner Capital	-	Owner Drawings	+	Revenues	-	Expenses	
1	(a)												1
2													2
3													3
4													4
5	(b)												5
6													6
7													7
8													8
9	(c)												9
10													10
11													11
12													12
13													13
14													14
15													15
16													16
17													17
18													18
19													19
20													20
21													21
22													22
23													23

Name

Section

Date

BE1-9

(a)		Received cash for services performed
(b)		Paid cash to purchase equipment
(c)		Paid employee salaries

BE1-10

Lopez Company

Balance Sheet

December 31, 2010

Assets

Liabilities and Owner's Equity

BE1-11

(a)		Notes payable
(b)		Advertising expense
(c)		Trent Buchanan, Capita;
(d)		Service revenue
(e)		

Name

Section

Date

Orlando Cabrera and Co.

DO IT! 1-3

	Assets				Liabilities	Owner's Equity							
	Cash	+	Accounts Receivable	=	Accounts Payable	+	O. Cabrera, Capital	-	O. Cabrera, Drawings	+	Revenues	-	Expenses
(1)													
(2)													
(3)													
(4)													

Name

Section

Date   Broadway Company

(a)

(b)

(c)

Name — Exercise 1-8

Section

Date — S. Moses & Co.

(a)

1

2.

3.

4.

5.

6.

7.

8.

9.

10.

(b)

(c)

Name Exercise 1-9

Section

Date S. Moses & Co.

S. Moses & Co.

Income Statement

For the Month Ended August 31, 2010

S. Moses & Co.

Owner's Equity Statement

For the Month Ended August 31, 2010

S. Moses & Co.

Balance Sheet

August 31, 2010

Assets

Liabilities and Owner's Equity

Name

Section

Date

Exercise 1-10

Lily Company

(a)

(b)

(c)

Name

Section

Date

Exercise 1-11

Craig Cantrel & Mills Enterprises

(a)

(b)

(c)

(d)

Name Exercise 1-12

Section

Date Linda Stanley Co.

Linda Stanley Co.

Income Statement

For the Year Ended December 31, 2010

Linda Stanley Co.

Owner's Equity Statement

For the Year Ended December 31, 2010

Name

Section

Date

E1-13

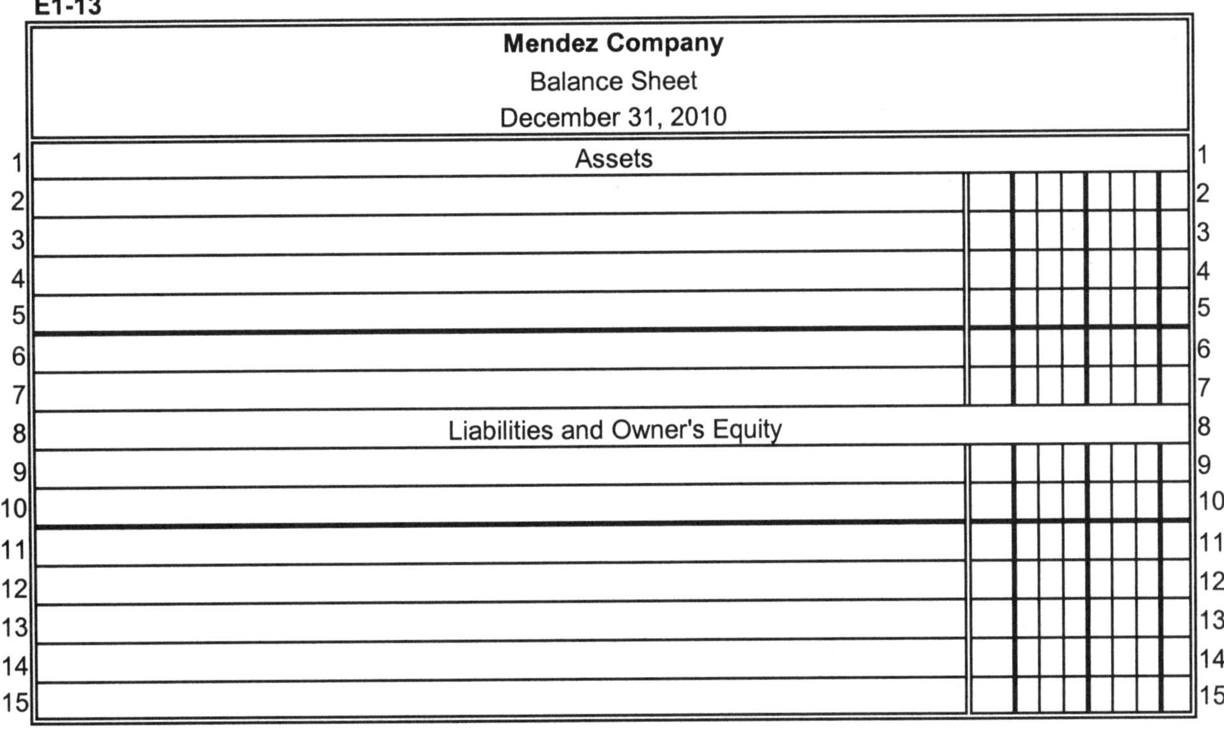

E1-15

Summers Cruise Company

Income Statement

For the Year Ended December 31, 2010

Name Exercise 1-14

Section

Date Deer Park

(a)

(b)

Deer Park

Balance Sheet

December 31, 2010

Assets

Liabilities and Owner's Equity

Name Exercise 1-16

Section

Date Kevin Johnson, Attorney

Kevin Johnson, Attorney

Owner's Equity Statement

For the Year Ended December 31, 2010

Supporting Computations

Problem 1-1A

Barone's Repair Shop

See Appendix

Name | Problem 1-1A Concluded

Section

Date | Barone's Repair Shop

(b)

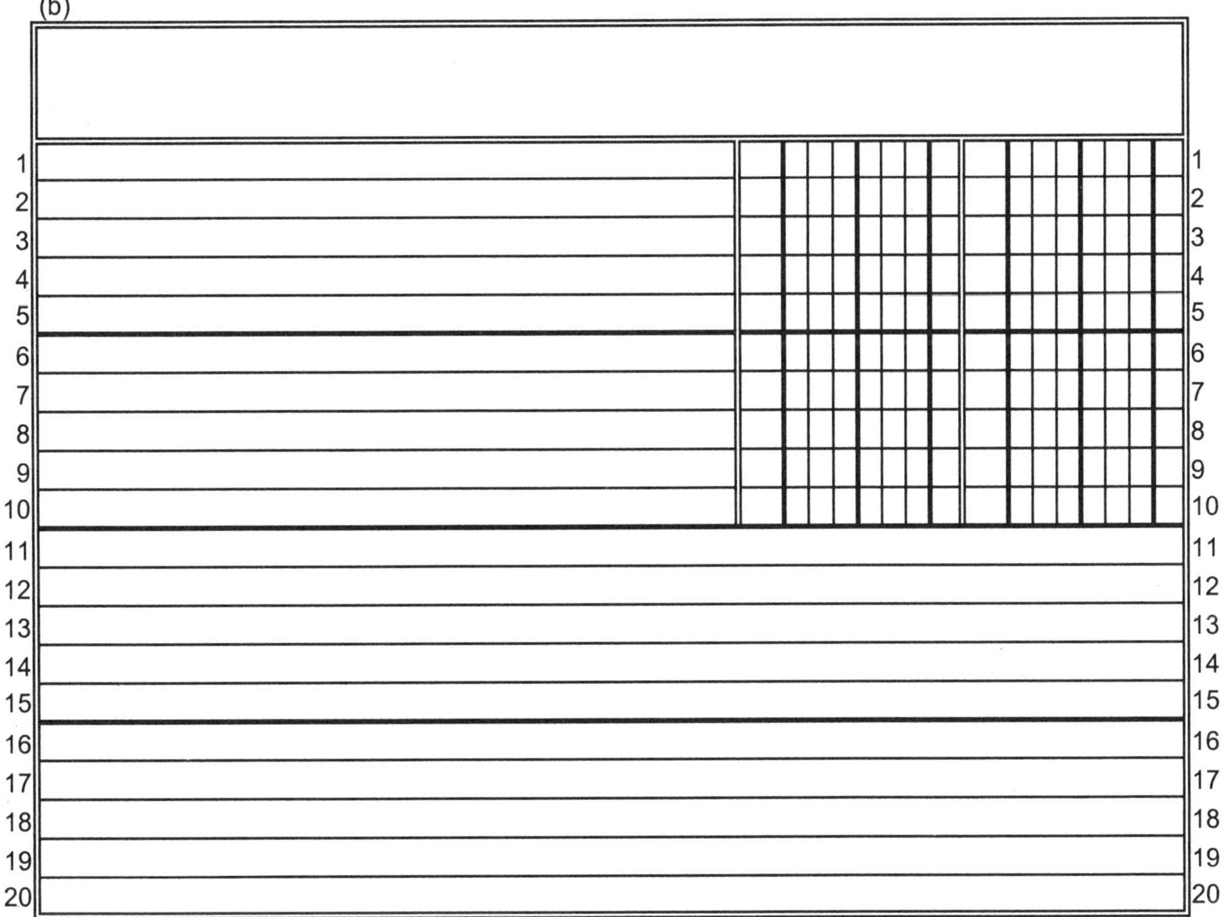

Problem 1-2A

Maria Gonzalez, Veterinarian

See Appendix

(b)

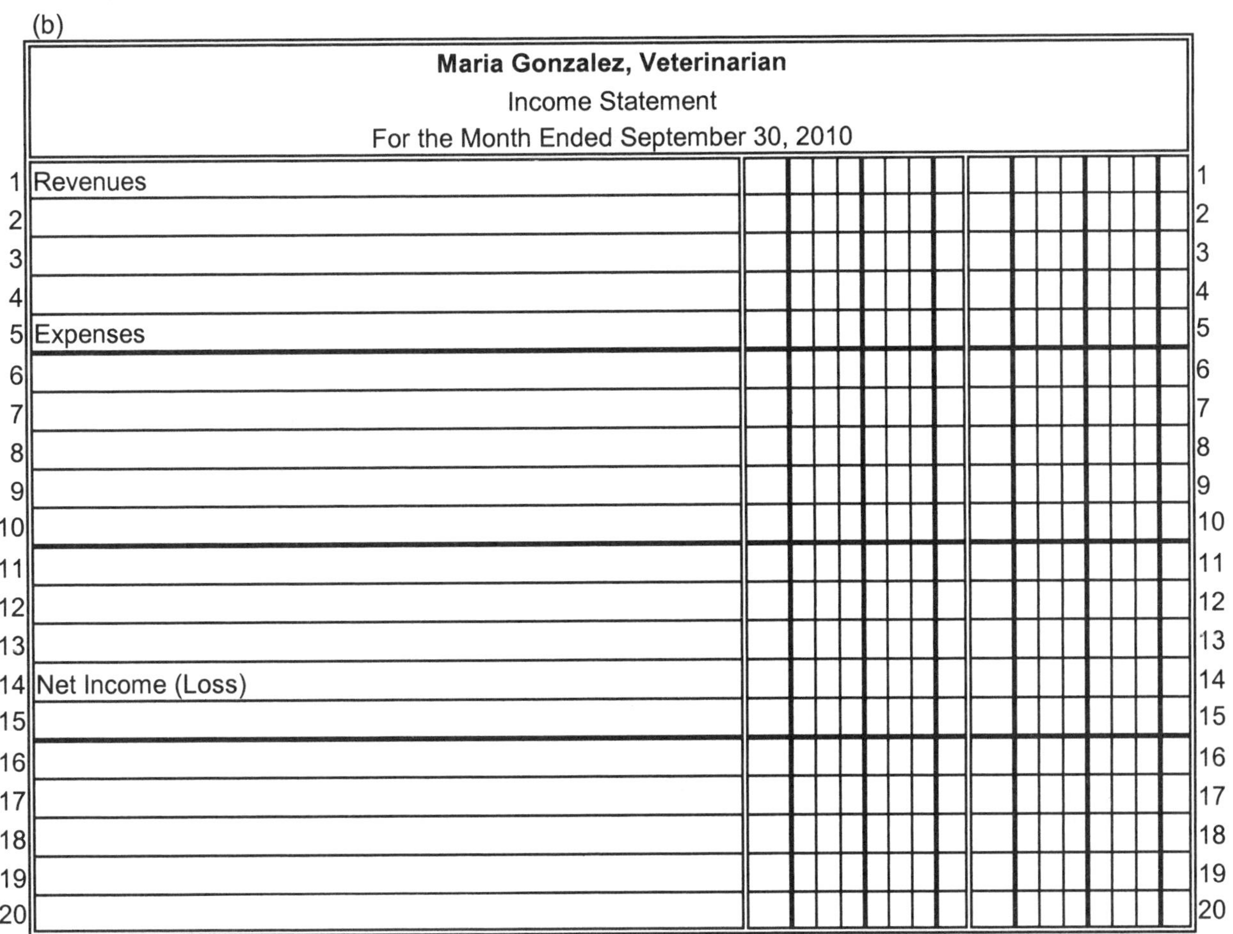

Maria Gonzalez, Veterinarian
Income Statement
For the Month Ended September 30, 2010

Revenues		
Expenses		
Net Income (Loss)		

Maria Gonzalez, Veterinarian
Owner's Equity Statement
For the Month Ended September 30, 2010

Name
Section
Date

Problem 1-2A Concluded

Maria Gonzalez, Veterinarian

(b) (Continued)

Maria Gonzalez, Veterinarian
Balance Sheet
September 30, 2010

Assets

Liabilities and Owner's Equity

Name | Problem 1-3A
Section
Date | Skyline Flying School

(a)

Skyline Flying School
Income Statement
For the Month Ended May 31, 2010

Revenues		
Expenses		
Net Income (Loss)		

Skyline Flying School
Owner's Equity Statement
For the Month Ended May 31, 2010

(a) Continued

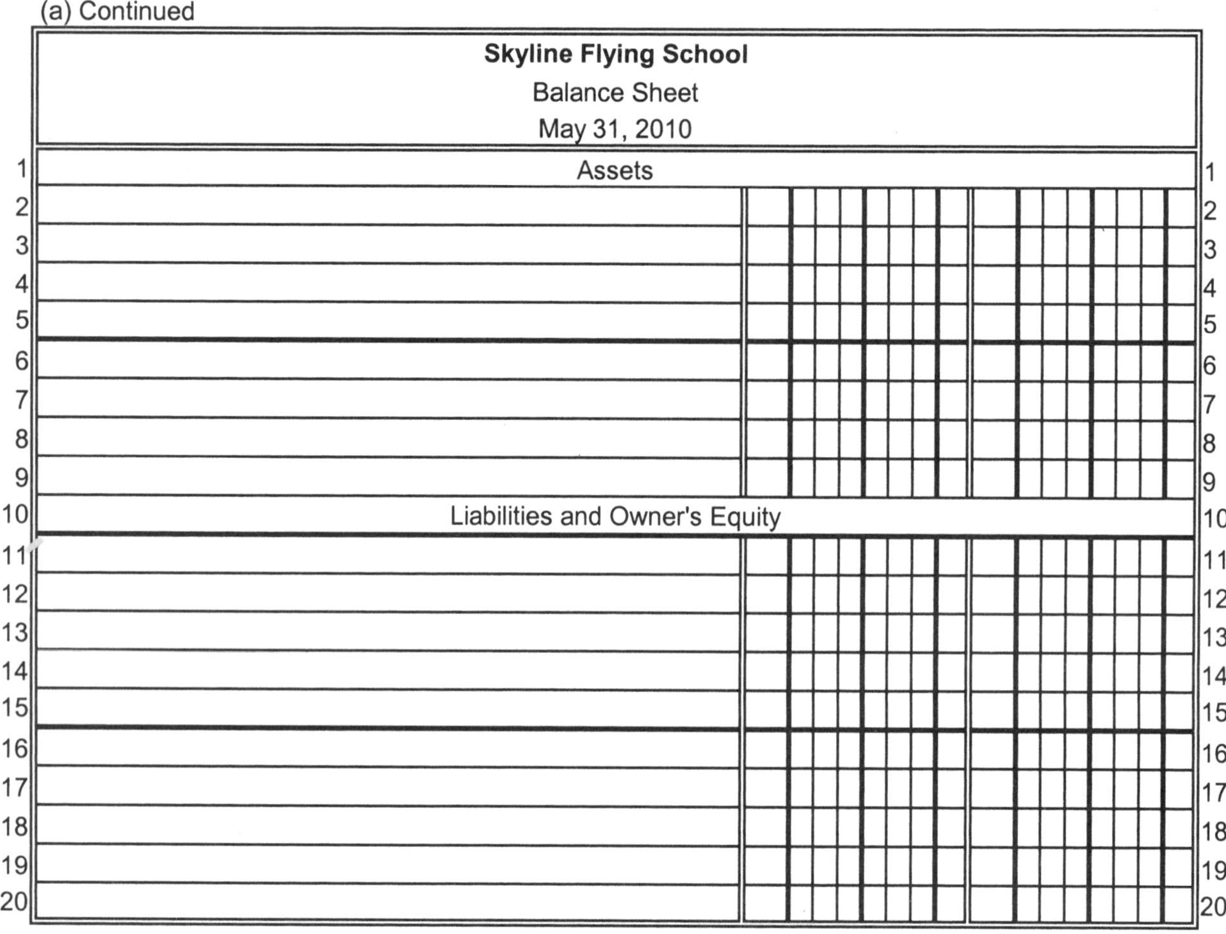

Skyline Flying School
Balance Sheet
May 31, 2010

Assets

Liabilities and Owner's Equity

(b)

Skyline Flying School
Income Statement
For the Month Ended May 31, 2010

Revenues

Expenses

Net Income (Loss)

Name

Section

Date

(b) Continued

Skyline Flying School

Owner's Equity Statement

For the Month Ended May 31, 2010

Problem 1-4A

Miller Deliveries

See Appendix

Name

Section

Date

Problem 1-4A Concluded

Miller Deliveries

(b)

Miller Deliveries

Income Statement

For the Month Ended June 30, 2010

1	Revenues			1
2				2
3				3
4	Expenses			4
5				5
6				6
7				7
8				8
9				9
10				10
11				11
12	Net income			12
13				13
14				14

Miller Deliveries

Balance Sheet

June 30, 2010

1	Assets			1
2				2
3				3
4				4
5				5
6				6
7				7
8	Liabilities and Owner's Equity			8
9				9
10				10
11				11
12				12
13				13
14				14
15				15
16				16
17				17
18				18

(a)

	Karma Company	Yates Company	McCain Company	Dench Company
January 1, 2008				
Assets	$ 95000	$ 110000		$ 170000
Liabilities	50000		75000	
Owner's Equity		60000	40000	90000
December 31, 2008				
Assets		137000	200000	
Liabilities	55000	75000		80000
Owner's Equity	60000		130000	170000
Owner's equity changes in year				
Add'l investment		15000	10000	15000
Drawings	25000		14000	20000
Total revenues	350000	420000		520000
Total expenses	320000	385000	342000	

(b)

Yates Company
Owner's Equity Statement
For the Year Ended December 31, 2010

(c)

Problem 1-1B

Vinnie's Travel Agency

See Appendix

(b)

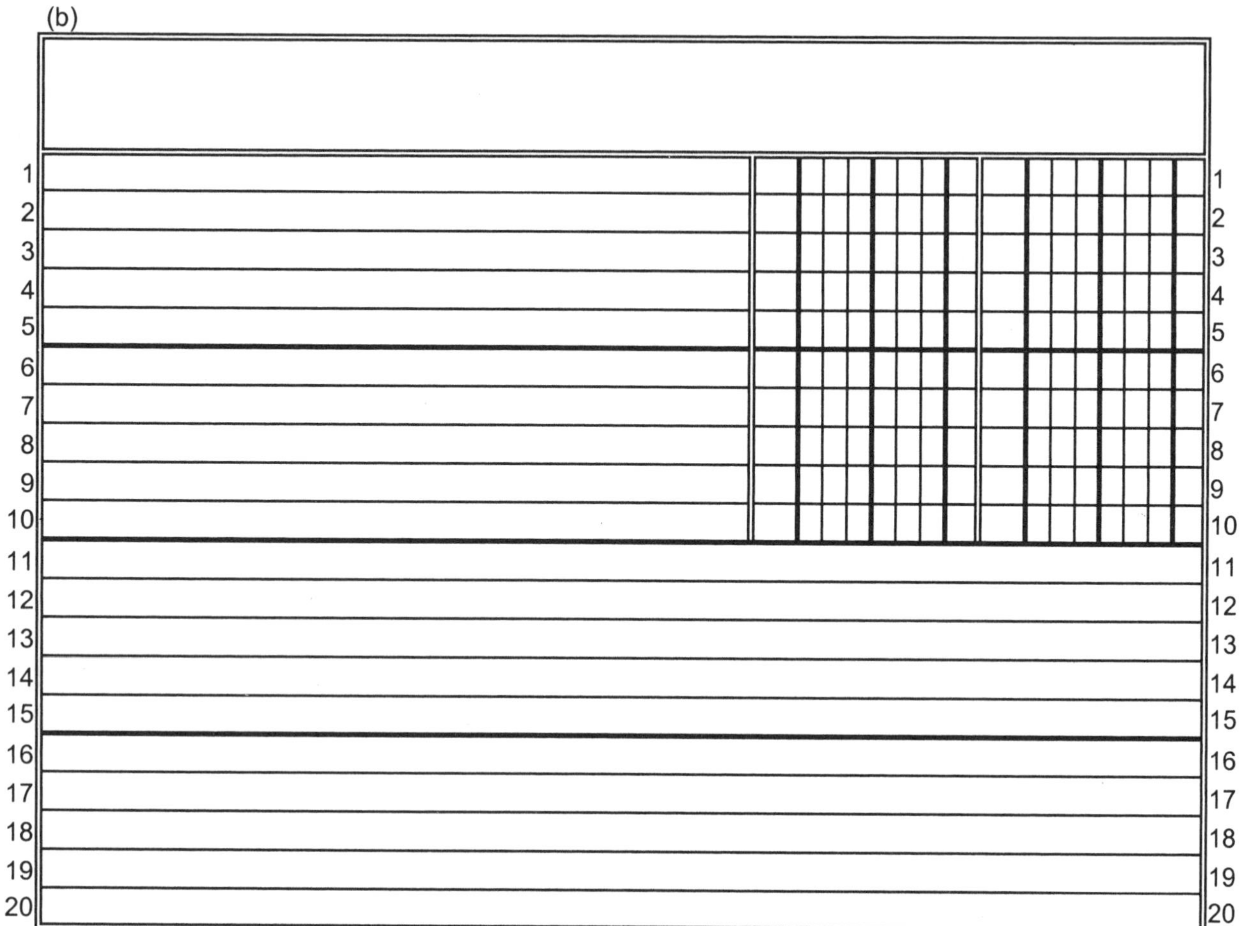

Problem 1-2B

Jenny Brown, Attorney at Law

See Appendix

(b)

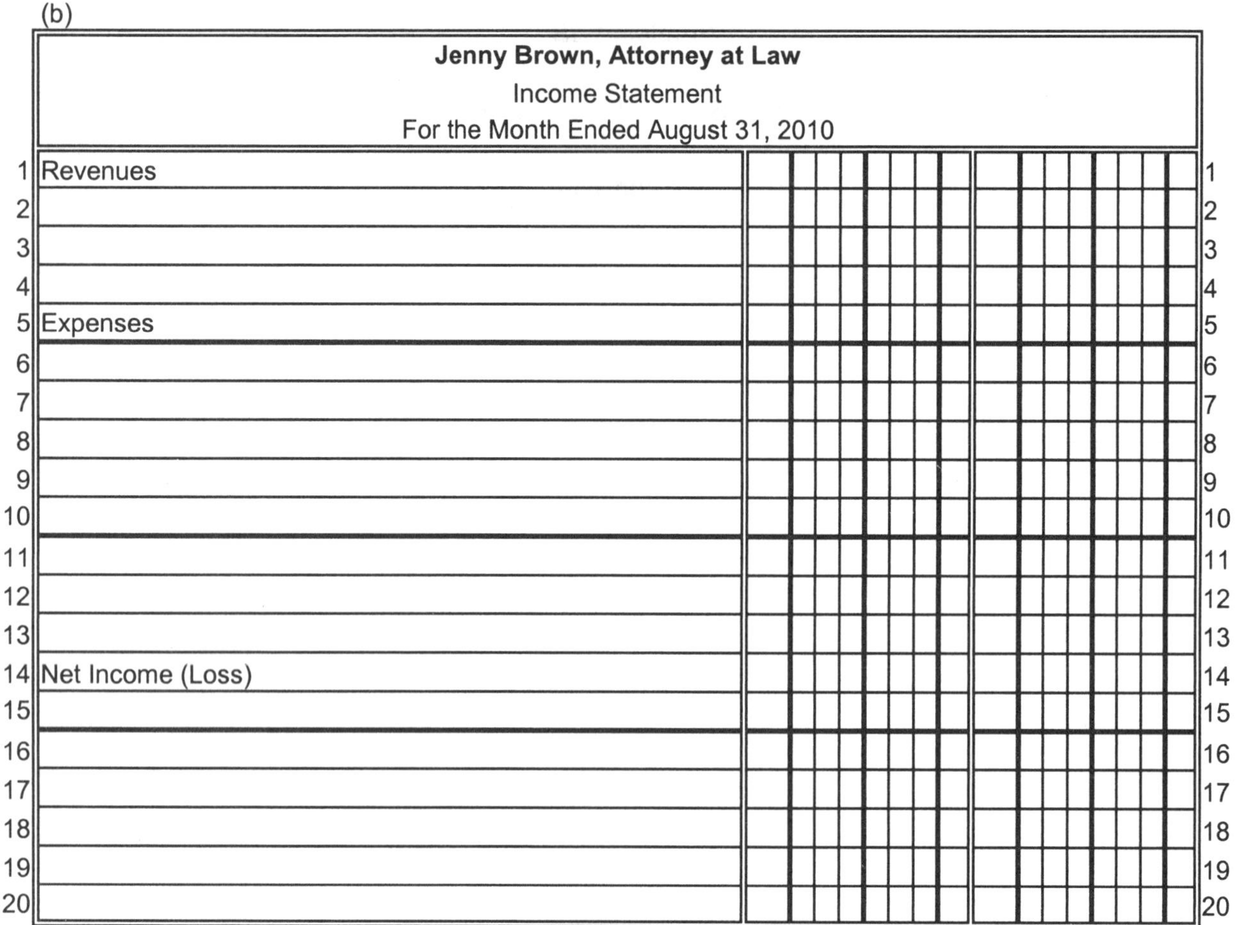

Jenny Brown, Attorney at Law
Income Statement
For the Month Ended August 31, 2010

Revenues		
Expenses		
Net Income (Loss)		

Jenny Brown, Attorney at Law
Owner's Equity Statement
For the Month Ended August 31, 2010

(b) (Continued)

Jenny Brown, Attorney at Law

Balance Sheet

August 31, 2010

Assets

Liabilities and Owner's Equity

Name Problem 1-3B

Section

Date Divine Cosmetics Co.

(a)

Divine Cosmetics Co.

Income Statement

For the Month Ended June 30, 2010

Revenues		
Expenses		
Net Income (Loss)		

Divine Cosmetics Co.

Owner's Equity Statement

For the Month Ended June 30, 2010

Name | Problem 1-3B Continued

Section

Date | Divine Cosmetics Co.

(a) Continued

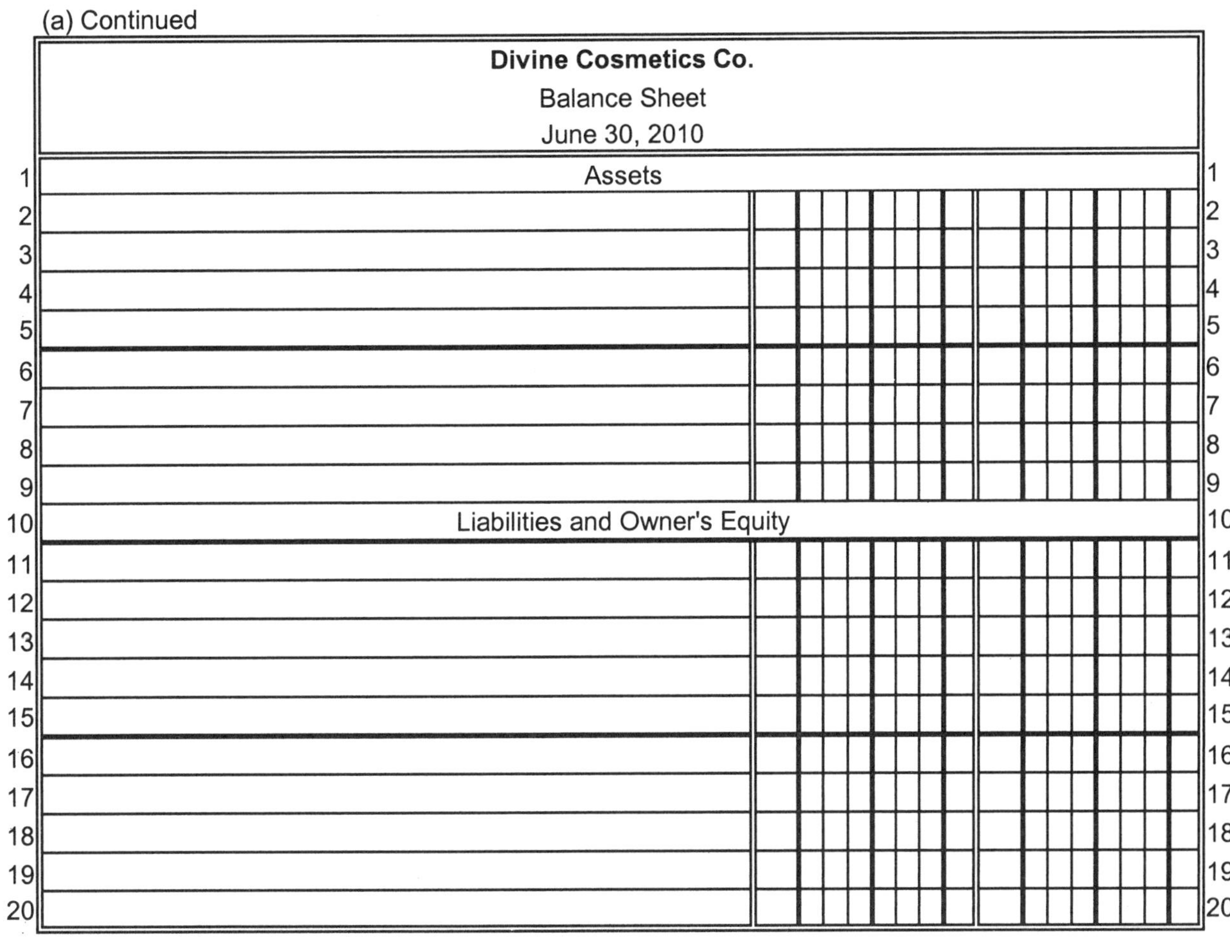

Divine Cosmetics Co.

Balance Sheet

June 30, 2010

Assets

Liabilities and Owner's Equity

(b)

Divine Cosmetics Co.

Income Statement

For the Month Ended June 30, 2010

Revenues

Expenses

Net Income (Loss)

(b) Continued

Divine Cosmetics Co.
Owner's Equity Statement
For the Month Ended June 30, 2010

Problem 1-4B

Rodriguez Consulting

See Appendix

(b)

Rodriguezr Consulting

Income Statement

For the Month Ended May 31, 2010

Revenues		
Expenses		
Net income		

(c)

Rodriguez Consulting

Balance Sheet

May 31, 2010

Assets		
Liabilities and Owner's Equity		

Name | Problem 1-5B

Section

Date | Donatello Company

(a)

	Donatello Company	Raphael Company	Michelangelo Company	Leonardo Company
January 1, 2010				
Assets	$ 80000	$ 90000		$ 150000
Liabilities	48000		80000	
Owner's Equity		40000	49000	90000
December 31, 2010				
Assets		112000	180000	
Liabilities	60000	72000		100000
Owner's Equity	40000		70000	145000
Owner's equity changes in year				
Add'l investment		8000	10000	15000
Drawings	15000		12000	10000
Total revenues	350000	410000		500000
Total expenses	333000	385000	350000	

(b)

Donatello Company

Owner's Equity Statement

For the Year Ended December 31, 2010

(c)

Name

Section

Date

Chapter 1 Financial Reporting Problem

PepsiCo, Inc.

(a)

(b)

(c)

(d) Net sales - 2005:

2006:

2007:

(e)

Name

Section

Date

Chapter 1 Comparative Analysis Problem

PepsiCo, Inc. versus Coca-Cola Company

	PepsiCo	Coca-Cola
(a) (in millions)		
1. Total assets		
2. Accounts receivable(net)		
3. Net sales		
4. Net income		

(b)

Name

Section

Date

(a)

(b)

Chip-Shot Driving Range

Balance Sheet

3/31/20010

Assets

Liabilities and Owner's Equity

(c)

(d)

Name

Section

Date

New York Company

Section

Date

New York Company

Balance Sheet

December 31, 2010

Assets

Liabilities and Owner's Equity

Name

Section

Date

BE2-1	(a) Debit Effect	(b) Credit Effect	(c) Normal Balance
1. Accounts Payable			
2. Advertising Expense			
3. Service Revenue			
4. Accounts Receivable			
5. A.J. Ritter, Capital			
6. A.J. Ritter, Drawing			

BE2-2	Account Debited	Account Credited
June 1		
2		
3		
12		

BE2-3

	Date	Account Titles	Debit	Credit
	June 1			
	2			
	3			
	12			

BE2-4

Name

Section

Date

BE2-5

Date	(a) Effect on Accounting Equation	(b) Debit - Credit Analysis
Aug. 1		
4		
16		
27		

BE2-6

Date	Account Titles	Debit	Credit
Aug. 1			
4			
16			
27			

Name

Section

Date

BE2-7

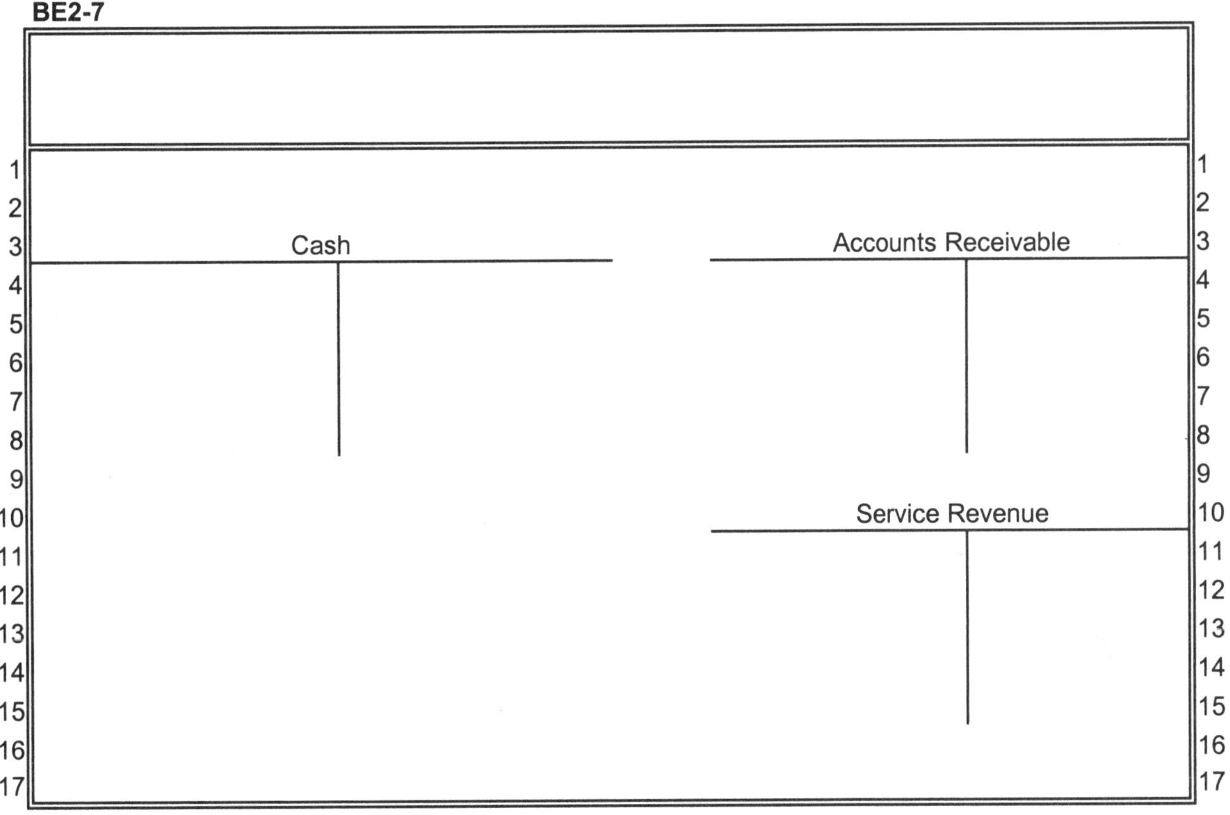

BE2-8

Cash

Date	Explanation	Ref	Debit	Credit	Balance

Accounts Receivable

Date	Explanation	Ref	Debit	Credit	Balance

Service Revenue

Date	Explanation	Ref	Debit	Credit	Balance

Name

Section

Date

BE2-9

Cleland Company
Trial Balance
June 30, 2010

	Debit	Credit

BE2-10

Kwun Company
Trial Balance
December 31, 2010

	Debit	Credit

Name

Section

Date

DO IT! 2-2

	Trans.	Account Titles	Debit	Credit	
1	1.				1
2					2
3					3
4	2.				4
5					5
6					6
7					7
8	3.				8
9					9

DO IT 2-3

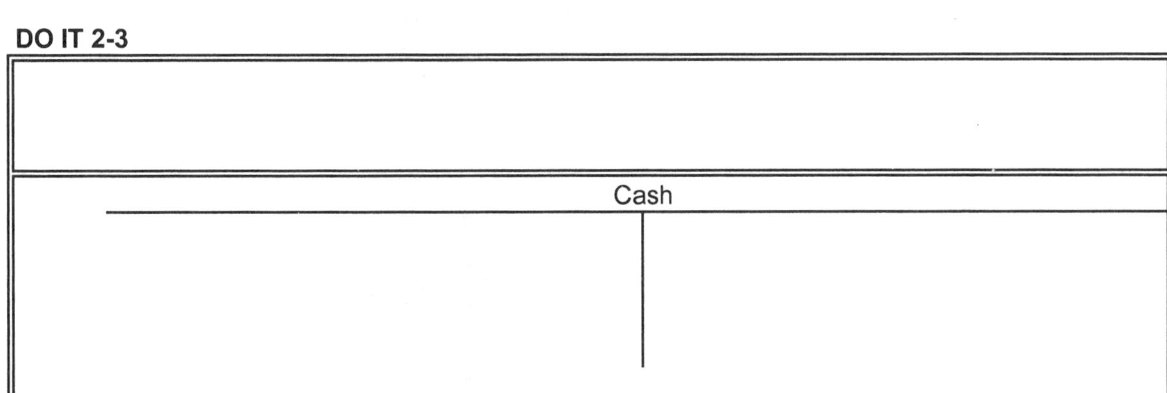

DO IT 2-4

Boardin' Company

Trial Balance

December 31, 2010

1				1
2				2
3				3
4				4
5				5
6				6
7				7
8				8
9				9
10				10
11				11
12				12
13				13
14				14
15				15

Name

Section

Date

E2-1

1.	
2.	
3.	
4.	
5.	

E2-3 General Journal J1

Date	Account Titles	Ref.	Debit	Credit
Jan. 2				
3				
9				
11				
16				
20				
23				
28				

Name

Section

Date

Exercise 2-2

D. Reyes

Trans-action No.	Account Debited				Account Credited			
	(a) Basic Type	(b) Specific Account	(c) Effect	(d) Normal Balance	(a) Basic Type	(b) Specific Account	(c) Effect	(d) Normal Balance
Jan. 2	Asset	Cash	Increase	Debit	Owner's	D. Reyes,	Increase	Credit
					Equity	Capital		
3								
9								
11								
16								
20								
23								
28								

Name

Section

Date

Exercises 2-4 and 2-5

E2-4

Date	
Oct. 1	
2	
3	
6	
27	
30	

E2-5

Date	Account Titles	Ref.	Debit	Credit
Oct. 1				
2				
3				
6				
27				
30				

Name — Exercises 2-6 and 2-8

Section

Date

E2-6

(a)	
1.	
2.	
3.	

(b)	Account Titles	Debit	Credit
1.			
2.			
3.			

E2-8

1.

2.

3.

4.

5.

Name Exercise 2-7

Section

Date Rowand Enterprises

(a)		Assets =	Liabilities +	Owners' Equity
1.				
2.				
3.				
4.				

(b)	Account Titles	Debit	Credit
1.			
2.			
3.			
4.			

Name | Exercise 2-9

Section

Date | Teresa Gonzalez, Investment Broker

(a)

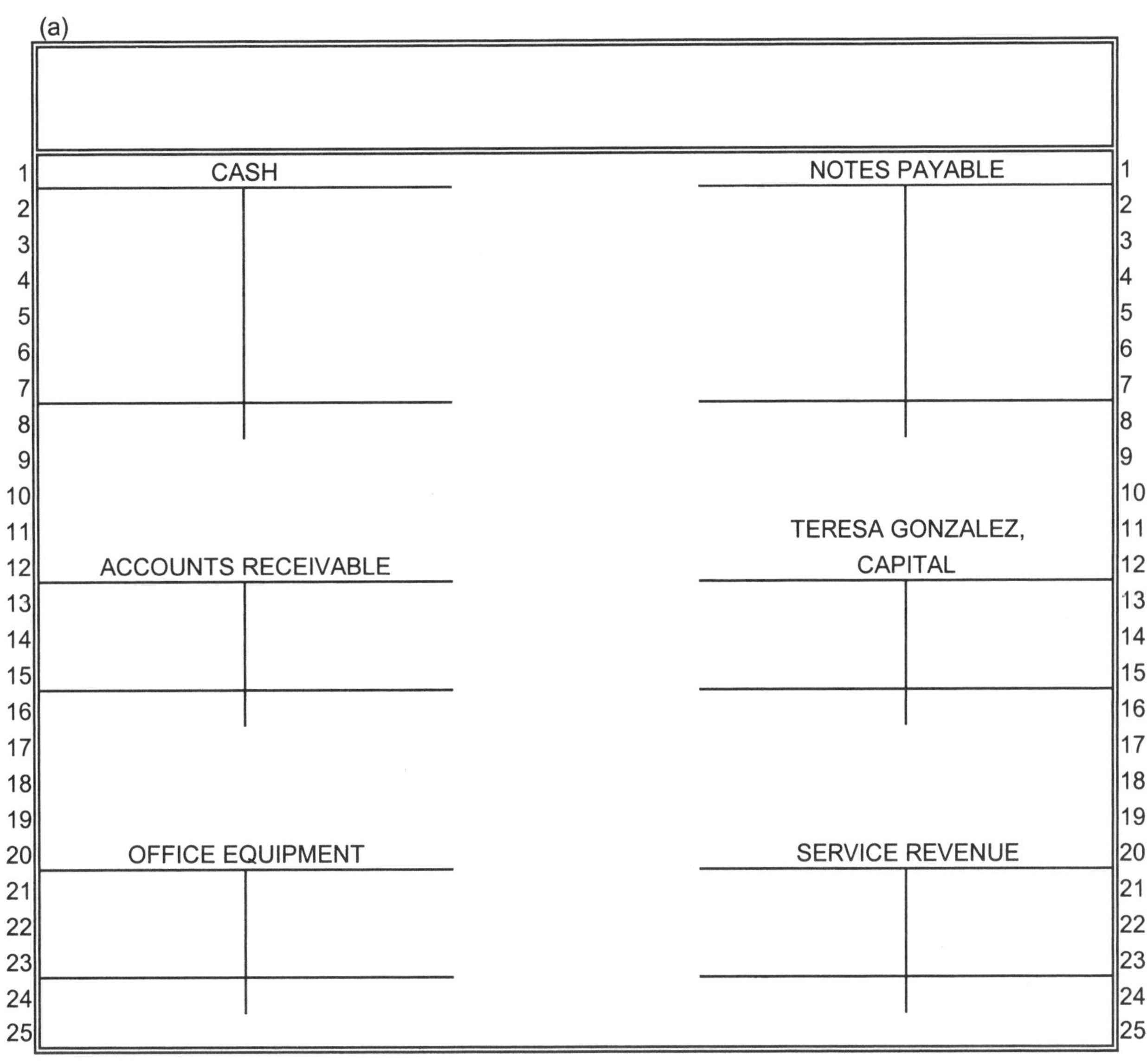

(b)

Teresa Gonzalez, Investment Broker

Trial Balance

August 31, 2010

	Debit	Credit

Name Exercise 2-10

Section

Date Simon Landscaping Company

(a)

General Journal

Date	Account Titles	Ref.	Debit	Credit
Apr. 1				
12				
15				
25				
29				
30				

(b)

Simon Landscaping Company
Trial Balance
April 30, 2010

	Debit	Credit

Name Exercise 2-11

Section

Date Heerey Co.

(a) General Journal

Date	Account Titles	Ref.	Debit	Credit
Oct. 1				
10				
10				
20				
20				

(b)

Heerey Co.
Trial Balance
October 31, 2010

	Debit	Credit

Name Exercise 2-12

Section

Date Tina Cordero Company

(a) General Journal J1

	Date	Account Titles	Ref.	Debit	Credit	
1	Sept. 1					1
2						2
3						3
4	5					4
5						5
6						6
7						7
8	25					8
9						9
10						10
11	30					11
12						12

(b)

Cash No. 101

Date	Explanation	Ref.	Debit	Credit	Balance

Equipment No. 157

Date	Explanation	Ref.	Debit	Credit	Balance

Accounts Payable No. 201

Date	Explanation	Ref.	Debit	Credit	Balance

Tina Cordero, Capital No. 301

Date	Explanation	Ref.	Debit	Credit	Balance

Tina Cordero, Drawing No. 306

Date	Explanation	Ref.	Debit	Credit	Balance

Name

Section

Date

E2-13

Error	(a) In Balance	(b) Difference	(c) Larger Column
1. A credit posting of $400 to Accounts Receivable was omitted.	No	$400	Debit
2. A debit posting of $750 for Prepaid Insurance was debited to Insurance Expense.			
3. A collection from a customer of $100 in payment of its account owed was journalized and posted as a debit to Cash for $100 and a credit to Service Revenue $100.			
4. A credit posting of $300 to Property Taxes Payable was made twice			
5. A cash purchase of supplies for $250 was journalized and posted as a debit to Supplies $25 and a credit to Cash $25.			
6. A debit of $475 to Advertising Expense was posted as $457.			

E2-14

Sanford Delivery Service

Trial Balance

July 31, 2010

	Debit	Credit

Name | Problem 2-1A

Section

Date | Frontier Park

General Journal

J1

Date	Account Titles	Ref.	Debit	Credit
Apr. 1				
4				
8				
11				
12				
13				
17				
20				
25				
30				
30				

Name Problem 2-2A

Section

Date Jane Kent, CPA

(a) General Journal J1

Date	Account Titles	Ref.	Debit	Credit
May 1				
2				
3				
7				
11				
12				
17				
31				
31				

Name Problem 2-2A Continued

Section

Date Jane Kent, CPA

(b)

Cash No. 101

Date	Explanation	Ref.	Debit	Credit	Balance

Accounts Receivable No. 112

Date	Explanation	Ref.	Debit	Credit	Balance

Supplies No. 126

Date	Explanation	Ref.	Debit	Credit	Balance

Accounts Payable No. 201

Date	Explanation	Ref.	Debit	Credit	Balance

Unearned Revenue No. 205

Date	Explanation	Ref.	Debit	Credit	Balance

Jane Kent, Capital No. 301

Date	Explanation	Ref.	Debit	Credit	Balance

(b) (Continued)

Service Revenue No. 400

Date	Explanation	Ref.	Debit	Credit	Balance

Salaries Expense No. 726

Date	Explanation	Ref.	Debit	Credit	Balance

Rent Expense No. 729

Date	Explanation	Ref.	Debit	Credit	Balance

(c)

Jane Kent, CPA
Trial Balance
May 31, 2010

		Debit	Credit	
1	Cash			1
2	Accounts Receivable			2
3	Supplies			3
4	Accounts Payable			4
5	Unearned Revenue			5
6	Jane Kent, Capital			6
7	Service Revenue			7
8	Salaries Expense			8
9	Rent Expense			9
10				10
11				11

Name	Problem 2-3A
Section	
Date	Byte Repair Service

(a) & (c)

Cash

Bal. 8,000	

Accounts Receivable

Bal. 15,000	

Parts Inventory

Bal. 13,000	

Prepaid Rent

Bal. 3,000	

Shop Equipment

Bal. 21,000	

Accounts Payable

	Bal. 19,000

Jack Shellenkamp, Capital

	Bal. 41,000

Jack Shellenkamp, Drawings

Repair Services Revenue

Advertising Expense

Miscellaneous Expense

Repair Parts Expense

Wage Expense

(b) General Journal J1

Date	Account Titles	Ref.	Debit	Credit
1.				
2.				
3.				
4.				
5.				
6.				
7.				
8.				
9.				

(d)

Byte Repair Service
Trial Balance
January 31, 2010

		Debit	Credit	
1	Cash			1
2	Accounts Receivable			2
3	Parts Inventory			3
4	Prepaid Rent			4
5	Shop Equipment			5
6	Accounts Payable			6
7	Jack Shellenkamp, Capital			7
8	Jack Shellenkamp, Drawings			8
9	Repair Services Revenue			9
10	Advertising Expense			10
11	Miscellaneous Expense			11
12	Repair Parts Expense			12
13	Wage Expense			13
14	Totals			14
15				15
16				16
17				17

Name | Problem 2-4A

Section

Date | Sterling Company

Sterling Company

Trial Balance

May 31, 2010

	Debit	Credit

Journal Entry Aids:

Name Problem 2-5A

Section

Date Lake Theater

(a) and (c)

Cash No. 101

Date	Explanation	Ref.	Debit	Credit	Balance
Apr. 1	Balance	√			6000

Accounts Receivable No. 112

Date	Explanation	Ref.	Debit	Credit	Balance

Prepaid Rentals No. 136

Date	Explanation	Ref.	Debit	Credit	Balance

Land No. 140

Date	Explanation	Ref.	Debit	Credit	Balance
Apr. 1	Balance	√			10000

Buildings No. 145

Date	Explanation	Ref.	Debit	Credit	Balance
Apr. 1	Balance	√			8000

Equipment No. 157

Date	Explanation	Ref.	Debit	Credit	Balance
Apr. 1	Balance	√			6000

Accounts Payable No. 201

Date	Explanation	Ref.	Debit	Credit	Balance
Apr. 1	Balance	√			2000

(a) and (c) (Continued)

Mortgage Payable No. 275

Date	Explanation	Ref.	Debit	Credit	Balance
Apr. 1	Balance	√			8000

Tony Carpino, Capital No. 301

Date	Explanation	Ref.	Debit	Credit	Balance
Apr. 1	Balance	√			20000

Admission Revenue No. 405

Date	Explanation	Ref.	Debit	Credit	Balance

Concession Revenue No. 406

Date	Explanation	Ref.	Debit	Credit	Balance

Advertising Expense No. 610

Date	Explanation	Ref.	Debit	Credit	Balance

Film Rental Expense No. 632

Date	Explanation	Ref.	Debit	Credit	Balance

Salaries Expense No. 726

Date	Explanation	Ref.	Debit	Credit	Balance

(b) General Journal J1

Date	Account Titles	Ref.	Debit	Credit
Apr. 2				
3				
9				
10				
11				
12				
20				
25				
29				
30				
30				

(d)

Lake Theater
Trial Balance
April 30, 2010

	Debit	Credit
Cash		
Accounts Receivable		
Prepaid Rentals		
Land		
Buildings		
Equipment		
Accounts Payable		
Mortgage Payable		
Tony Carpino, Capital		
Admission Revenue		
Concession Revenue		
Advertising Expense		
Film Rental Expense		
Salaries Expense		

Name

Section

Date

Problem 2-1B

Hyzer Disc Golf Course

General Journal

J1

Date	Account Titles	Ref.	Debit	Credit
Mar. 1				
3				
5				
6				
10				
18				
19				
25				
30				

Name | Problem 2-1B Concluded

Section

Date | Hyzer Disc Golf Course

General Journal

J1

Date	Account Titles	Ref.	Debit	Credit
Mar. 30				
31				

Name

Section

Date

Problem 2-2B

Maria Juarez, Dentist

(a) General Journal J1

Date	Account Titles	Ref.	Debit	Credit
Apr. 1				
1				
2				
3				
10				
11				
20				
30				
30				

Name

Section

Date

Problem 2-2B Continued

Maria Juarez, Dentist

(b)

Cash — No. 101

Date	Explanation	Ref.	Debit	Credit	Balance

Accounts Receivable — No. 112

Date	Explanation	Ref.	Debit	Credit	Balance

Supplies — No. 126

Date	Explanation	Ref.	Debit	Credit	Balance

Accounts Payable — No. 201

Date	Explanation	Ref.	Debit	Credit	Balance

Unearned Revenue — No. 205

Date	Explanation	Ref.	Debit	Credit	Balance

Maria Juarez, Capital — No. 301

Date	Explanation	Ref.	Debit	Credit	Balance

(b) (Continued)

Service Revenue No. 400

Date	Explanation	Ref.	Debit	Credit	Balance

Salaries Expense No. 726

Date	Explanation	Ref.	Debit	Credit	Balance

Rent Expense No. 729

Date	Explanation	Ref.	Debit	Credit	Balance

(c)

Maria Juarez, Dentist
Trial Balance
April 30, 2010

		Debit	Credit	
1	Cash			1
2	Accounts Receivable			2
3	Supplies			3
4	Accounts Payable			4
5	Unearned Revenue			5
6	Maria Juarez, Dentist			6
7	Service Revenue			7
8	Salaries Expense			8
9	Rent Expense			9
10				10
11				11

Name Problem 2-3B

Section

Date Slowhand Services

(a) General Journal

Trans.	Account Titles	Ref.	Debit	Credit
1.				
2.				
3.				
4.				
5.				
6.				
7.				
8.				
9.				
10.				
11.				
12.				

Name

Section

Date

(b)

Cash

Accounts Payable

Accounts Receivable

Eric Clapton, Capital

Office Supplies

Service Revenue

Prepaid Insurance

Salaries Expense

Prepaid Rent

Utility Expense

Furniture & Equipment

Name

Section

Date

(c)

Slowhand Services

Trial Balance

May 31, 2010

	Debit	Credit
Cash		
Accounts Receivable		
Office Supplies		
Prepaid Insurance		
Prepaid Rent		
Furniture and Equipment		
Accounts Payable		
Eric Clapton, Capital		
Service Revenue		
Salaries Expense		
Utility Expense		

Name Problem 2-4B

Section

Date Syed Moiz Co.

Syed Moiz Co.

Trial Balance

June 30, 2010

	Debit	Credit

Journal Entry Aids:

Name Problem 2-5B

Section

Date Josie Theater

(a) and (c)

Cash No. 101

Date	Explanation	Ref.	Debit	Credit	Balance
Mar. 1	Balance	√			9000

Accounts Receivable No. 112

Date	Explanation	Ref.	Debit	Credit	Balance

Land No. 140

Date	Explanation	Ref.	Debit	Credit	Balance
Mar. 1	Balance	√			24000

Buildings No. 145

Date	Explanation	Ref.	Debit	Credit	Balance
Mar. 1	Balance	√			10000

Equipment No. 157

Date	Explanation	Ref.	Debit	Credit	Balance
Mar. 1	Balance	√			10000

Accounts Payable No. 201

Date	Explanation	Ref.	Debit	Credit	Balance
Mar. 1	Balance	√			7000

J. Micheals, Capital No. 301

Date	Explanation	Ref.	Debit	Credit	Balance
Mar. 1	Balance	√			46000

(a) and (c) (Continued)

Admission Revenue No. 405

Date	Explanation	Ref.	Debit	Credit	Balance

Concession Revenue No. 406

Date	Explanation	Ref.	Debit	Credit	Balance

Advertising Expense No. 610

Date	Explanation	Ref.	Debit	Credit	Balance

Film Rental Expense No. 632

Date	Explanation	Ref.	Debit	Credit	Balance

Salaries Expense No. 726

Date	Explanation	Ref.	Debit	Credit	Balance

Name Problem 2-5B Continued

Section

Date Josie Theater

(b) General Journal J1

Date	Account Titles	Ref.	Debit	Credit
Mar. 2				
3				
9				
10				
11				
12				
20				
20				
31				

(b) General Journal J1

	Date	Account Titles	Ref.	Debit	Credit	
1	Mar. 31					1
2						2
3						3
4						4
5						5
6						6
7	31					7
8						8
9						9
10						10
11						11
12						12
13						13
14						14
15						15
16						16

(d)

Josie Theater
Trial Balance
March 31, 2010

		Debit	Credit	
1	Cash			1
2	Accounts Receivable			2
3	Land			3
4	Buildings			4
5	Equipment			5
6	Accounts Payable			6
7	J. Micheals, Capital			7
8	Admission Revenue			8
9	Concession Revenue			9
10	Advertising Expense			10
11	Film Rental Expense			11
12	Salaries Expense			12
13				13
14				14
15				15
16				16
17				17

Name | Chapter 2 Decision Making Across the Organization

Section

Date | Ortega Riding Academy

(a)

Date	Account Titles	Debit	Credit
May 1			
5			
7			
14			
15			
20			
30			
31			

(b)

(c)

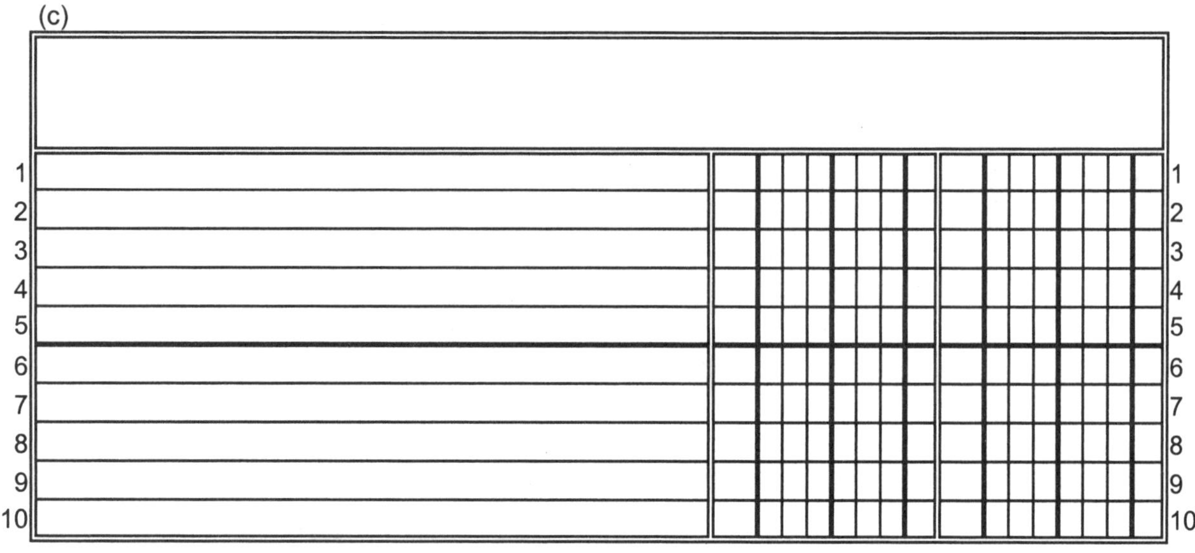

(d)

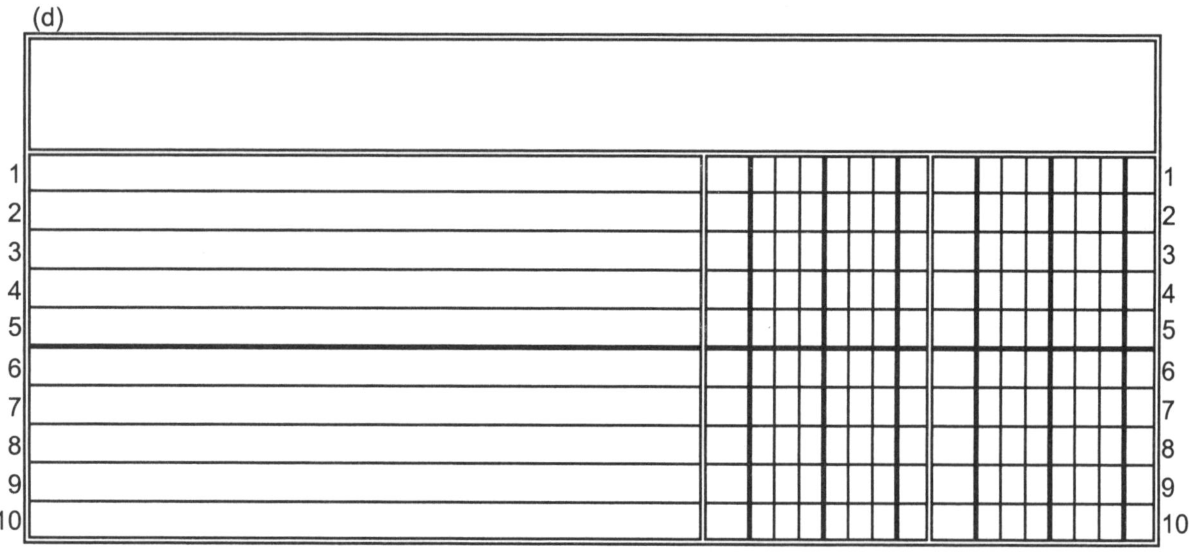

Name

Section

Date

BE3-3

Date	Account Titles	Debit	Credit
Dec. 31			

Advertising Supplies

Advertising Supplies Expense

BE3-4

Date	Account Titles	Debit	Credit
Dec. 31			

Depr. Expense - Equipment

Accum. Depreciation - Equipment

Balance Sheet:		

BE3-5

Date	Account Titles	Debit	Credit
July 1			
Dec. 31			

Prepaid Insurance

Insurance Expense

Name

Section

Date

BE3-6

Date	Account Titles	Debit	Credit
July 1			
Dec. 31			

Unearned Insurance Revenue		Insurance Revenue	

BE3-7

Date	Account Titles	Debit	Credit
Dec. 31			
31			
31			

BE3-8

Account	(a) Type of Adjustment	(b) Related Account
Accounts Receivable		
Prepaid Insurance		
Accum. Depr. - Equipment		
Interest Payable		
Unearned Service Revenue		

Name

Section

Date

BE3-9

Harmony Company
Income Statement
For the Year Ended December 31, 2010

BE3-10

Harmony Company
Owner's Equity Statement
For the Year Ended December 31, 2010

***BE3-11**

Date	Account Titles	Debit	Credit
(a)			
Apr. 30			
(b)			
Apr. 30			

Name

Section

Date

DO IT! 3-2

Trans.	Account Titles	Debit	Credit
1.			
2.			
3.			
4.			

DO IT! 3-3

Trans.	Account Titles	Debit	Credit
1.			
2.			
3.			

(a)

Revenues:

Expenses:

Net income (loss)

(b)

Assets:

Liabilities:

(c)

Name

Section

Date

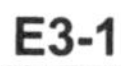

E3-1

E3-3

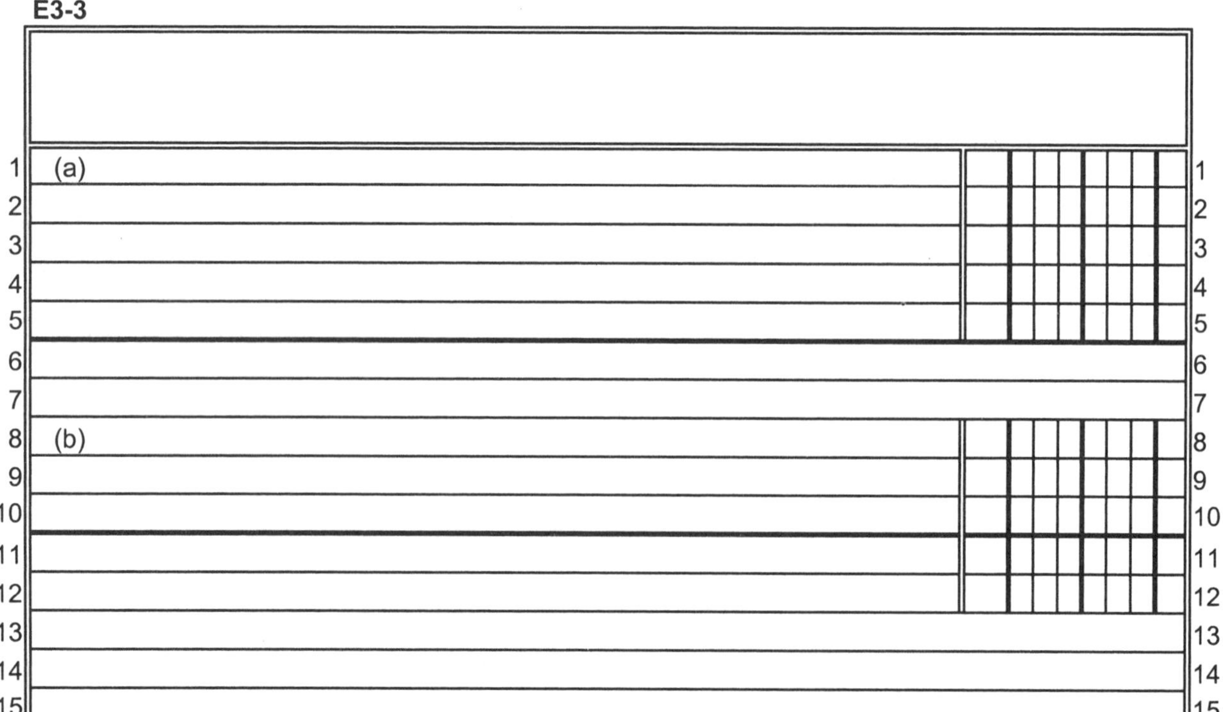

Name ______________________ Exercises 3-4 and 3-5

Section ______________________

Date ______________________

E3-4

Item	Type of Adjustment
1.	
2.	
3.	
4.	
5.	
6.	
7.	
8.	
9.	
10.	
11.	

E3-5

Item	Account Titles	Debit	Credit
1.			
2.			
3.			
4.			
5.			
6.			
7.			

Name

Section

Date

E3-6

Item	(a) Type of Adjustment	(b) Accounts before Adjustment
1.		
2.		
3.		
4.		
5.		
6.		

E3-7

Date	Account Titles	Debit	Credit
Mar. 31			
31			
31			
31			
31			

Name

Section

Date

E3-8

Date	Account Titles	Debit	Credit
Jan. 31			
31			
31			
31			
31			
31			

E3-9

Date	Account Titles	Debit	Credit
Oct. 31			
31			
31			
31			
31			
31			
31			

Name

Exercises 3-10 and 3-11

Section

Date

E3-10

Benning Co.
Income Statement
For the Month Ended July 31, 2010

Revenues:		
Expenses:		

E3-11

Answer	Computation	
(a)		
(b)		
(c)		
(d)		

Name Exercise 3-12

Section

Date Tabor Company

Date	Account Titles	Debit	Credit
(a)			
July 10			
14			
15			
20			
(b)			
July 31			
31			
31			
31			

Name

Section

Date

E3-13

Date	Account Titles	Debit	Credit
Aug. 31			
31			
31			
31			
31			
31			

E3-14

Garcia Company
Income Statement
For the Year Ended August 31, 2010

Revenues:		
Expenses:		

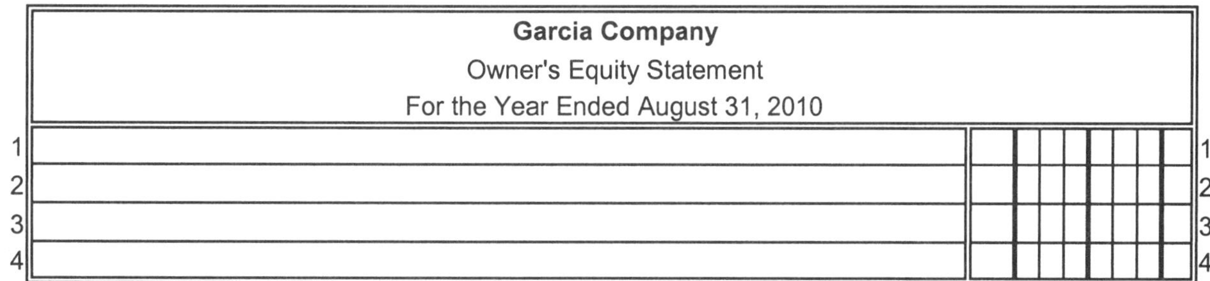

Garcia Company

Owner's Equity Statement

For the Year Ended August 31, 2010

Garcia Company

Balance Sheet

August 31, 2010

Assets

Liabilities and Owner's Equity

Name

Section

Date

E3-15

	Account Titles	Debit	Credit
(a)			
1.			
2.			
3. (a)			
(b)			
4.			
5.			

(b)

***E3-16**

	Account Titles	Debit	Credit
1.			
2.			
3.			

Name *Exercise 3-17

Section

Date Natasha Company

(a)

Date	Account Titles	Debit	Credit
Jan. 2			
10			
15			

(b)

Date	Account Titles	Debit	Credit
Jan. 31			
31			
31			

CASH

PREPAID INSURANCE

INSURANCE EXPENSE

SUPPLIES

SUPPLIES EXPENSE

UNEARNED REVENUE

SERVICE REVENUE

Name *Exercise 3-17 Concluded

Section

Date Natasha Company

(c)

1	Insurance Expense		1
2	Supplies Expense		2
3	Service Revenue		3
4	Prepaid Insurance		4
5	Supplies		5
6	Unearned Revenue		6
7			7
8			8
9			9
10			10

Name Problem 3-1A

Section

Date Masasi Company

(a) General Journal J3

Date	Account Titles	Ref.	Debit	Credit
2010				
June 30				
30				
30				
30				
30				
30				
30				

Name Problem 3-1A Continued

Section

Date Masasi Company

(b)

Cash No. 101

Date	Explanation	Ref.	Debit	Credit	Balance
2010					
June 30	Balance	√			7150

Accounts Receivable No. 112

Date	Explanation	Ref.	Debit	Credit	Balance
2010					
June 30	Balance	√			6000

Supplies No. 126

Date	Explanation	Ref.	Debit	Credit	Balance
2010					
June 30	Balance	√			2000

Prepaid Insurance No. 130

Date	Explanation	Ref.	Debit	Credit	Balance
2010					
June 30	Balance	√			3000

Office Equipment No. 157

Date	Explanation	Ref.	Debit	Credit	Balance
2010					
June 30	Balance	√			15000

Accumulated Depreciation - Office Furniture No, 158

Date	Explanation	Ref.	Debit	Credit	Balance

Accounts Payable No. 201

Date	Explanation	Ref.	Debit	Credit	Balance
2010					
June 30	Balance	√			4500

Name | Problem 3-1A Continued
Section
Date | Masasi Company

(b) (Continued)

Unearned Service Revenue — No. 209

Date	Explanation	Ref.	Debit	Credit	Balance
2010					
June 30	Balance	√			4000

Salaries Payable — No. 212

Date	Explanation	Ref.	Debit	Credit	Balance

Utilities Payable — No. 244

Date	Explanation	Ref.	Debit	Credit	Balance

T. Masasi, Capital — No. 301

Date	Explanation	Ref.	Debit	Credit	Balance
2010					
June 30	Balance	√			21750

Service Revenue — No. 400

Date	Explanation	Ref.	Debit	Credit	Balance
2010					
June 30	Balance	√			7900

Supplies Expense — No. 631

Date	Explanation	Ref.	Debit	Credit	Balance

Depreciation Expense — No. 711

Date	Explanation	Ref.	Debit	Credit	Balance

(b) (Continued)

Insurance Expense No. 722

Date	Explanation	Ref.	Debit	Credit	Balance

Salaries Expense No. 726

Date	Explanation	Ref.	Debit	Credit	Balance
2010					
June 30	Balance	√			4000

Rent Expense No. 729

Date	Explanation	Ref.	Debit	Credit	Balance
2010					
June 30	Balance	√			1000

Utilities Expense No. 732

Date	Explanation	Ref.	Debit	Credit	Balance

Name Problem 3-1A Concluded

Section

Date Masasi Company

(c)

Masasi Company

Adjusted Trial Balance

June 30, 2010

	Debit	Credit
Cash		
Accounts Receivable		
Supplies		
Prepaid Insurance		
Office Equipment		
Accumulated Depreciation - Office Equipment		
Accounts Payable		
Unearned Service Revenue		
Salaries Payable		
Utilities Payable		
T. Masasi, Capital		
Service Revenue		
Supplies Expense		
Depreciation Expense		
Insurance Expense		
Salaries Expense		
Rent Expense		
Utilities Expense		
Totals		

Name Problem 3-2A

Section

Date Neosho River Resort

(a) General Journal J1

Date	Account Titles	Ref.	Debit	Credit
Aug. 31				
31				
31				
31				
31				
31				
31				
31				

(b)

Cash No. 101

Date	Explanation	Ref.	Debit	Credit	Balance
Aug. 31	Balance	√			19600

Accounts Receivable No. 112

Date	Explanation	Ref.	Debit	Credit	Balance

(b) (Continued)

Supplies No. 126

Date	Explanation	Ref.	Debit	Credit	Balance
Aug. 31	Balance	√			3300

Prepaid Insurance No. 130

Date	Explanation	Ref.	Debit	Credit	Balance
Aug.31	Balance	√			6000

Land No. 140

Date	Explanation	Ref.	Debit	Credit	Balance
Aug.31	Balance	√			25000

Cottages No. 143

Date	Explanation	Ref.	Debit	Credit	Balance
Aug. 31	Balance	√			125000

Accumulated Depreciation - Cottages No. 144

Date	Explanation	Ref.	Debit	Credit	Balance

Furniture No. 149

Date	Explanation	Ref.	Debit	Credit	Balance
Aug. 31	Balance	√			26000

Accumulated Depreciation - Furniture No. 150

Date	Explanation	Ref.	Debit	Credit	Balance

Accounts Payable No. 201

Date	Explanation	Ref.	Debit	Credit	Balance
Aug. 31	Balance	√			6500

Unearned Rent Revenue No. 209

Date	Explanation	Ref.	Debit	Credit	Balance
Aug. 31	Balance	√			7400

Salaries Payable No. 212

Date	Explanation	Ref.	Debit	Credit	Balance

(b) (Continued)

Interest Payable No. 230

Date	Explanation	Ref.	Debit	Credit	Balance

Mortgage Payable No. 275

Date	Explanation	Ref.	Debit	Credit	Balance
Aug. 31	Balance	√			80000

P. Harder, Capital No. 301

Date	Explanation	Ref.	Debit	Credit	Balance
Aug. 31	Balance	√			100000

P. Harder, Drawing No. 306

Date	Explanation	Ref.	Debit	Credit	Balance
Aug. 31	Balance	√			5000

Rent Revenue No. 429

Date	Explanation	Ref.	Debit	Credit	Balance
Aug. 31	Balance	√			80000

Depreciation Expense - Cottages No. 620

Date	Explanation	Ref.	Debit	Credit	Balance

Depreciation Expense - Furniture No. 621

Date	Explanation	Ref.	Debit	Credit	Balance

Repair Expense No. 622

Date	Explanation	Ref.	Debit	Credit	Balance
Aug. 31	Balance	√			3600

Supplies Expense No. 631

Date	Explanation	Ref.	Debit	Credit	Balance

Interest Expense No. 718

Date	Explanation	Ref.	Debit	Credit	Balance

(b) (Continued)

Insurance Expense No. 722

Date	Explanation	Ref.	Debit	Credit	Balance

Salaries Expense No. 726

Date	Explanation	Ref.	Debit	Credit	Balance
Aug. 31	Balance	√			5 1 0 0 0

Utilities Expense No. 732

Date	Explanation	Ref.	Debit	Credit	Balance
Aug. 31	Balance	√			9 4 0 0

(c)

Neosho River Resort
Adjusted Trial Balance
August 31, 2010

		Debit	Credit	
1	Cash			1
2	Accounts Receivable			2
3	Supplies			3
4	Prepaid Insurance			4
5	Land			5
6	Cottages			6
7	Accumulated Depreciation - Cottages			7
8	Furniture			8
9	Accumulated Depreciation - Furniture			9
10	Accounts Payable			10
11	Unearned Rent			11
12	Salaries Payable			12
13	Interest Payable			13
14	Mortgage Payable			14
15	P. Harder, Capital			15
16	P. Harder, Drawing			16
17	Rent Revenue			17
18	Depreciation Expense - Cottages			18
19	Depreciation Expense - Furniture			19
20	Repair Expense			20
21	Supplies Expense			21
22	Interest Expense			22
23	Insurance Expense			23
24	Salaries Expense			24
25	Utilities Expense			25
26	Totals			26

(d)

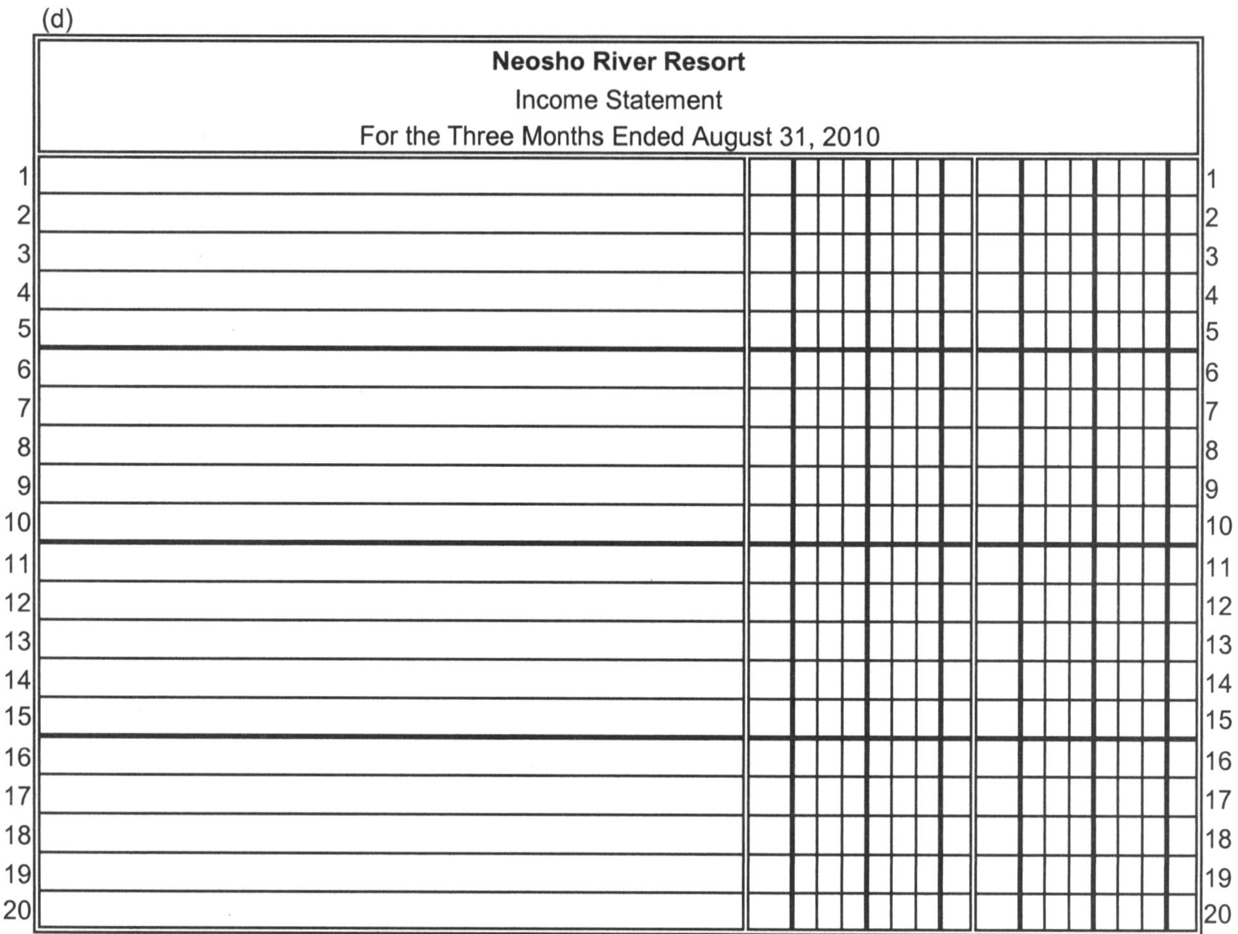

Neosho River Resort

Income Statement

For the Three Months Ended August 31, 2010

Neosho River Resort

Owner's Equity Statement

For the Three Months Ended August 31, 2010

(d) (Continued)

Neosho River Resort

Balance Sheet

August 31, 2010

Assets

Liabilities and Owner's Equity

Name Problem 3-3A

Section

Date Fernetti Advertising Agency

(a)

	Date	Accounts Titles	Debit	Credit	
1	Dec. 31				1
2					2
3					3
4	31				4
5					5
6					6
7	31				7
8					8
9					9
10	31				10
11					11
12					12
13	31				13
14					14
15					15
16	31				16
17					17
18					18
19	31				19
20					20
21					21

(b)

Fernetti Advertising Agency

Income Statement

For the Year Ended December 31, 2010

1				1
2				2
3				3
4				4
5				5
6				6
7				7
8				8
9				9
10				10
11				11
12				12
13				13
14				14

(b) (Continued)

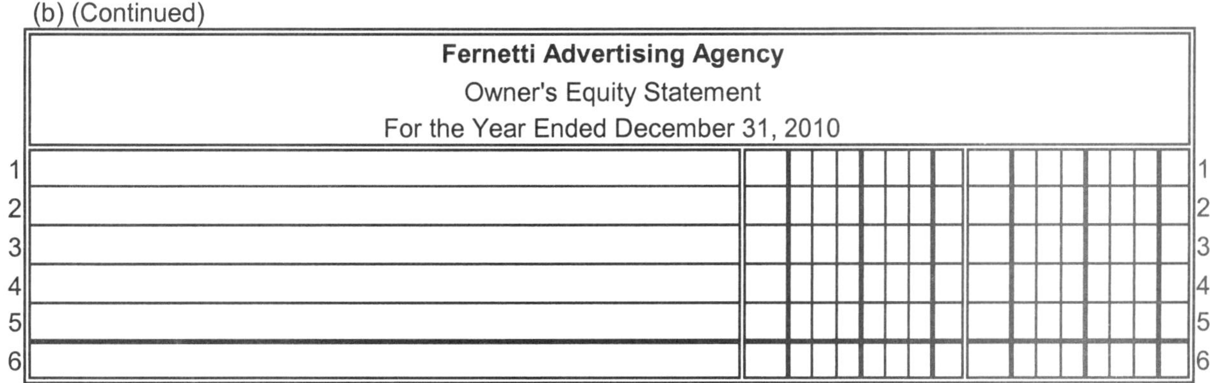

Fernetti Advertising Agency
Owner's Equity Statement
For the Year Ended December 31, 2010

Fernetti Advertising Agency
Balance Sheet
December 31, 2010

Assets

Liabilities and Owner's Equity

Name | Problem 3-4A

Section

Date | Remington Company

General Journal

	Date	Accounts Titles	Debit	Credit	
1	1.				1
2	Dec. 31				2
3					3
4					4
5					5
6	2.				6
7	Dec. 31				7
8					8
9					9
10					10
11	3.				11
12	Dec. 31				12
13					13
14					14
15					15
16	4.				16
17	Dec. 31				17
18					18
19					19
20					20
21					21
22					22
23					23
24					24
25					25
26					26
27					27
28					28
29					29
30					30
31					31
32					32
33					33
34					34
35					35
36					36
37					37
38					38
39					39
40					40

Name | Problem 3-5A
Section
Date | Rand Equipment Repair

(a), (c) and (e)

Cash | No. 101

Date	Explanation	Ref.	Debit	Credit	Balance
Sept. 1	Balance	√			4880

Accounts Receivable | No. 112

Date	Explanation	Ref.	Debit	Credit	Balance
Sept. 1	Balance	√			3520

Supplies | No. 126

Date	Explanation	Ref.	Debit	Credit	Balance
Sept. 1	Balance	√			2000

Store Equipment | No. 153

Date	Explanation	Ref.	Debit	Credit	Balance
Sept. 1	Balance	√			15000

Accumulated Depreciation - Equipment | No. 154

Date	Explanation	Ref.	Debit	Credit	Balance
Sept. 1	Balance	√			1500

Accounts Payable | No. 201

Date	Explanation	Ref.	Debit	Credit	Balance
Sept. 1	Balance	√			3400

Name | Problem 3-5A Continued
Section
Date | Rand Equipment Repair

(a), (c) and (e) (Continued)

Unearned Service Revenue — No. 209

Date	Explanation	Ref.	Debit	Credit	Balance
Sept. 1	Balance	√			1400

Salaries Payable — No. 212

Date	Explanation	Ref.	Debit	Credit	Balance
Sept. 1	Balance	√			500

J. Rand, Capital — No. 301

Date	Explanation	Ref.	Debit	Credit	Balance
Sept. 1	Balance	√			18600

Service Revenue — No. 407

Date	Explanation	Ref.	Debit	Credit	Balance

Depreciation Expense — No. 615

Date	Explanation	Ref.	Debit	Credit	Balance

Supplies Expense — No. 631

Date	Explanation	Ref.	Debit	Credit	Balance

Salaries Expense — No. 726

Date	Explanation	Ref.	Debit	Credit	Balance

Rent Expense — No. 729

Date	Explanation	Ref.	Debit	Credit	Balance

Name | Problem 3-5A Continued

Section

Date | Rand Equipment Repair

(b) General Journal J1

Date	Account Titles	Ref.	Debit	Credit
Sept. 8				
10				
12				
15				
17				
20				
22				
25				
27				
29				

(d) & (f)

Rand Equipment Repair
Trial Balances
September 30, 2010

		Before Adjustment		After Adjustment		
		Dr.	Cr.	Dr.	Cr.	
1	Cash					1
2	Accounts Receivable					2
3	Supplies					3
4	Store Equipment					4
5	Accumulated Depreciation					5
6	Accounts Payable					6
7	Unearned Service Revenue					7
8	Salaries Payable					8
9	J. Rand, Capital					9
10	Service Revenue					10
11	Depreciation Expense					11
12	Supplies Expense					12
13	Salaries Expense					13
14	Rent Expense					14
15	Totals					15
16						16
17						17
18						18
19						19
20						20

Name | Problem 3-5A Continued

Section

Date | Rand Equipment Repair

(e) General Journal J1

Date	Account Titles	Ref	Debit	Credit
1.				
Sept. 30				
2.				
Sept. 30				
3.				
Sept. 30				
4.				
Sept. 30				

Name | Problem 3-5A Continued

Section

Date | Rand Equipment Repair

(g)

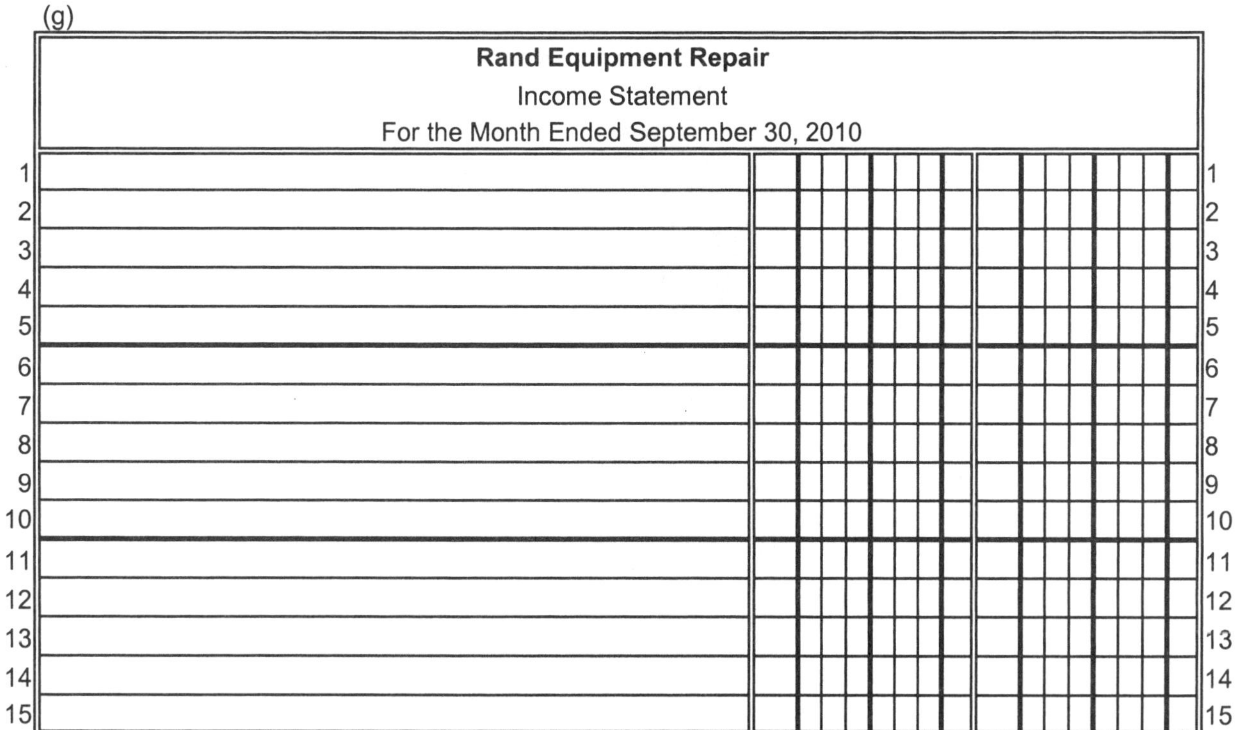

Rand Equipment Repair

Income Statement

For the Month Ended September 30, 2010

Rand Equipment Repair

Owner's Equity Statement

For the Month Ended September 30, 2010

(g) (Continued)

Rand Equipment Repair

Balance Sheet

September 30, 2010

Assets

Liabilities and Owner's Equity

Name

Section

Date

*Problem 3-6A

Givens Graphics Company

(a)

Date	Account Titles	Debit	Credit
1.			
June 30			
2.			
June 30			
3.			
June 30			
4.			
June 30			
5.			
June 30			
6.			
June 30			

Name *Problem 3-6A Continued

Section

Date Givens Graphics Company

(b)

Givens Graphics Company
Adjusted Trial Balance
June 30, 2010

	Debit	Credit

(c)

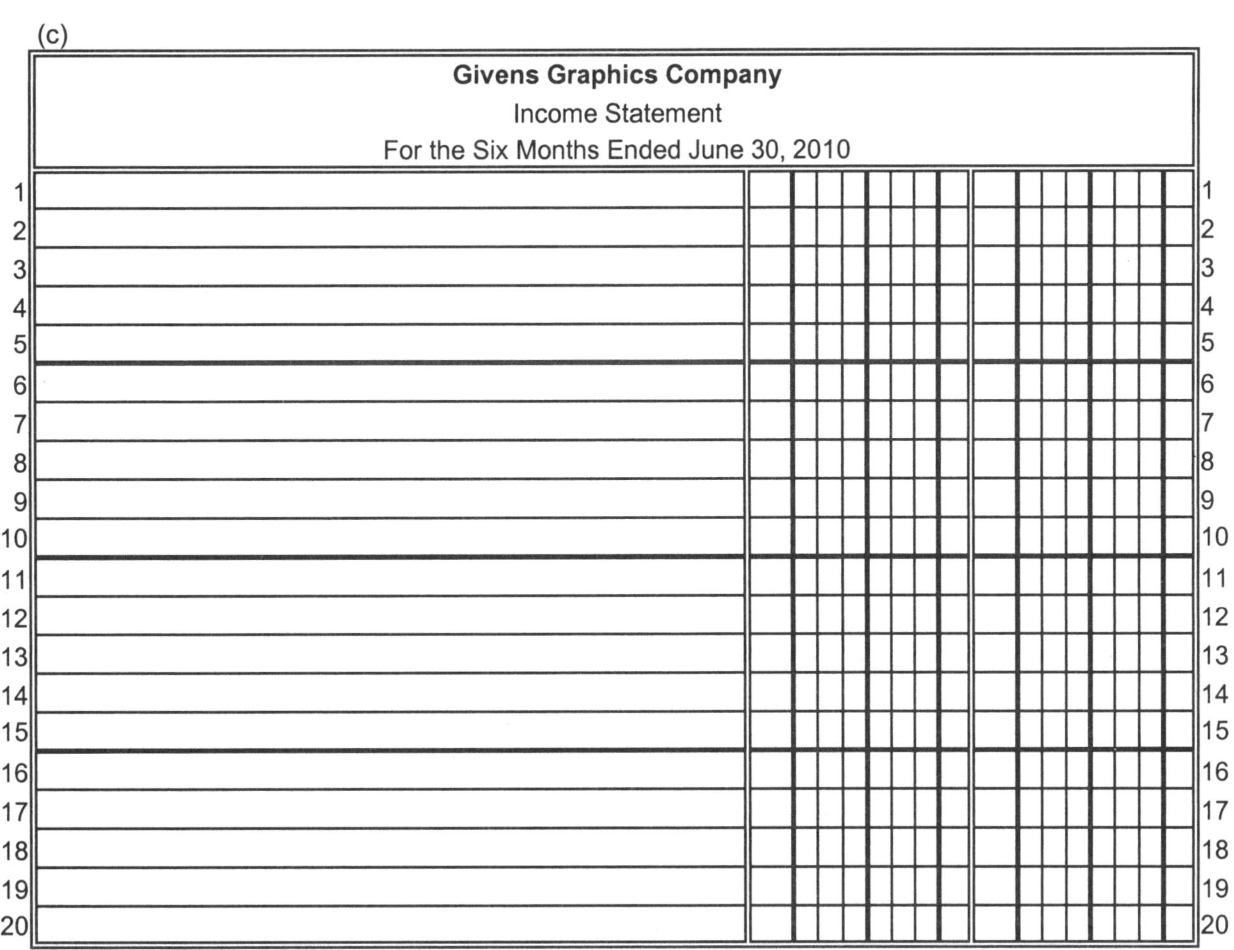

Givens Graphics Company

Owner's Equity Statement

For the Six Months Ended June 30, 2010

(c) (Continued)

Givens Graphics Company
Balance Sheet
June 30, 2010

Assets

Liabilities and Owner's Equity

Name Problem 3-1B

Section

Date Hambone Consulting

(a) General Journal J4

	Date	Account Titles	Ref.	Debit	Credit	
1	2010					1
2	May 31					2
3						3
4						4
5	31					5
6						6
7						7
8						8
9	31					9
10						10
11						11
12						12
13	31					13
14						14
15						15
16						16
17	31					17
18						18
19						19
20						20
21	31					21
22						22
23						23
24						24
25	31					25
26						26
27						27
28						28
29						29
30						30
31						31
32						32
33						33
34						34
35						35
36						36
37						37
38						38
39						39
40						40

(b)

Cash — No. 101

Date	Explanation	Ref.	Debit	Credit	Balance
2010					
May 31	Balance	√			5700

Accounts Receivable — No. 112

Date	Explanation	Ref.	Debit	Credit	Balance
2010					
May 31	Balance	√			6000

Supplies — No. 126

Date	Explanation	Ref.	Debit	Credit	Balance
2010					
May 31	Balance	√			1900

Prepaid Insurance — No. 130

Date	Explanation	Ref.	Debit	Credit	Balance
2010					
May 31	Balance	√			3600

Office Furniture — No. 149

Date	Explanation	Ref.	Debit	Credit	Balance
2008					
May 31	Balance	√			10200

Accumulated Depreciation - Office Furniture — No, 150

Date	Explanation	Ref.	Debit	Credit	Balance

Accounts Payable — No. 201

Date	Explanation	Ref.	Debit	Credit	Balance
2010					
May 31	Balance	√			4500

(b) (Continued)

Unearned Service Revenue No. 209

Date	Explanation	Ref.	Debit	Credit	Balance
2010					
May 31	Balance	√			2000

Salaries Payable No. 212

Date	Explanation	Ref.	Debit	Credit	Balance

Travel Payable No. 229

Date	Explanation	Ref.	Debit	Credit	Balance

K. Ham, Capital No. 301

Date	Explanation	Ref.	Debit	Credit	Balance
2010					
May 31	Balance	√			17700

Service Revenue No. 400

Date	Explanation	Ref.	Debit	Credit	Balance
2010					
May 31	Balance	√			7500

Supplies Expense No. 631

Date	Explanation	Ref.	Debit	Credit	Balance

Depreciation Expense No. 717

Date	Explanation	Ref.	Debit	Credit	Balance

(b) (Continued)

Insurance Expense No. 722

Date	Explanation	Ref.	Debit	Credit	Balance

Salaries Expense No. 726

Date	Explanation	Ref.	Debit	Credit	Balance
2010					
May 31	Balance	√			3400

Rent Expense No. 729

Date	Explanation	Ref.	Debit	Credit	Balance
2010					
May 31	Balance	√			900

Travel Expense No. 736

Date	Explanation	Ref.	Debit	Credit	Balance

(c)

Hambone Consulting
Adjusted Trial Balance
May 31, 2010

	Debit	Credit
Cash		
Accounts Rdeceivable		
Prepaid Insurance		
Supplies		
Office Furniture		
Accumulated Depreciation - Office Furniture		
Accounts Payable		
Travel Payable		
Salaries Payable		
Unearned Service Revenue		
K. Ham, Capital		
Service Revenue		
Salaries Expense		
Rent Expense		
Depreciation Expense		
Insurance Expense		
Travel Expense		
Supplies Expense		
Totals		

Name Problem 3-2B

Section

Date Mound View Motel

(a) General Journal J1

Date	Account Titles	Ref.	Debit	Credit
May 31				
31				
31				
31				
31				
31				
31				

(b)

Cash No. 101

Date	Explanation	Ref.	Debit	Credit	Balance
May 31	Balance	√			3500

Supplies No. 126

Date	Explanation	Ref.	Debit	Credit	Balance
May 31	Balance	√			2200

Name | Problem 3-2B Continued

Section

Date | Mound View Motel

(b)

Prepaid Insurance | No. 130

Date	Explanation	Ref.	Debit	Credit	Balance
May 31	Balance	√			2280

Land | No. 140

Date	Explanation	Ref.	Debit	Credit	Balance
May 31	Balance	√			12000

Lodge | No. 141

Date	Explanation	Ref.	Debit	Credit	Balance
May 31	Balance	√			60000

Accumulated Depreciation - Lodge | No. 142

Date	Explanation	Ref.	Debit	Credit	Balance

Furniture | No. 149

Date	Explanation	Ref.	Debit	Credit	Balance
May 31	Balance	√			15000

Accumulated Depreciation - Furniture | No. 150

Date	Explanation	Ref.	Debit	Credit	Balance

Accounts Payable | No. 201

Date	Explanation	Ref.	Debit	Credit	Balance
May 31	Balance	√			4800

Unearned Rent Revenue | No. 209

Date	Explanation	Ref.	Debit	Credit	Balance
May 31	Balance	√			3300

Salaries Payable | No. 212

Date	Explanation	Ref.	Debit	Credit	Balance

Interest Payable | No. 230

Date	Explanation	Ref.	Debit	Credit	Balance

(b) (Continued)

Mortgage Payable No. 275

Date	Explanation	Ref.	Debit	Credit	Balance
May 31	Balance	√			35000

Kevin Henry, Capital No. 301

Date	Explanation	Ref.	Debit	Credit	Balance
May 31	Balance	√			46380

Rent Revenue No. 429

Date	Explanation	Ref.	Debit	Credit	Balance
May 31	Balance	√			10300

Advertising Expense No. 610

Date	Explanation	Ref.	Debit	Credit	Balance
May 31	Balance	√			600

Depreciation Expense - Lodge No. 619

Date	Explanation	Ref.	Debit	Credit	Balance

Depreciation Expense - Furniture No. 621

Date	Explanation	Ref.	Debit	Credit	Balance

Supplies Expense No. 631

Date	Explanation	Ref.	Debit	Credit	Balance

Interest Expense No. 718

Date	Explanation	Ref.	Debit	Credit	Balance

Insurance Expense No. 722

Date	Explanation	Ref.	Debit	Credit	Balance

Salaries Expense No. 726

Date	Explanation	Ref.	Debit	Credit	Balance
May 31	Balance	√			3300

(b) (Continued)

Utilities Expense — No. 732

Date	Explanation	Ref.	Debit	Credit	Balance
May 31	Balance	√			900

(c)

Mound View Motel
Adjusted Trial Balance
May 31, 2010

	Debit	Credit
Cash		
Supplies		
Prepaid Insurance		
Land		
Lodge		
Accum. Depreciation - Lodge		
Furniture		
Accum. Depreciation - Furniture		
Accounts Payable		
Unearned Rent Revenue		
Salaries Payable		
Interest Payable		
Mortgage Payable		
Kevin Henry, Capital		
Rent Revenue		
Advertising Expense		
Depr. Expense - Lodge		
Depr. Expense - Furniture		
Supplies Expense		
Interest Expense		
Insurance Expense		
Salaries Expense		
Utilities Expense		
Totals		

Name

Section

Date

(d)

Mound View Motel

Income Statement

For the Month Ended May 31, 2010

Mound View Motel

Owner's Equity Statement

For the Month Ended May 31, 2010

(d) (Continued)

Mound View Motel

Balance Sheet

May 31, 2010

Assets

Liabilities and Owner's Equity

Name | Problem 3-3B

Section

Date | Poblano Co.

(a)

Date	Accounts Titles	Debit	Credit
Sept. 30			
30			
30			
30			
30			
30			
30			

(b)

Poblano Co.

Income Statement

For the Quarter Ended September 30, 2010

Revenues:		
Expenses:		

(b) (Continued)

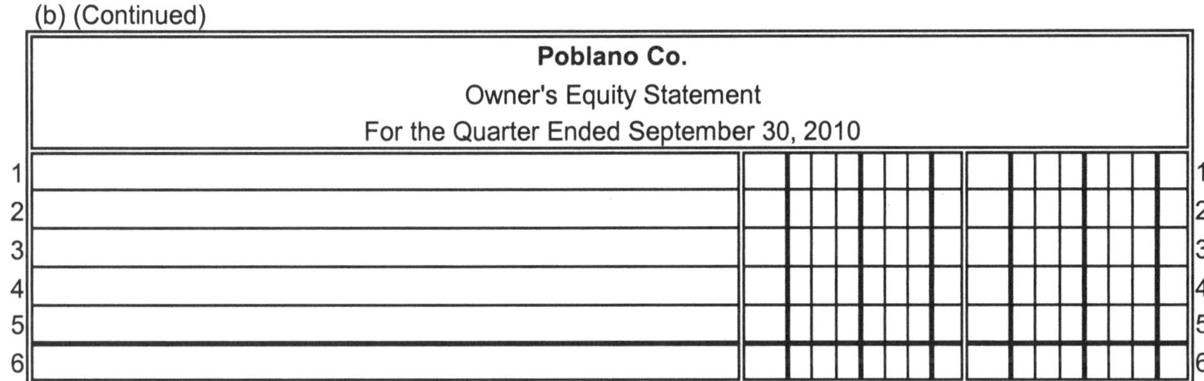

Poblano Co.

Balance Sheet

September 30, 2010

Assets

Liabilities and Owner's Equity

(c)

Name Problem 3-4B

Section

Date Obi Company

General Journal

Date	Accounts Titles	Debit	Credit
1.			
Dec. 31			
2.			
Dec. 31			
3.			
Dec. 31			
4.			
Dec. 31			

Name | Problem 3-5B

Section

Date | Morelli Equipment Repair

(a), (c) and (e)

Cash — No. 101

Date	Explanation	Ref.	Debit	Credit	Balance
Nov. 1	Balance	√			2400

Accounts Receivable — No. 112

Date	Explanation	Ref.	Debit	Credit	Balance
Nov. 1	Balance	√			4250

Supplies — No. 126

Date	Explanation	Ref.	Debit	Credit	Balance
Nov. 1	Balance	√			1800

Store Equipment — No. 153

Date	Explanation	Ref.	Debit	Credit	Balance
Nov. 1	Balance	√			12000

Accumulated Depreciation - Store Equipment — No. 154

Date	Explanation	Ref.	Debit	Credit	Balance
Nov. 1	Balance	√			2000

Accounts Payable — No. 201

Date	Explanation	Ref.	Debit	Credit	Balance
Nov. 1	Balance	√			2600

Name
Section
Date

Problem 3-5B Continued

Morelli Equipment Repair

(a), (c) and (e) (Continued)

Unearned Service Revenue — No. 209

Date	Explanation	Ref.	Debit	Credit	Balance
Nov. 1	Balance	√			1200

Salaries Payable — No. 212

Date	Explanation	Ref.	Debit	Credit	Balance
Nov. 1	Balance	√			700

V. Morelli, Capital — No. 301

Date	Explanation	Ref.	Debit	Credit	Balance
Nov. 1	Balance	√			13950

Service Revenue — No. 407

Date	Explanation	Ref.	Debit	Credit	Balance

Depreciation Expense — No. 615

Date	Explanation	Ref.	Debit	Credit	Balance

Supplies Expense — No. 631

Date	Explanation	Ref.	Debit	Credit	Balance

Salaries Expense — No. 726

Date	Explanation	Ref.	Debit	Credit	Balance

Rent Expense — No. 729

Date	Explanation	Ref.	Debit	Credit	Balance

Name | Problem 3-5B Continued

Section

Date | Morelli Equipment Repair

(b) General Journal J1

Date	Account Titles	Ref	Debit	Credit
Nov. 8				
10				
12				
15				
17				
20				
22				
25				
27				
29				

(d) & (f)

Morelli Equipment Repair
Trial Balances
November 30, 2010

		Before Adjustment		After Adjustment		
		Dr.	Cr.	Dr.	Cr.	
1	Cash					1
2	Accounts Receivable					2
3	Supplies					3
4	Equipment					4
5	Accumulated Depreciation					5
6	Accounts Payable					6
7	Unearned Service Revenue					7
8	Salaries Payable					8
9	V. Morelli, Capital					9
10	Service Revenue					10
11	Depreciation Expense					11
12	Supplies Expense					12
13	Salaries Expense					13
14	Rent Expense					14
15	Totals					15
16						16
17						17
18						18
19						19
20						20

Name Problem 3-5B Continued

Section

Date Morelli Equipment Repair

(e) General Journal J1

Date	Account Titles	Ref	Debit	Credit
1.				
Nov. 30				
2.				
Nov. 30				
3.				
Nov. 30				
4.				
Nov. 30				

(g)

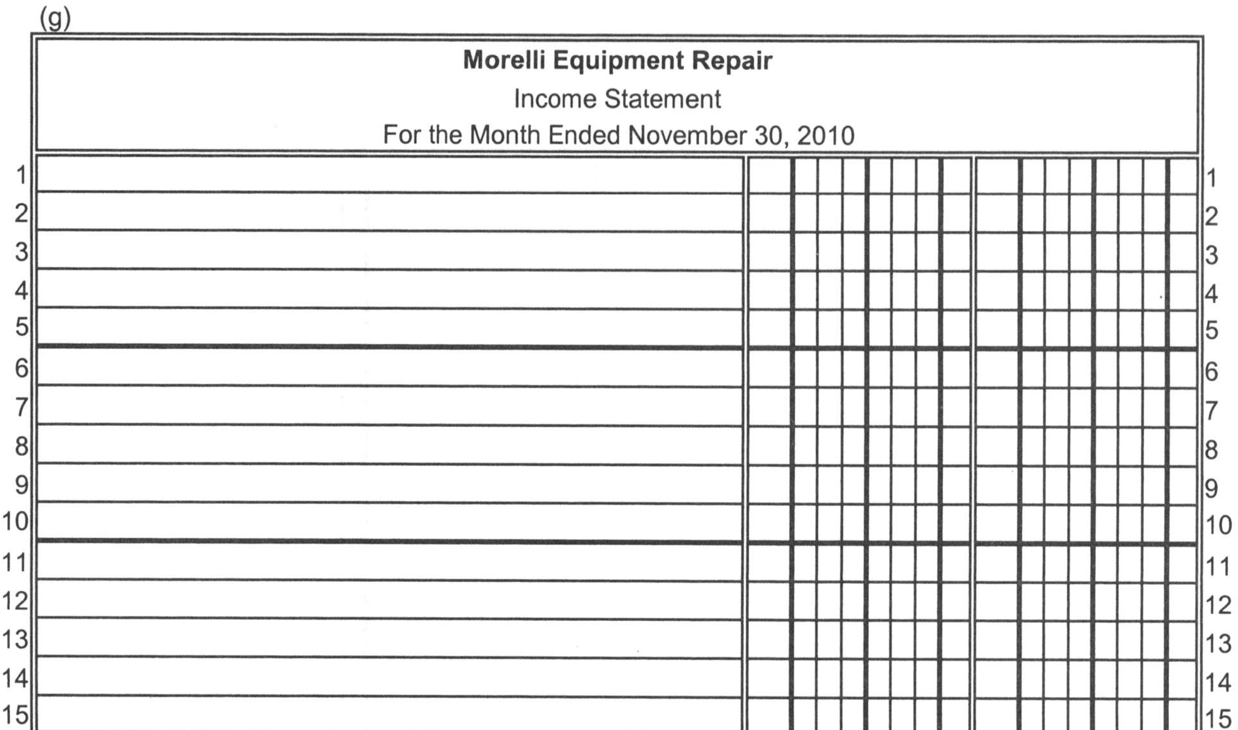

Morelli Equipment Repair
Income Statement
For the Month Ended November 30, 2010

Morelli Equipment Repair
Owner's Equity Statement
For the Month Ended November 30, 2010

(g) (Continued)

Morelli Equipment Repair

Balance Sheet

November 30, 2010

Assets

Liabilities and Owner's Equity

Name

Section

Date

Chapter 3 Comparative Analysis Problem

PepsiCo, Inc. versus Coca-Cola Company

	PepsiCo	Coca-Cola
Increase (decrease) from 2006 to 2007 in:		
(a) Property, plant, and equipment, net		
(b) Selling, general, and administrative expenses		
(c) Long-term debt (obligations)		
(d) Net income		
(e) Cash and cash equivalents		

Name

Section

Date

(a)

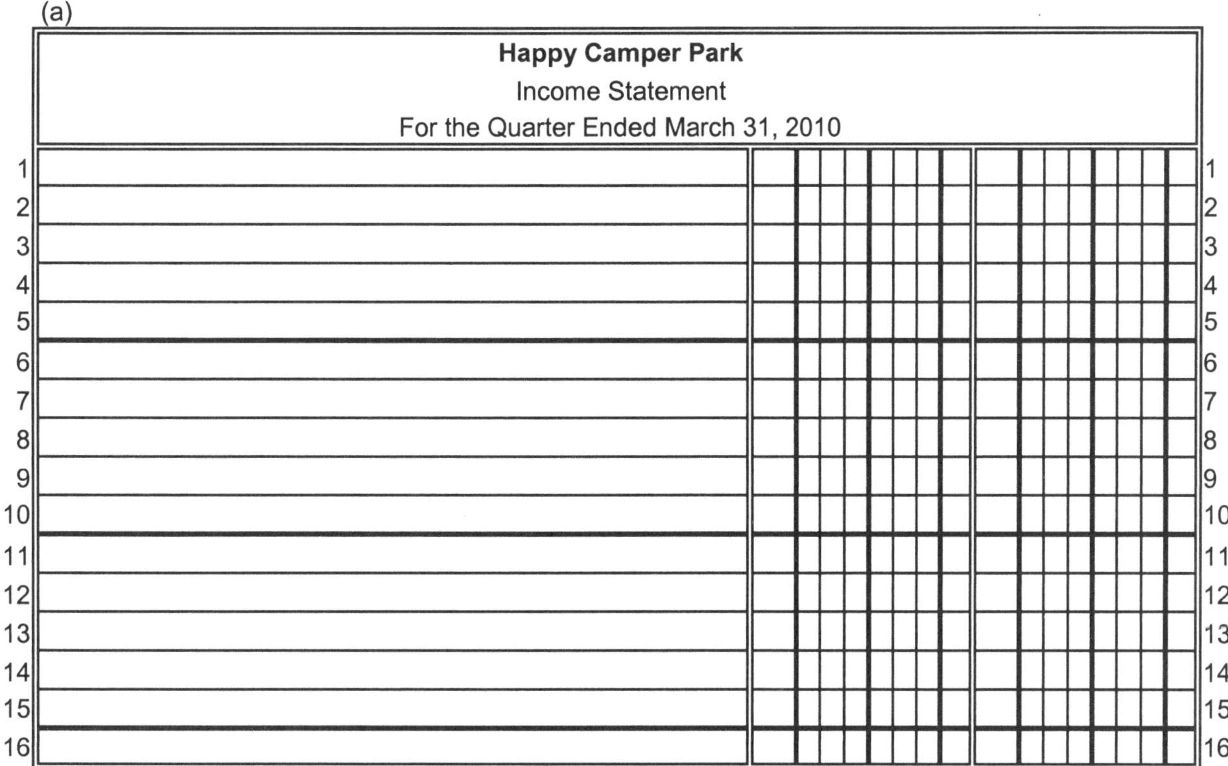

(b)

Name

Section

Date

BE4-1

(a) Prepare a trial balance on the worksheet.

(b) Enter adjusted balances.

(c) Extend adjusted balances to appropriate statement columns.

(d) Total the statement columns, compute net income (loss), and complete worksheet.

(e) Enter adjustment data.

BE4-2 is on the next page

BE4-3

Account	Income Statement Debit	Income Statement Credit	Balance Sheet Debit	Balance Sheet Credit
Accum. Depreciation				
Depreciation Expense				
N. Batan, Capital				
N. Batan, Drawing				
Service Revenue				
Supplies				
Accounts Payable				

BE4-4

Date	Account Titles	Debit	Credit
Dec. 31			
31			
31			
31			

Brief Exercise 4-2

Ley Company

See Appendix

Name

Section

Date

BE4-5

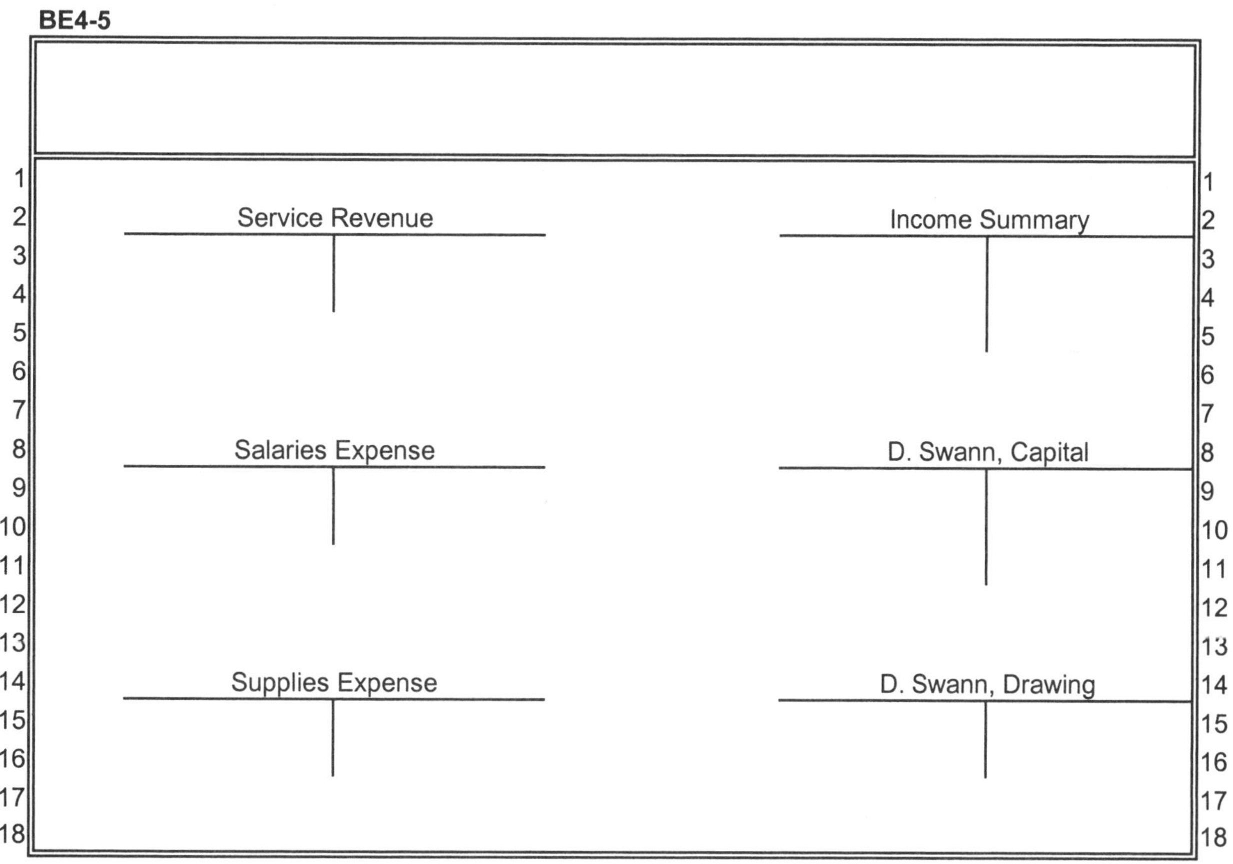

Section

Date

BE4-6

	Date	Account Titles	Debit	Credit	
1	July 31				1
2					2
3					3
4	31				4
5					5
6					6

Green Fee Revenue

Date	Explanation	Ref.	Debit	Credit	Balance

Salaries Expense

Date	Explanation	Ref.	Debit	Credit	Balance

Maintenenace Expense

Date	Explanation	Ref.	Debit	Credit	Balance

Name

Section

Date

BE4-9

	Account Titles	Debit	Credit
1.			
2.			

BE4-10

Diaz Company

Partial Balance Sheet

Current assets		

BE4-11

	Accounts payable
	Accounts receivable
	Accumulated depreciation
	Building
	Cash
	Copyrights
	Income tax payable
	Investment in long-term bonds
	Land
	Merchandise inventory
	Patent
	Supplies

***BE4-12**

Date	Account Titles	Debit	Credit
Nov. 1			

Name

Section

Date

DO IT! 4-2

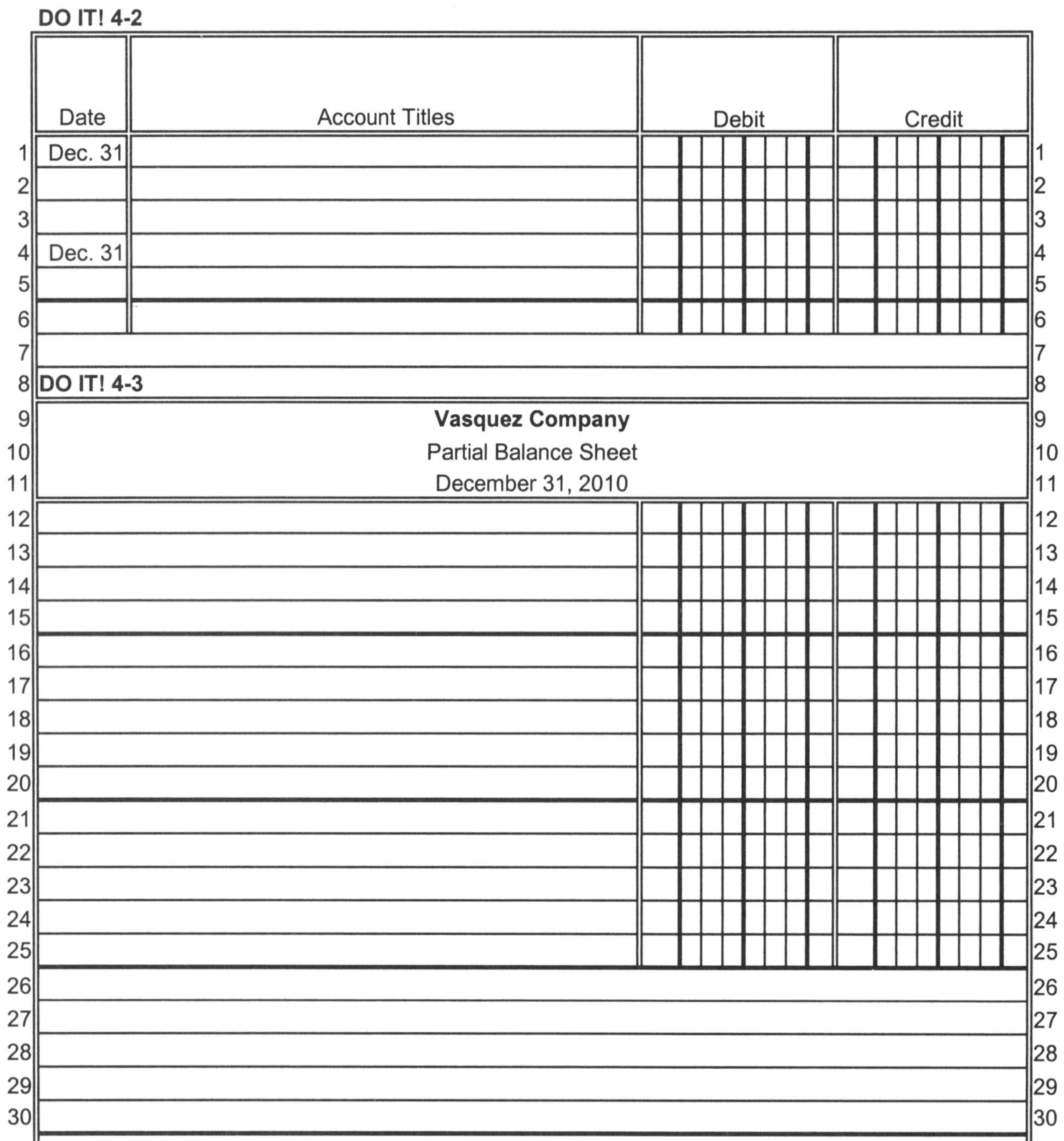

Date	Account Titles	Debit	Credit
Dec. 31			
Dec. 31			

DO IT! 4-3

Vasquez Company

Partial Balance Sheet

December 31, 2010

Exercise 4-1

Briscoe Company

See Appendix

Name

Section

Date

Exercise 4-2

Goode Company

Goode Company
(Partial) Worksheet
For the Month Ended April 30, 2010

	Account Titles	Adjusted Trial Balance		Income Statement		Balance Sheet		
		Dr.	Cr.	Dr.	Cr.	Dr.	Cr.	
1	Cash	13752						1
2	Accounts Receivable	7840						2
3	Prepaid Rent	2280						3
4	Equipment	23050						4
5	Accumulated Depreciation		4921					5
6	Notes Payable		5700					6
7	Accounts Payable		5672					7
8	T. Goode, Capital		30960					8
9	T. Goode, Drawing	3650						9
10	Service Revenue		15590					10
11	Salaries Expense	10840						11
12	Rent Expense	760						12
13	Depreciation Expense	671						13
14	Interest Expense	57						14
15	Interest Payable		57					15
16	Totals	62900	62900					16
17	Net Income							17
18	Totals							18
19								19
20								20

Name Exercise 4-3

Section

Date Goode Company

Goode Company

Income Statement

For the Month Ended April 30, 2010

Goode Company

Owner's Equity Statement

For the Month Ended April 30, 2010

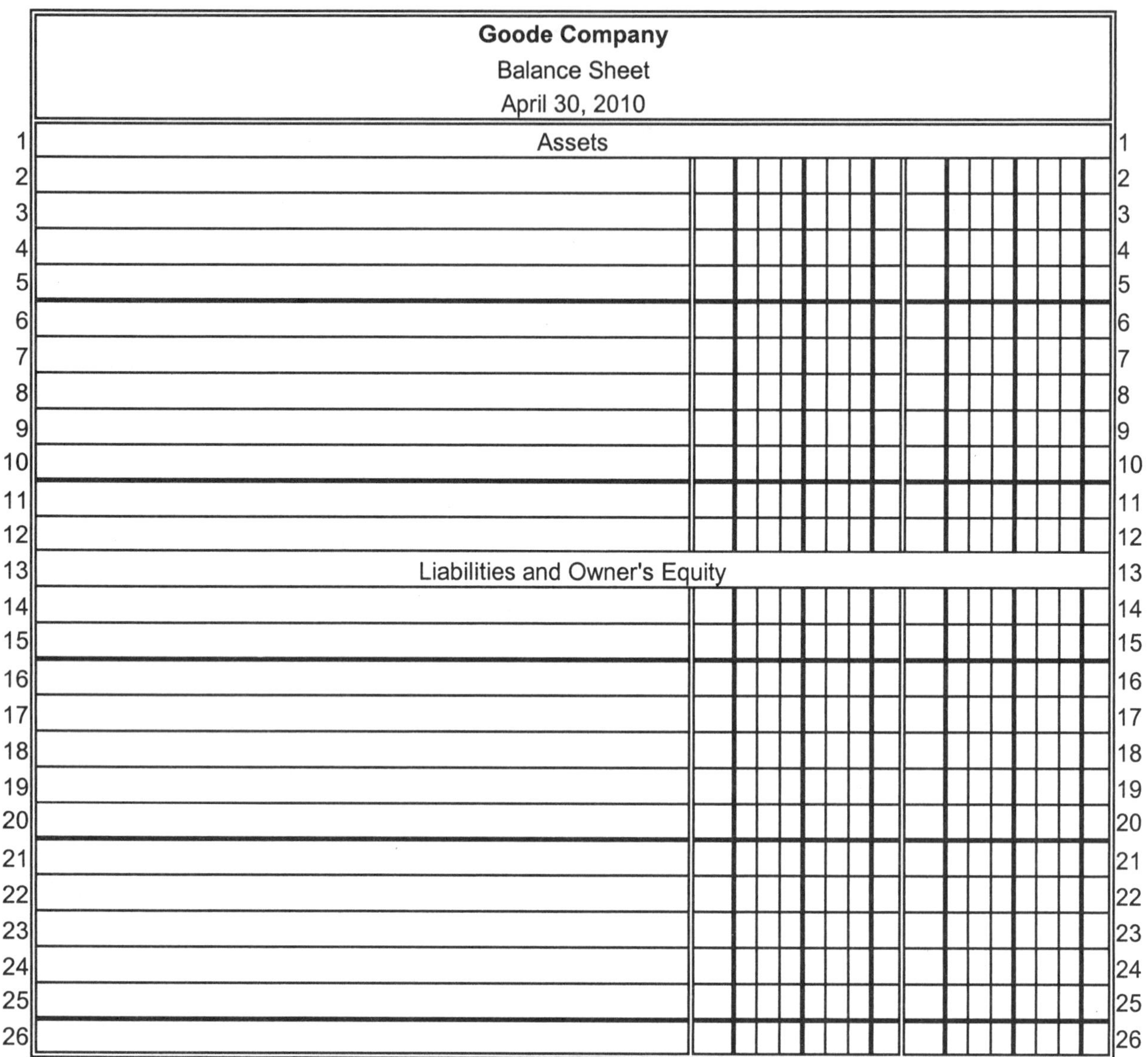

Goode Company
Balance Sheet
April 30, 2010

Assets

Liabilities and Owner's Equity

Name | Exercise 4-4

Section

Date | Goode Company

(a)

Date	Account Titles	Debit	Credit
Apr. 30			
30			
30			
30			

(b)

INCOME SUMMARY

T. GOODE, CAPITAL

(c)

Goode Company
Post-Closing Trial Balance
April 30, 2010

	Debit	Credit

Name	Exercise 4-5
Section	
Date	Mears Company

(a)

	Account Titles	Debit	Credit	
1				1
2				2
3				3
4				4
5				5
6				6
7				7
8				8
9				9
10				10
11				11
12				12

(b)

		Income Statement		Balance Sheet		
		Debit	Credit	Debit	Credit	
1	Accounts Receivable					1
2	Prepaid Insurance					2
3	Accum. Depreciation					3
4	Salaries Payable					4
5	Service Revenue					5
6	Salaries Expense					6
7	Insurance Expense					7
8	Depr. Expense					8
9						9

Name | Exercise 4-6

Section

Date | Nicholson Company

(a)

	Account Titles	Trial Balance		Adjustments		Adjusted Trial Balance		
		Debit	Credit	Debit	Credit	Debit	Credit	
1	Accounts Receivable					34000		1
2	Prepaid Insurance	26000				20000		2
3	Supplies	7000						3
4	Accumulated Depreciation		12000					4
5	Salaries Payable						5000	5
6	Service Revenue		88000				97000	6
7	Insurance Expense							7
8	Depreciation Expense					10000		8
9	Supplies Expense					5000		9
10	Salaries Expense					49000		10

(b)

	Account Titles	Debit	Credit	
1				1
2				2
3				3
4				4
5				5
6				6
7				7
8				8
9				9
10				10
11				11
12				12
13				13
14				14

Name Exercise 4-7

Section

Date Emil Skoda Company

(a)

Account Titles	Debit	Credit

(b)

Emil Skoda Company

Post-Closing Trial Balance

For the Month Ended June 30, 2010

Account Titles	Debit	Credit

Name | Exercise 4-8

Section

Date | Apachi Company

(a)

General Journal | J15

Date	Account Titles	Ref.	Debit	Credit
July 31				
31				
31				
31				

(b)

B. J. Apachi, Capital | No. 301

Date	Explanation	Ref.	Debit	Credit	Balance

Income Summary | No. 350

Date	Explanation	Ref.	Debit	Credit	Balance

(c)

Apachi Company
Post-Closing Trial Balance
July 31, 2010

	Debit	Credit

Name

Section

Date

Exercise 4-9

Apachi Company

(a)

Apachi Company

Income Statement

For The Year Ended July 31, 2010

Apachi Company

Owner's Equity Statement

For the Year Ended July 31, 2010

(b)

Apachi Company

Balance Sheet

July 31, 2010

Assets

Liabilities and Owner's Equity

Name

Section

Date

Exercises 4-11 and 4-13

E4-11

Date	Account Titles	Debit	Credit
(a)			
June 30			
30			
30			
30			

(b)

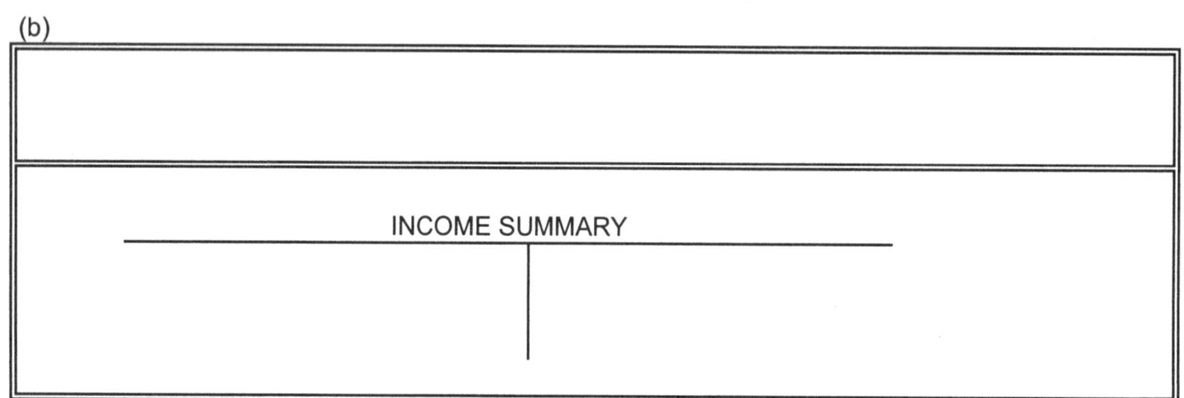

E4-13

Item	Account Titles	Debit	Credit
1.			
2.			
3.			

Name Exercise 4-12

Section

Date Max Weinberg Company

Item	Account Titles	Debit	Credit
(a)			
1.			
2.			
3.			
(b)			
1.			
2.			
3.			

Name
Section
Date

Exercise 4-14

Karr Bowling Alley

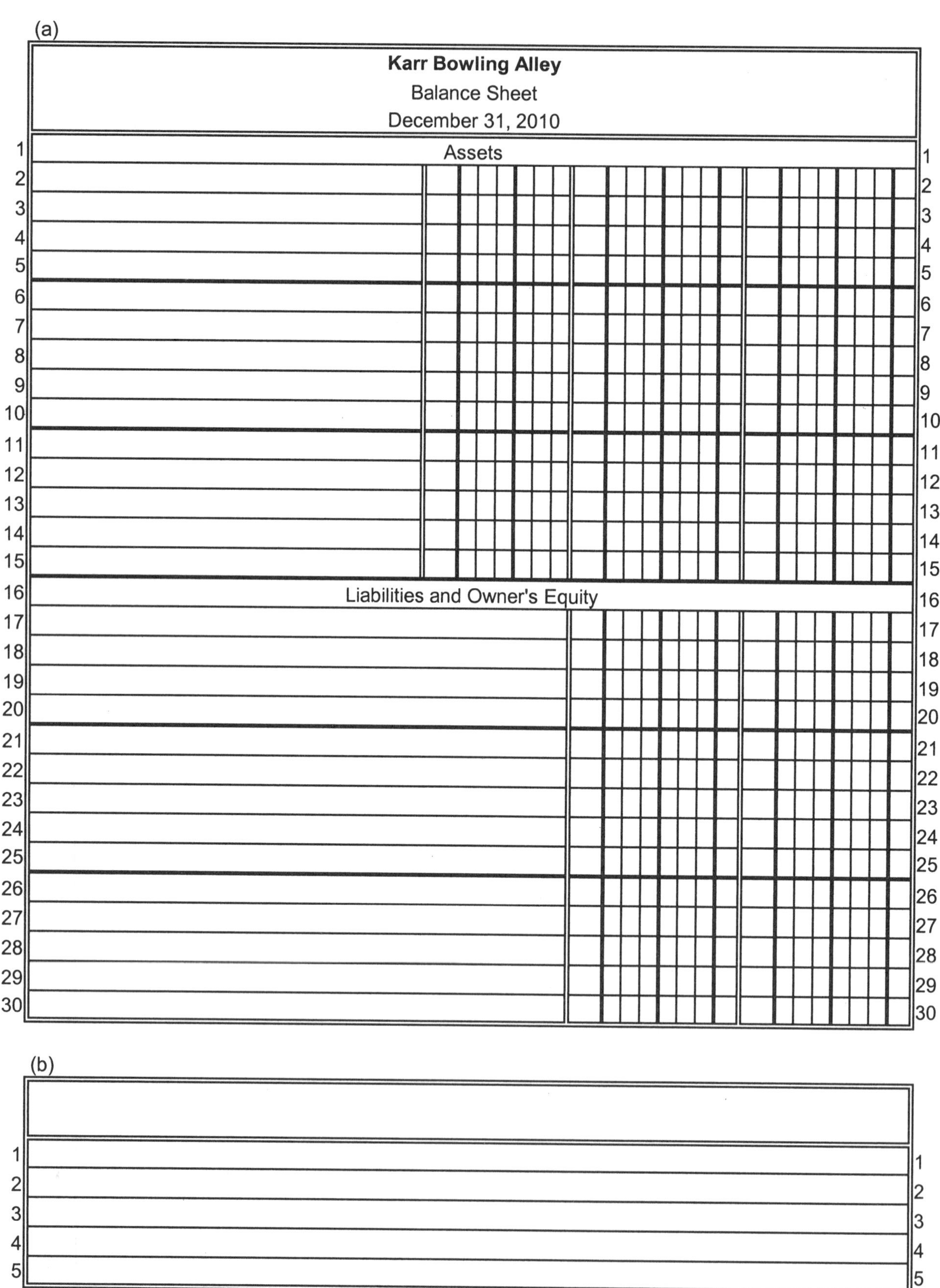

(a)

Karr Bowling Alley

Balance Sheet

December 31, 2010

Assets

Liabilities and Owner's Equity

(b)

Name

Section

Date

E4-15

	Accounts Payable
	Accounts Receivable
	Accumulated Depreciation
	Buildings
	Cash
	Roberts, Capital
	Patents
	Salaries Payable
	Inventories
	Investments
	Land
	Long-term Debt
	Supplies
	Office Equipment
	Prepaid Expenses

***E4-18**

Date	Account Titles	Debit	Credit
(a)			
Dec. 31			
Jan. 6			
(b)			
Dec. 31			
Jan. 1			
6			

Name

Exercise 4-16

Section

Date

R. Stevens Company

R. Stevens Company

Balance Sheet

December 31, 2010

(in thousands)

Assets

Liabilities and Owner's Equity

Name | Exercise 4-17

Section

Date | B. Snyder Company

(a)

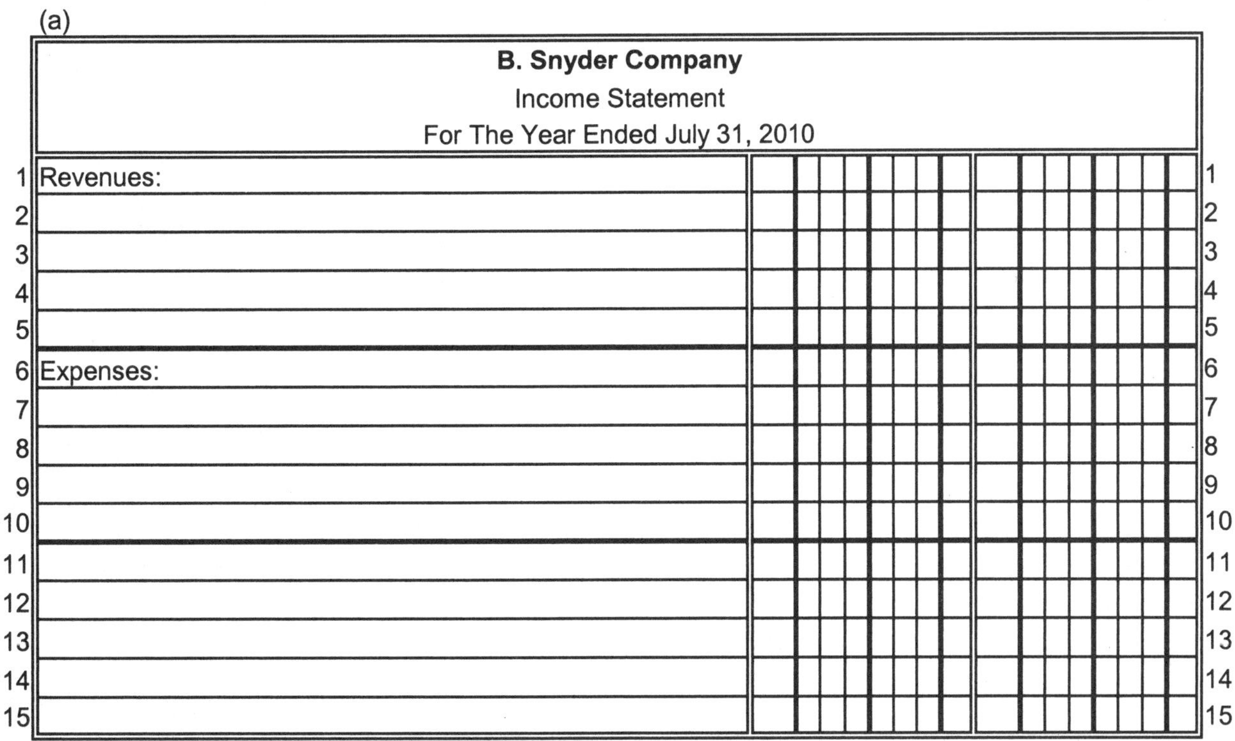

B. Snyder Company

Income Statement

For The Year Ended July 31, 2010

Revenues:

Expenses:

B. Snyder Company

Owner's Equity Statement

For the Year Ended July 31, 2010

(b)

B. Snyder Company
Balance Sheet
July 31, 2010

Assets

Liabilities and Owner's Equity

Name *Exercise 4-19

Section

Date Oslo Employment Agency

(a) & (b)

Date	Account Titles	Debit	Credit
Dec. 31			
31			
Jan. 1			
1			

(c) & (e)

ACCOUNTS RECEIVABLE

Debit	Credit
Dec 31 Bal 19,500	

COMMISSION REVENUE

Debit	Credit
	Dec 31 Bal 87,500

INTEREST PAYABLE

Debit	Credit

INTEREST EXPENSE

Debit	Credit
Dec 31 Bal 6,300	

(d)

Date	Account Titles		Debit	Credit
	(1)			
Jan. 10				
	(2)			
15				

Problem 4-1A

Thomas Magnum, P.I.

See Appendix

Name

Section

Date

(b)

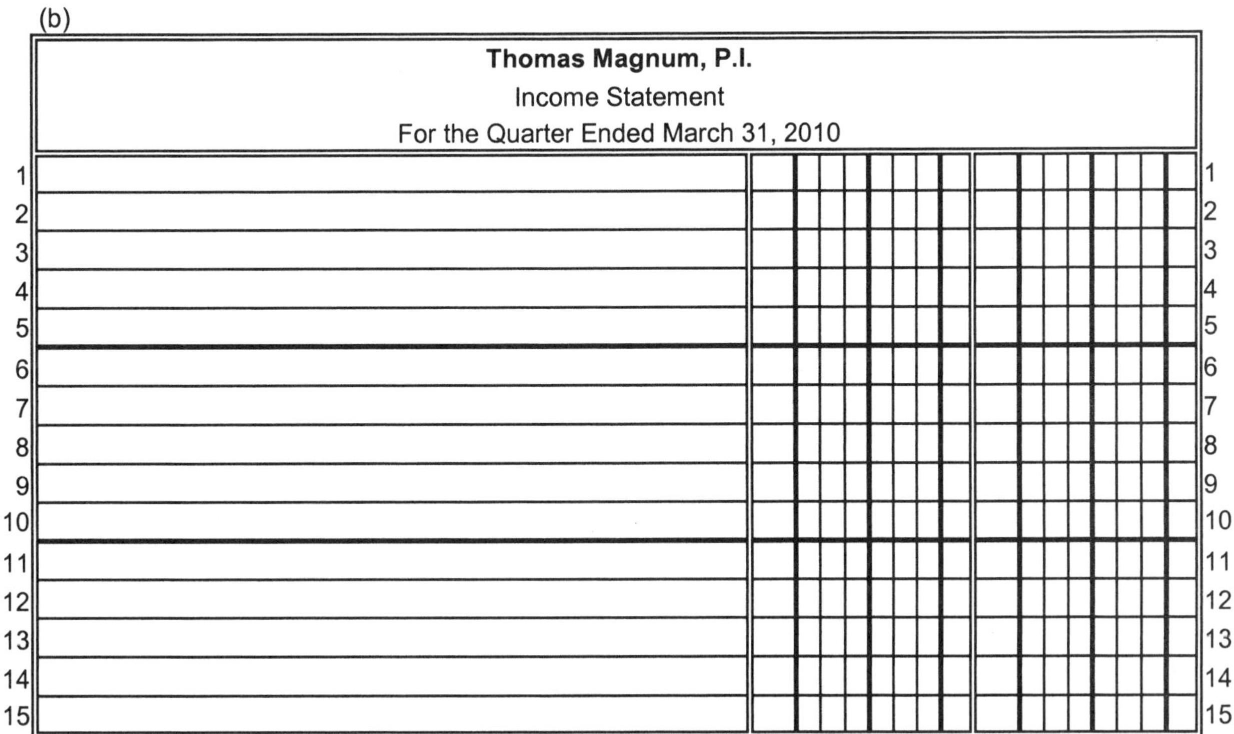

Thomas Magnum, P.I.

Income Statement

For the Quarter Ended March 31, 2010

Thomas Magnum, P.I.

Owner's Equity Statement

For the Quarter Ended March 31, 2010

(b) (Continued)

Thomas Magnum, P.I.
Balance Sheet
March 31, 2010

Assets

Liabilities and Owner's Equity

(c)

General Journal

Date	Account Titles	Debit	Credit
	Adjusting Entries		
Mar. 31			
31			
31			
31			
31			

(d)

General Journal

Date	Account Titles	Debit	Credit
	Closing Entries		
Mar. 31			
31			
31			
31			

Name Problem 4-2A

Section

Date Porter Company

(a)

Porter Company
Worksheet (Partial)
For the Year Ended December 31, 2010

	Account		Adjusted Trial Balance		Income Statement		Balance Sheet		
	No.	Titles	Dr.	Cr.	Dr.	Cr.	Dr.	Cr.	
1	101	Cash	18800						1
2	112	Accounts Receivable	16200						2
3	126	Supplies	2300						3
4	130	Prepaid Insurance	4400						4
5	151	Office Equipment	44000						5
6	152	Accum. Depr. - Office Equip.		20000					6
7	200	Notes Payable		20000					7
8	201	Accounts Payable		8000					8
9	212	Salaries Payable		2600					9
10	230	Interest Payable		1000					10
11	301	B. Porter, Capital		36000					11
12	306	B. Porter, Drawing	12000						12
13	400	Service Revenue		77800					13
14	610	Advertising Expense	12000						14
15	631	Supplies Expense	3700						15
16	711	Depreciation Expense	8000						16
17	722	Insurance Expense	4000						17
18	726	Salaries Expense	39000						18
19	905	Interest Expense	1000						19
20		Totals	165400	165400					20
21		Net Income							21
22		Totals							22
23									23

(b)

Porter Company
Income Statement
For the Year Ended December 31, 2010

Porter Company
Owner's Equity Statement
For the Year Ended December 31, 2010

(b) (Continued)

Porter Company
Balance Sheet
December 31, 2010

Assets

Liabilities and Owner's Equity

Name	Problem 4-2A Continued
Section	
Date	Porter Company

(c)

General Journal J14

Date	Account Titles	Ref.	Debit	Credit
Dec. 31				
31				
31				
31				

(d)

B. Porter, Capital No.301

Date	Explanation	Ref.	Debit	Credit	Balance
Dec 31	Balance	√			36000

B. Porter, Drawing No. 306

Date	Explanation	Ref.	Debit	Credit	Balance
Dec 31	Balance	√			12000

Income Summary No. 350

Date	Explanation	Ref.	Debit	Credit	Balance

(d) (Continued)

Service Revenue No. 400

Date	Explanation	Ref.	Debit	Credit	Balance
Dec 31	Balance	√			77800

Advertising Expense No. 610

Date	Explanation	Ref.	Debit	Credit	Balance
Dec 31	Balance	√			12000

Supplies Expense No. 631

Date	Explanation	Ref.	Debit	Credit	Balance
Dec 31	Balance	√			3700

Depreciation Expense No. 711

Date	Explanation	Ref.	Debit	Credit	Balance
Dec 31	Balance	√			8000

Insurance Expense No. 722

Date	Explanation	Ref.	Debit	Credit	Balance
Dec 31	Balance	√			4000

Salaries Expense No. 726

Date	Explanation	Ref.	Debit	Credit	Balance
Dec 31	Balance	√			39000

Interest Expense No. 905

Date	Explanation	Ref.	Debit	Credit	Balance
Dec 31	Balance	√			1000

(e)

Porter Company
Post-Closing Trial Balance
December 31, 2010

	Debit	Credit

Name | Problem 4-3A
Section
Date | Woods Company

(a)

Woods Company
Income Statement
For the Year Ended December 31, 2010

Woods Company
Owner's Equity Statement
For the Year Ended December 31, 2010

(a) (Continued)

Woods Company
Balance Sheet
December 31, 2010

Assets

Liabilities and Owner's Equity

Name Problem 4-3A Continued

Section

Date Woods Company

(b) General Journal

Date	Accounts Titles	Ref.	Debit	Credit
	Closing Entries			
Dec. 31				
31				
31				
31				

(c)

S. Woods, Capital No. 301

	12/31 Bal 34,000

S. Woods, Drawing No.306

12/31 Bal 7,200	

Income Summary No. 350

Service Revenue No. 400

	12/31 Bal 44,000

Repair Expense No. 622

12/31 Bal 5,400	

Depreciation Expense No. 711

12/31 Bal 2,800	

Insurance Expense No. 722

12/31 Bal 1,200	

Salaries Expense No. 726

12/31 Bal 35,200	

Utilities Expense No. 732

12/31 Bal 4,000	

(d)

Woods Company
Post-Closing Trial Balance
December 31, 2010

		Debit	Credit	
1				1
2				2
3				3
4				4
5				5
6				6
7				7
8				8
9				9
10				10

Problem 4-4A

Disney Amusement Park

See Appendix

(b)

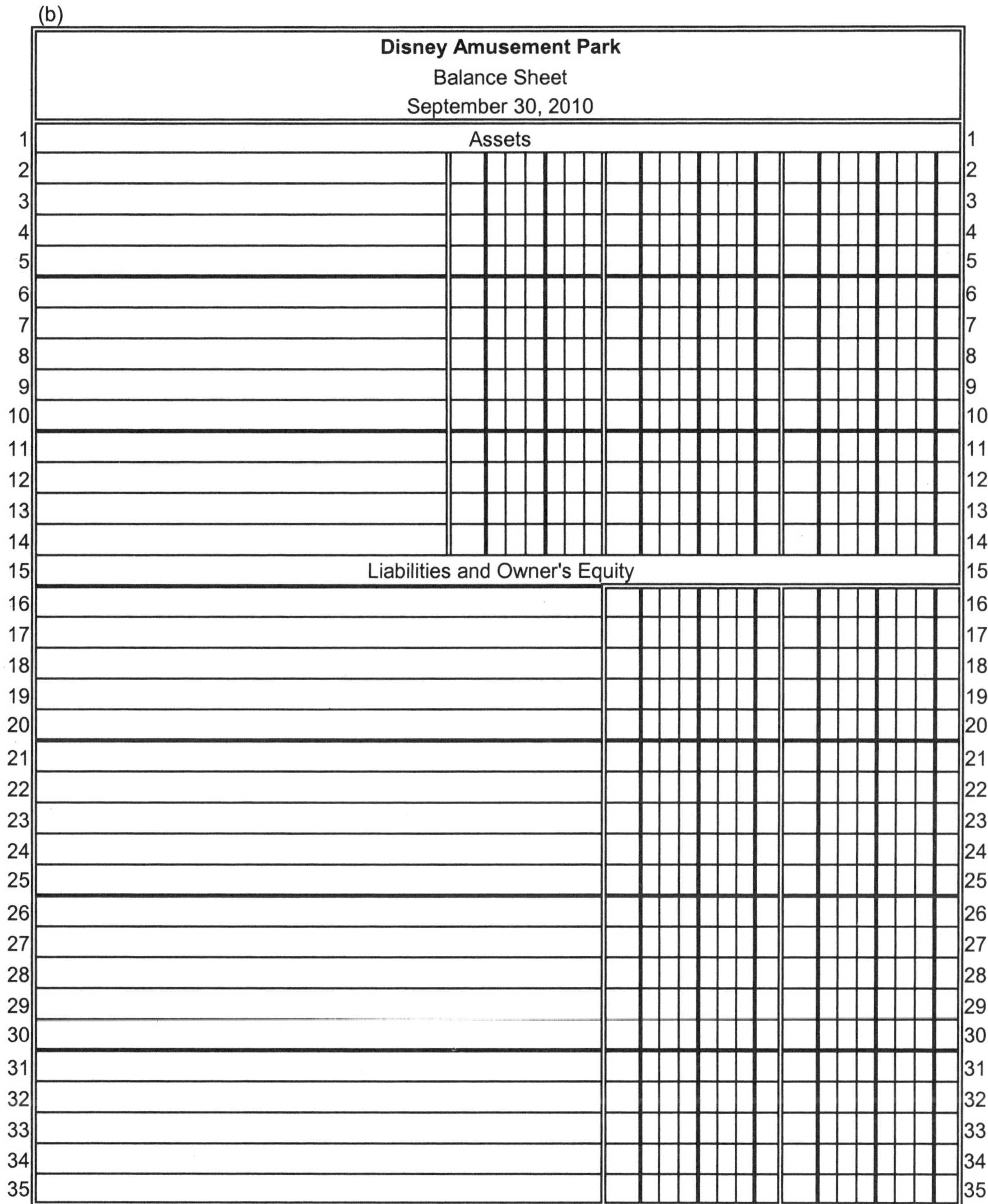

Disney Amusement Park

Balance Sheet

September 30, 2010

Assets

Liabilities and Owner's Equity

Name | Problem 4-4A Continued

Section

Date | Disney Amusement Park

(c) & (d)

Date	Accounts Titles	Debit	Credit
(c)	Adjusting Entries		
Sept. 30			
30			
30			
30			
30			
30			
(d)	Closing Entries		
Sept. 30			
30			
30			
30			

(e)

Disney Amusement Park
Post-Closing Trial Balance
September 30, 2010

	Debit	Credit

Name

Section

Date

Problem 4-5A

Eddy's Carpet Cleaners

(a)

General Journal

J1

Date	Accounts Titles	Ref.	Debit	Credit
Mar. 1				
1				
3				
5				
14				
18				
20				
21				
28				
31				
31				

Problem 4-5A

Eddy's Carpet Cleaners

See Appendix

(a), (e) and (f)

Cash No. 101

Date	Explanation	Ref.	Debit	Credit	Balance

Accounts Receivable No. 112

Date	Explanation	Ref.	Debit	Credit	Balance

Cleaning Supplies No. 128

Date	Explanation	Ref.	Debit	Credit	Balance

Prepaid Insurance No. 130

Date	Explanation	Ref.	Debit	Credit	Balance

Equipment No. 157

Date	Explanation	Ref.	Debit	Credit	Balance

(a), (e) and (f) (Continued)

Accumulated Depreciation - Equipment No. 158

Date	Explanation	Ref.	Debit	Credit	Balance

Accounts Payable No. 201

Date	Explanation	Ref.	Debit	Credit	Balance

Salaries Payable No. 212

Date	Explanation	Ref.	Debit	Credit	Balance
			Debit	Credit	Balance

L. Eddy, Capital No. 301

Date	Explanation	Ref.	Debit	Credit	Balance

L. Eddy, Drawing No. 306

Date	Explanation	Ref.	Debit	Credit	Balance

Income Summary No. 350

Date	Explanation	Ref.	Debit	Credit	Balance

Service Revenue No. 400

Date	Explanation	Ref.	Debit	Credit	Balance

Name
Section
Date

Problem 4-5A Continued

Eddy's Carpet Cleaners

(a), (e) and (f) (Continued)

Gas & Oil Expense — No. 633

Date	Explanation	Ref.	Debit	Credit	Balance

Cleaning Supplies E — No. 634

Date	Explanation	Ref.	Debit	Credit	Balance

Depreciation Expens — No. 711

Date	Explanation	Ref.	Debit	Credit	Balance

Insurance Expense — No. 722

Date	Explanation	Ref.	Debit	Credit	Balance

Salaries Expense — No. 726

Date	Explanation	Ref.	Debit	Credit	Balance

(d)

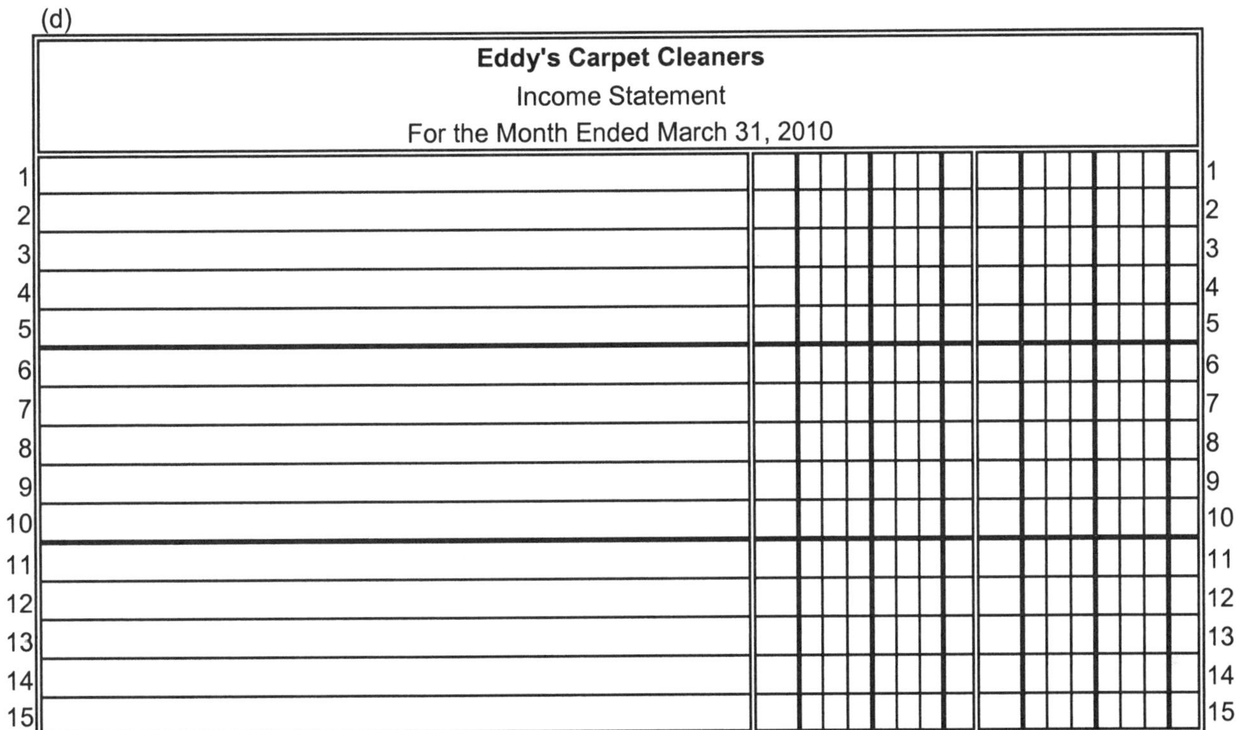

Eddy's Carpet Cleaners

Owner's Equity Statement

For the Month Ended March 31, 2010

Name

Section

Date

Problem 4-5A Continued

Eddy's Carpet Cleaners

(d) (Continued)

Eddy's Carpet Cleaners

Balance Sheet

March 31, 2010

Assets

Liabilities and Owner's Equity

Name Problem 4-5A Continued

Section

Date Eddy's Carpet Cleaners

(e) General Journal J2

Date	Accounts Titles	Ref.	Debit	Credit
	Adjusting Entries			
Mar. 31				
31				
31				
31				
31				

(f) General Journal J3

Date	Account Titles	Ref.	Debit	Credit
	Closing Entries			
Mar. 31				
31				
31				
31				

(g)

Eddy's Carpet Cleaners
Post-Closing Trial Balance
March 31, 2010

	Debit	Credit

Problem 4-6A

Fox Cable

See Appendix

(b)

Fox Cable
Trial Balance
April 30, 2010

	Debit	Credit
Cash		
Accounts Receivable		
Supplies		
Equipment		
Accumulated Depreciation		
Accounts Payable		
Salaries Payable		
Unearned Revenue		
A. Manion, Capital		
Service Revenue		
Salaries Expense		
Advertising Expense		
Miscellaneous Expense		
Repair Expense		
Depreciation Expense		

Problem 4-1B

Sasse Roofing

See Appendix

(b)

Sasse Roofing
Income Statement
For the Month Ended March 31, 2010

1			1
2			2
3			3
4			4
5			5
6			6
7			7
8			8
9			9
10			10
11			11
12			12
13			13
14			14
15			15

Sasse Roofing
Owner's Equity Statement
For the Month Ended March 31, 2010

1		1
2		2
3		3
4		4
5		5
6		6
7		7
8		8
9		9
10		10

(b) (Continued)

Sasse Roofing
Balance Sheet
March 31, 2010

Assets

Liabilities and Owner's Equity

Name

Section

Date

Problem 4-1B Concluded

Sasse Roofing

(c) General Journal

Date	Account Titles	Debit	Credit
	Adjusting Entries		
Mar. 31			
31			
31			
31			

(d) General Journal

Date	Account Titles	Debit	Credit
	Closing Entries		
Mar. 31			
31			
31			
31			

Name

Section

Date

Problem 4-2B

Rachel Company

(a)

Rachel Company
Partial Worksheet
For the Year Ended December 31, 2010

	Account No.	Account Titles	Adjusted Trial Balance Dr.	Adjusted Trial Balance Cr.	Income Statement Dr.	Income Statement Cr.	Balance Sheet Dr.	Balance Sheet Cr.	
1	101	Cash	8100						1
2	112	Accounts Receivable	10800						2
3	126	Supplies	1500						3
4	130	Prepaid Insurance	2000						4
5	151	Office Equipment	24000						5
6	152	Accum. Depr. - Office Equip.		5600					6
7	200	Notes Payable		15000					7
8	201	Accounts Payable		6100					8
9	212	Salaries Payable		2400					9
10	230	Interest Payable		600					10
11	301	T. Rachel, Capital		15800					11
12	306	T. Rachel, Drawing	7000						12
13	400	Service Revenue		61000					13
14	610	Advertising Expense	8400						14
15	631	Supplies Expense	4000						15
16	711	Depreciation Expense	5600						16
17	722	Insurance Expense	3500						17
18	726	Salaries Expense	31000						18
19	905	Interest Expense	600						19
20		Totals	106500	106500					20
21		Net Income							21
22		Totals							22
23									23

Name

Section

Date

Problem 4-2B Continued

Rachel Company

(b)

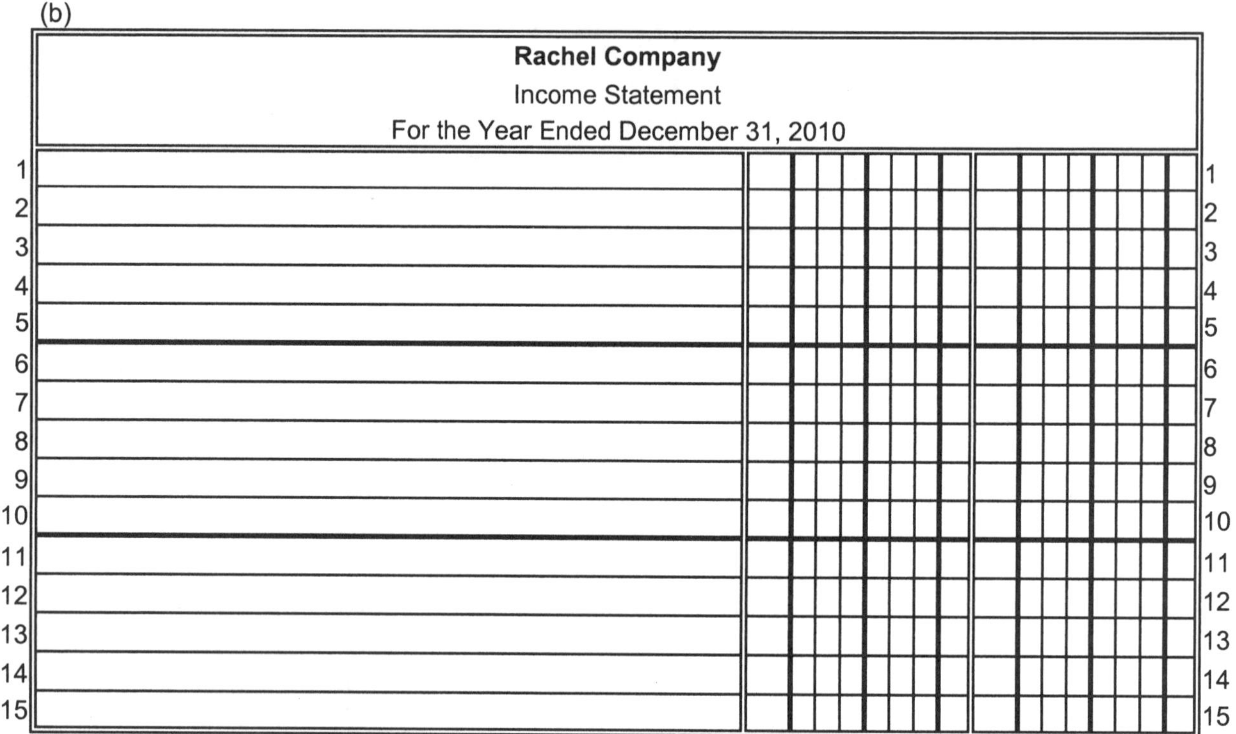

Rachel Company

Owner's Equity Statement

For the Year Ended December 31, 2010

(b) (Continued)

Rachel Company
Balance Sheet
December 31, 2010

Assets

Liabilities and Owner's Equity

Name

Section

Date

Problem 4-2B Continued

Rachel Company

(c)

General Journal J14

Date	Account Titles	Ref.	Debit	Credit
Dec. 31				
31				
31				
31				

(d)

T. Rachel, Capital No.301

Date	Explanation	Ref.	Debit	Credit	Balance
Jan 1	Balance	√			15800

T. Rachel, Drawing No. 306

Date	Explanation	Ref.	Debit	Credit	Balance
Dec 31	Balance	√			7000

Income Summary No. 350

Date	Explanation	Ref.	Debit	Credit	Balance

(d) (Continued)

Service Revenue No. 400

Date	Explanation	Ref.	Debit	Credit	Balance
Dec 31	Balance	√			61000

Advertising Expense No. 610

Date	Explanation	Ref.	Debit	Credit	Balance
Dec 31	Balance	√			8400

Supplies Expense No. 631

Date	Explanation	Ref.	Debit	Credit	Balance
Dec 31	Balance	√			4000

Depreciation Expense No. 711

Date	Explanation	Ref.	Debit	Credit	Balance
Dec 31	Balance	√			5600

Insurance Expense No. 722

Date	Explanation	Ref.	Debit	Credit	Balance
Dec 31	Balance	√			3500

Salaries Expense No. 726

Date	Explanation	Ref.	Debit	Credit	Balance
Dec 31	Balance	√			31000

Interest Expense No. 905

Date	Explanation	Ref.	Debit	Credit	Balance
Dec 31	Balance	√			600

Name Problem 4-2B Concluded

Section

Date Rachel Company

(e)

Rachel Company

Post-Closing Trial Balance

December 31, 2010

		Debit	Credit	
1				1
2				2
3				3
4				4
5				5
6				6
7				7
8				8
9				9
10				10
11				11
12				12
13				13
14				14
15				15
16				16
17				17
18				18
19				19
20				20

Name Problem 4-3B

Section

Date Muddy Company

(a)

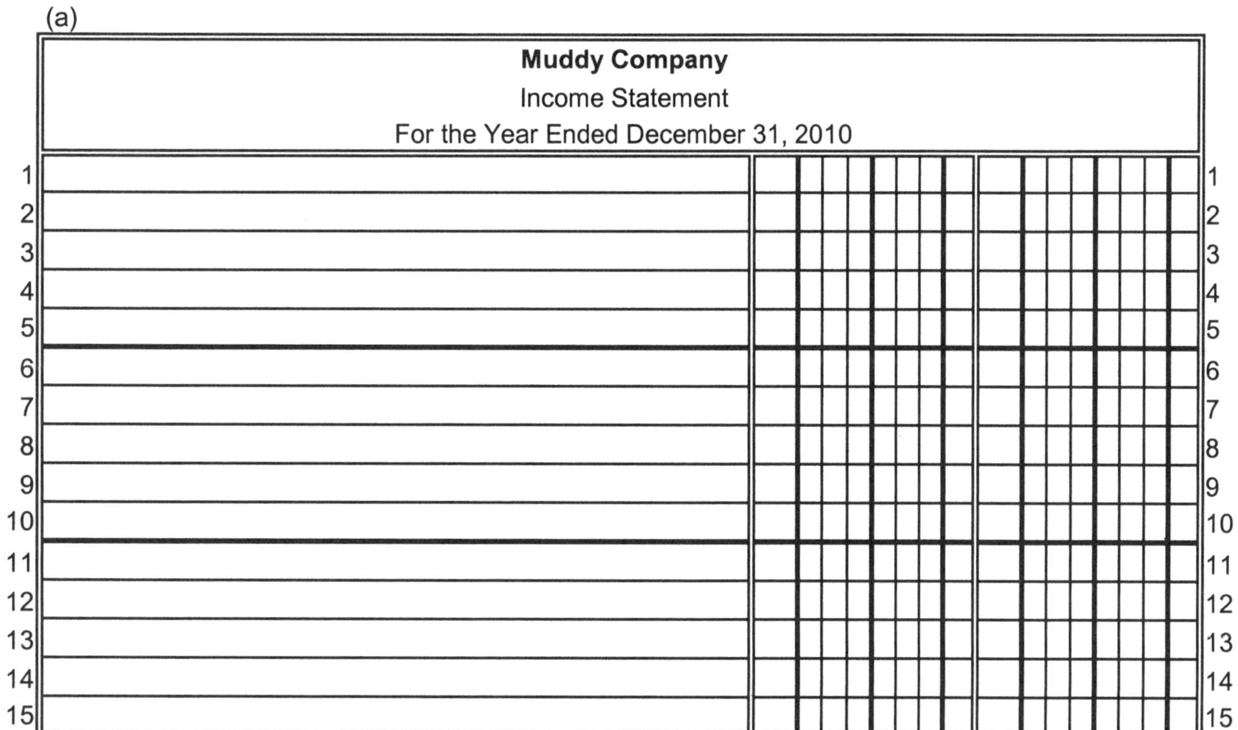

Muddy Company

Income Statement

For the Year Ended December 31, 2010

Muddy Company

Owner's Equity Statement

For the Year Ended December 31, 2010

(a) (Continued)

Muddy Company
Balance Sheet
December 31, 2010

1	Assets			1
2				2
3				3
4				4
5				5
6				6
7				7
8				8
9				9
10				10
11				11
12	Liabilities and Owner's Equity			12
13				13
14				14
15				15
16				16
17				17
18				18
19				19
20				20
21				21
22				22
23				23

Name Problem 4-3B Continued

Section

Date Muddy Company

(b) General Journal

Date	Accounts Titles	Ref.	Debit	Credit
	Closing Entries			
Dec. 31				
31				
31				
31				

(c)

Melissa Muddy, Capital	No. 301
	1/1 Bal 28,500

Melissa Muddy, Drawing	No.306
12/31 Bal 11,000	

Income Summary	No. 350

Service Revenue	No. 400

Repair Expense	No. 622

Depreciation Expense	No. 711

Insurance Expense	No. 722

Salaries Expense	No. 726

Utilities Expense	No. 732

(d)

Muddy Company
Post-Closing Trial Balance
December 31, 2010

		Debit	Credit	
1				1
2				2
3				3
4				4
5				5
6				6
7				7
8				8
9				9
10				10

Problem 4-4B

Rockford Management Services

See Appendix

Name | Problem 4-4B Continued
Section
Date | Rockford Management Services

(b)

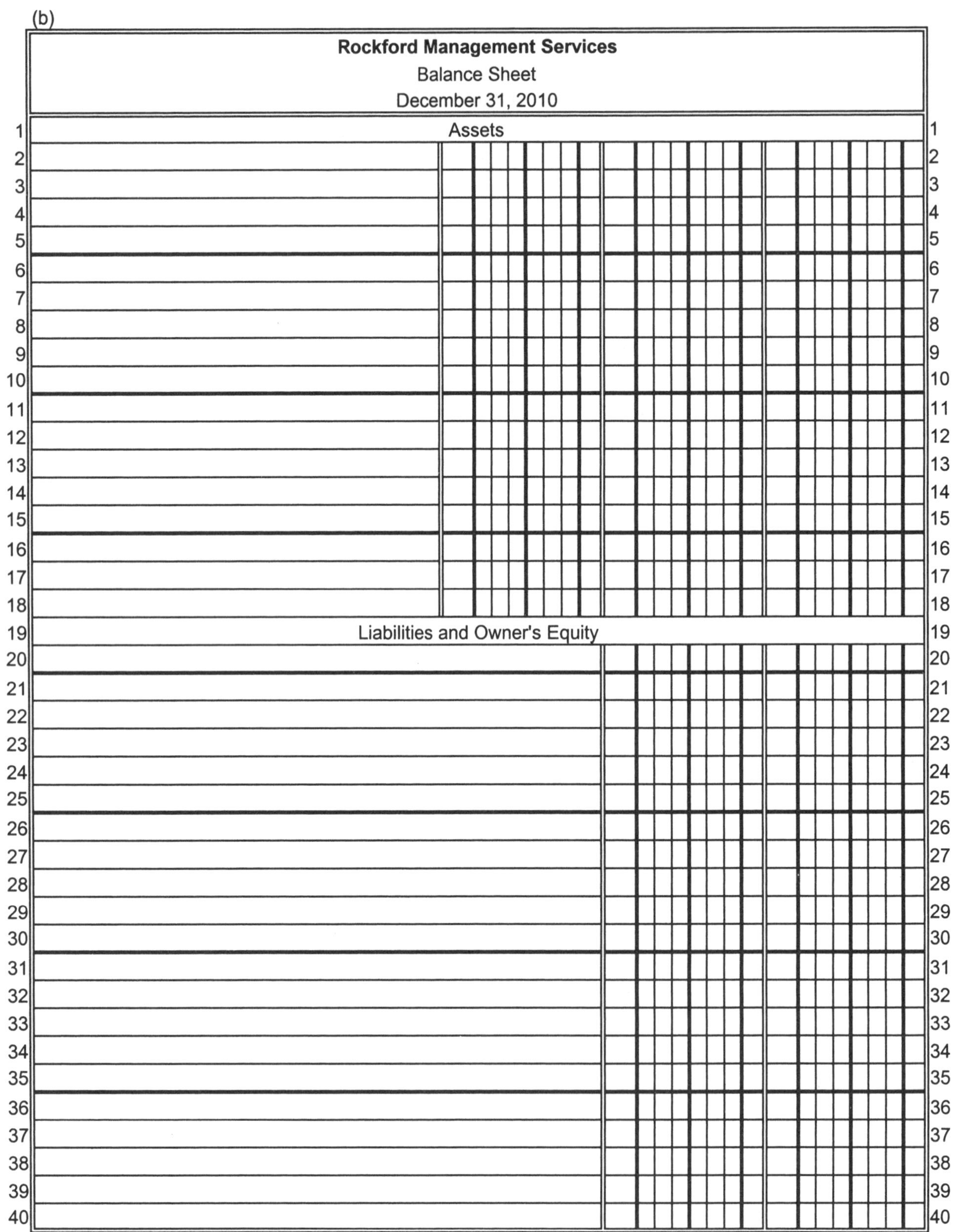

Rockford Management Services

Balance Sheet

December 31, 2010

Assets

Liabilities and Owner's Equity

Date	Accounts Titles	Debit	Credit
(c)	Adjusting Entries		
Dec. 31			
31			
31			
31			
31			
(d)	Closing Entries		
Dec. 31			
31			
31			
31			

(e)

Rockford Management Services

Post-Closing Trial Balance

December 31, 2010

	Debit	Credit

Name | Problem 4-5B

Section

Date | Chang's Cleaning Services

(a) General Journal J1

Date	Accounts Titles	Ref.	Debit	Credit
July 1				
1				
3				
5				
12				
18				
20				
21				
25				
31				
31				

Problem 4-5B

Chang's Cleaning Services

See Appendix

Name
Section
Date

Problem 4-5B Continued

Chang's Cleaning Services

(a), (e) and (f)

Cash No. 101

Date	Explanation	Ref.	Debit	Credit	Balance

Accounts Receivable No. 112

Date	Explanation	Ref.	Debit	Credit	Balance

Cleaning Supplies No. 128

Date	Explanation	Ref.	Debit	Credit	Balance

Prepaid Insurance No. 130

Date	Explanation	Ref.	Debit	Credit	Balance

Equipment No. 157

Date	Explanation	Ref.	Debit	Credit	Balance

(a), (e) and (f) (Continued)

Accumulated Depreciation - Equipment | No. 158

Date	Explanation	Ref.	Debit	Credit	Balance

Accounts Payable | No. 201

Date	Explanation	Ref.	Debit	Credit	Balance

Salaries Payable | No. 212

Date	Explanation	Ref.	Debit	Credit	Balance

Lee Chang, Capital | No. 301

Date	Explanation	Ref.	Debit	Credit	Balance

Lee Chang, Drawing | No. 306

Date	Explanation	Ref.	Debit	Credit	Balance

Income Summary | No. 350

Date	Explanation	Ref.	Debit	Credit	Balance

Service Revenue | No. 400

Date	Explanation	Ref.	Debit	Credit	Balance

(a), (e) and (f) (Continued)

Gas & Oil Expense No. 633

Date	Explanation	Ref.	Debit	Credit	Balance

Cleaning Supplies Expense No. 634

Date	Explanation	Ref.	Debit	Credit	Balance

Depreciation Expense No. 711

Date	Explanation	Ref.	Debit	Credit	Balance

Insurance Expense No. 722

Date	Explanation	Ref.	Debit	Credit	Balance

Salaries Expense No. 726

Date	Explanation	Ref.	Debit	Credit	Balance

(d)

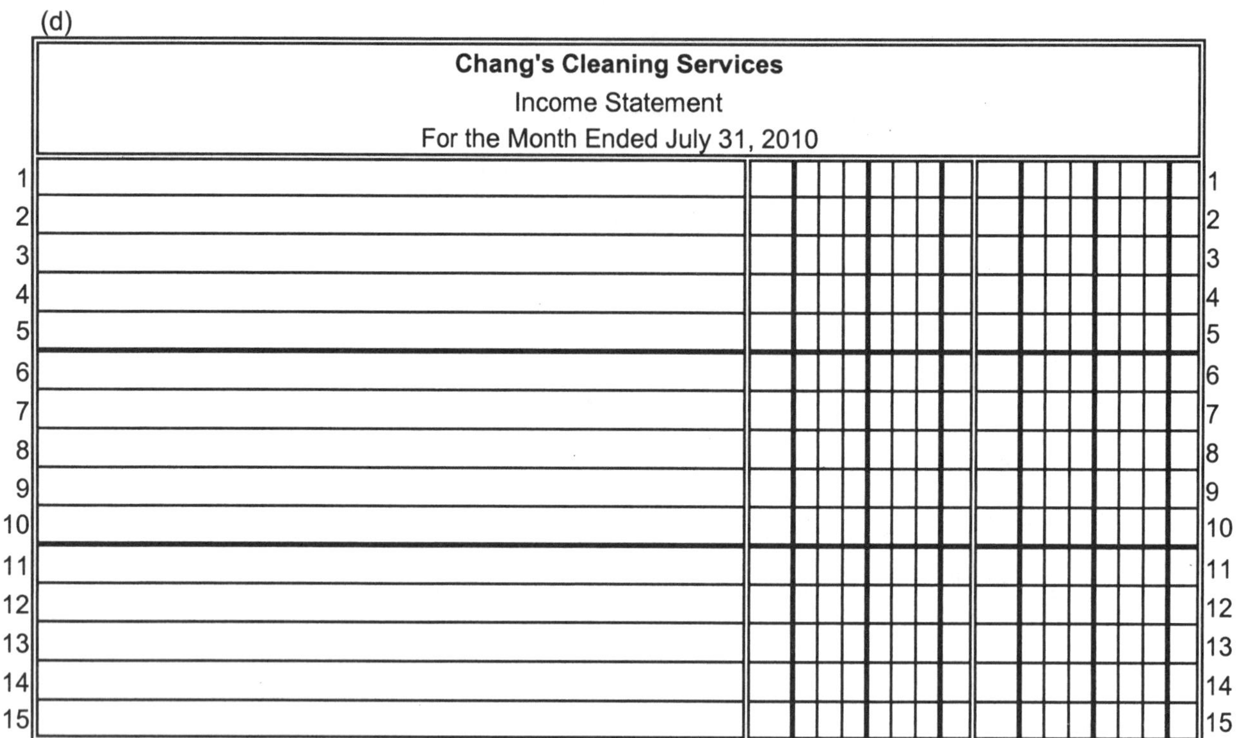

Chang's Cleaning Services

Income Statement

For the Month Ended July 31, 2010

Chang's Cleaning Services

Owner's Equity Statement

For the Month Ended July 31, 2010

Name Problem 4-5B Continued

Section

Date Chang's Cleaning Services

(d) (Continued)

Chang's Cleaning Services

Balance Sheet

July 31, 2010

Assets

Liabilities and Owner's Equity

Name

Section

Date

Problem 4-5B Continued

Chang's Cleaning Services

(e) General Journal J2

Date	Accounts Titles	Ref.	Debit	Credit
	Adjusting Entries			
July 31				
31				
31				
31				
31				

(f) General Journal J3

Date	Account Titles	Ref.	Debit	Credit
	Closing Entries			
July 31				
31				
31				
31				

(g)

Chang's Cleaning Services
Post-Closing Trial Balance
July 31, 2010

	Debit	Credit

Name

Comprehensive Problem: Chapters 2 to 4

Section

Date

Julie's Maids Cleaning Service

(a) General Journal J1

Date	Accounts Titles	Ref.	Debit	Credit
July 1				
1				
3				
5				
12				
18				
20				
21				
25				
31				
31				

Comprehensive Problem Ch 2 - 4

Julie's Maids Cleaning Service

See Appendix

(a), (e) and (f)

Cash No. 101

Date	Explanation	Ref.	Debit	Credit	Balance

Accounts Receivable No. 112

Date	Explanation	Ref.	Debit	Credit	Balance

Cleaning Supplies No. 128

Date	Explanation	Ref.	Debit	Credit	Balance

Prepaid Insurance No. 130

Date	Explanation	Ref.	Debit	Credit	Balance

Equipment No. 157

Date	Explanation	Ref.	Debit	Credit	Balance

Accumulated Depreciation - Equipment No. 158

Date	Explanation	Ref.	Debit	Credit	Balance

(a), (e) and (f) (Continued)

Accounts Payable No. 201

Date	Explanation	Ref.	Debit	Credit	Balance

Salaries Payable No. 212

Date	Explanation	Ref.	Debit	Credit	Balance

Julie Molony, Capital No. 301

Date	Explanation	Ref.	Debit	Credit	Balance

Julie Molony, Drawing No. 306

Date	Explanation	Ref.	Debit	Credit	Balance

Income Summary No. 350

Date	Explanation	Ref.	Debit	Credit	Balance

Service Revenue No. 400

Date	Explanation	Ref.	Debit	Credit	Balance

(a), (e) and (f) (Continued)

Gas & Oil Expense No. 633

Date	Explanation	Ref.	Debit	Credit	Balance

Cleaning Supplies Expense No. 634

Date	Explanation	Ref.	Debit	Credit	Balance

Depreciation Expense No. 711

Date	Explanation	Ref.	Debit	Credit	Balance

Insurance Expense No. 722

Date	Explanation	Ref.	Debit	Credit	Balance

Salaries Expense No. 726

Date	Explanation	Ref.	Debit	Credit	Balance

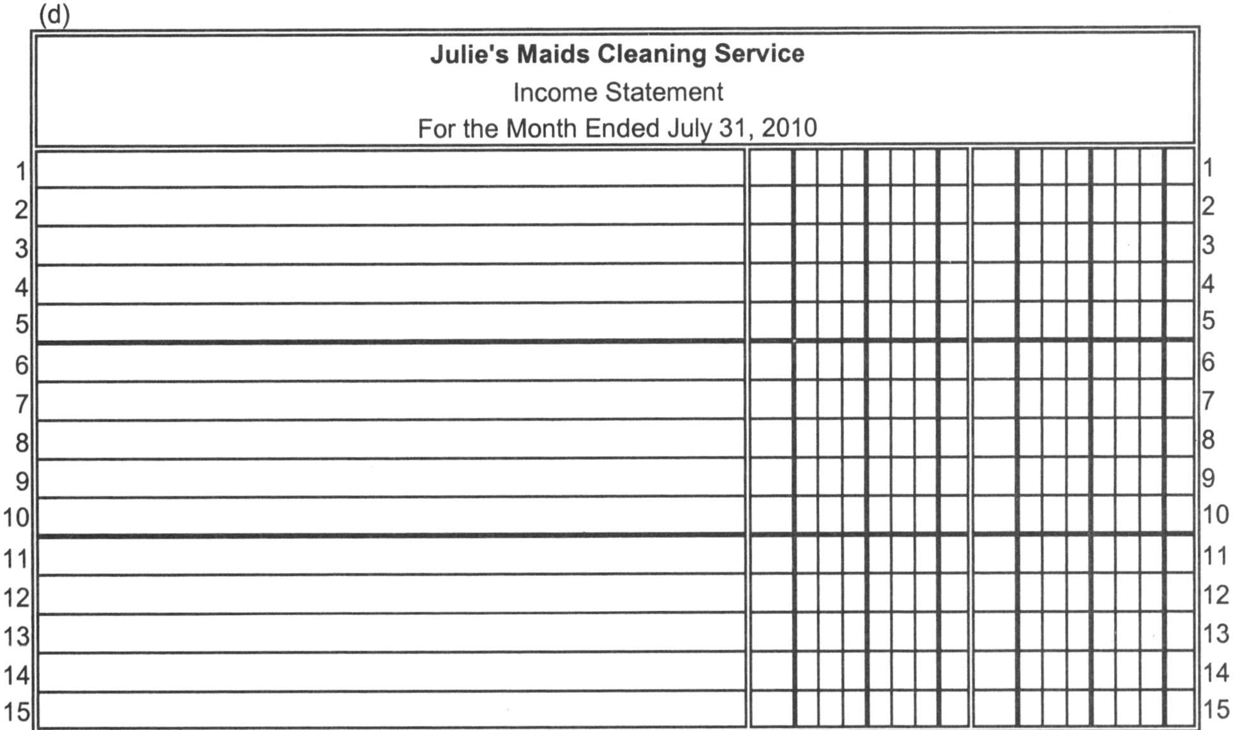
(d)

Julie's Maids Cleaning Service
Income Statement
For the Month Ended July 31, 2010

Julie's Maids Cleaning Service
Statement of Owner's Equity
For the Month Ended July 31, 2010

(d) (Continued)

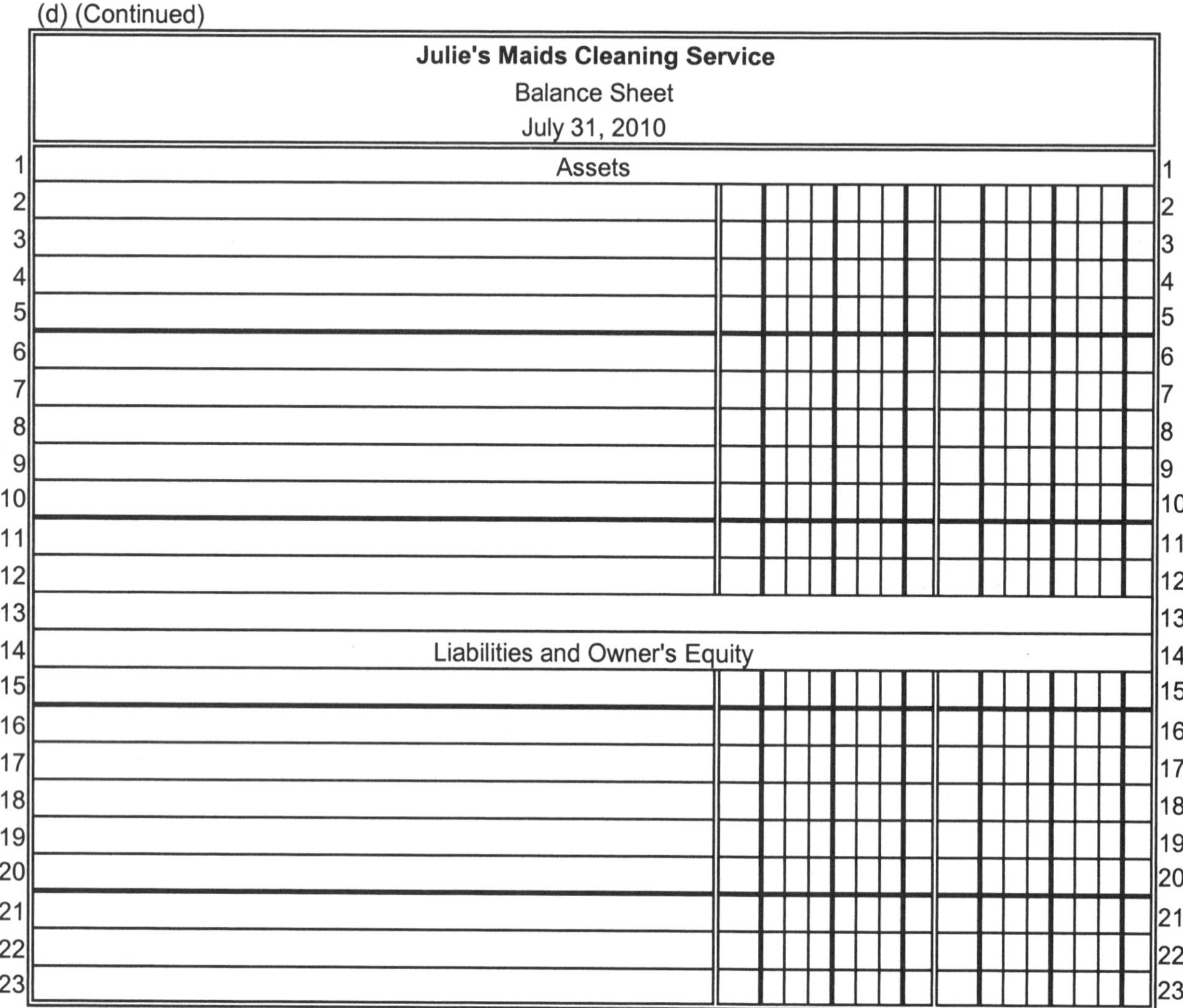

Julie's Maids Cleaning Service

Balance Sheet

July 31, 2010

Assets

Liabilities and Owner's Equity

(g)

Julie's Maids Cleaning Service

Post-Closing Trial Balance

July 31, 2010

	Debit	Credit

General Journal J2

Date	Accounts Titles	Ref.	Debit	Credit
(e)	Adjusting Entries			
July 31				
31				
31				
31				
31				

General Journal J3

Date	Account Titles	Ref.	Debit	Credit
(f)	Closing Entries			
July 31				
31				
31				
31				

Name — Chapter 4 Comparative Analysis Problem

Section

Date — PepsiCo, Inc. versus Coca-Cola Company

	PepsiCo	Coca-Cola
(a) (in millions)		
1. Total current assets		
2. Net property, plant, and equipment		
3. Total current liabilities		
4. Total stockholders' (shareholders') equity		

(b)

(a)

Whitegloves Janitorial Service

Balance Sheet

December 31, 2010

Assets

Liabilities and Owner's Equity

Whitegloves Janitorial Service

Capital Account Detail

December 31, 2010

Capital account balance as reported

(b)

Name

Section

Date

Personal Balance Sheet

Assets

Liabilities and Owner's Equity

Name

Section

Date

BE5-1

	Sales	Cost of Goods Sold	Gross Profit	Operating Expenses	Net Income
(a)	$ 75000		$ 30000		$ 10800
(b)	108000	70000			29500
(c)		71900	79600	39500	

BE5-2 Account Titles	Debit	Credit
Hollins Company		
Gordon Company		

BE5-3 Account Titles	Debit	Credit
(a)		
(b)		
(c)		

Name

Section

Date

BE5-4

	Account Titles	Debit	Credit
(a)			
(b)			
(c)			

BE5-5

	Account Titles	Debit	Credit

BE5-6

	Account Titles	Debit	Credit

BE5-7

Maulder Company

Income Statement (Partial)

For the Month Ended October 31, 2010

Name

Section

Date

BE5-10

***BE5-11**

***BE5-12**	Account Titles	Debit	Credit
(a)			
(b)			
(c)			

***BE5-13**

(a) Cash:

(b) Merchandise Inventory:

(c) Sales:

(d) Cost of Goods Sold

Name

Section

Date

DO IT! 5-1

Date	Account Titles	Debit	Credit
Oct. 5			
Oct. 8			

DO IT! 5-2

Date	Account Titles	Debit	Credit
Oct. 5			
Oct. 8			

Name　　　　Chapter 5 DO IT! 5-3

Section

Date　　　　Dionne's Boutique

Date	Account Titles	Debit	Credit
Dec. 31			

Name　　　　　　　　　　　　　　　　　　　　　　　　　　　　　　　　　　Exercises 5-2 and 5-3

Section

Date

E5-2

General Journal

Date	Account Titles	Debit	Credit
(a)			
Apr. 5			
6			
7			
8			
15			
(b)			
May 4			

E5-3

Date	Account Titles	Debit	Credit
Sept. 6			
9			
10			
12			

Name
Section
Date

E5-3 (Continued) General Journal

	Date	Account Titles	Debit	Credit	
1	Sept. 14				1
2					2
3					3
4					4
5					5
6	20				6
7					7
8					8
9					9
10					10
11					11
12					12

E5-4

	Date	Account Titles	Debit	Credit	
1	(a)				1
2	June 10				2
3					3
4					4
5	11				5
6					6
7					7
8	12				8
9					9
10					10
11	19				11
12					12
13					13
14					14
15	(b)				15
16	June 10				16
17					17
18					18
19					19
20					20
21					21
22					22
23					23

E5-4 (Continued) General Journal

Date	Account Titles	Debit	Credit
June 12			
19			

E5-5

Date	Account Titles	Debit	Credit
(a)			
Dec. 3			
8			
13			
(b)			
Jan. 2			

Name

Section

Date

E5-6 (a)

Zambrana Company
Income Statement (Partial)
For the Year Ended October 31, 2010

(b)

Date	Account Titles	Debit	Credit
Oct. 31			
31			

E5-7

Account Titles	Debit	Credit
(a)		
(b)		

Name Exercise 5-8

Section

Date Rogers Co.

	Account Titles	Debit	Credit
(a)			
(b)			

Name Exercise 5-9

Section

Date Obley Company

(a)

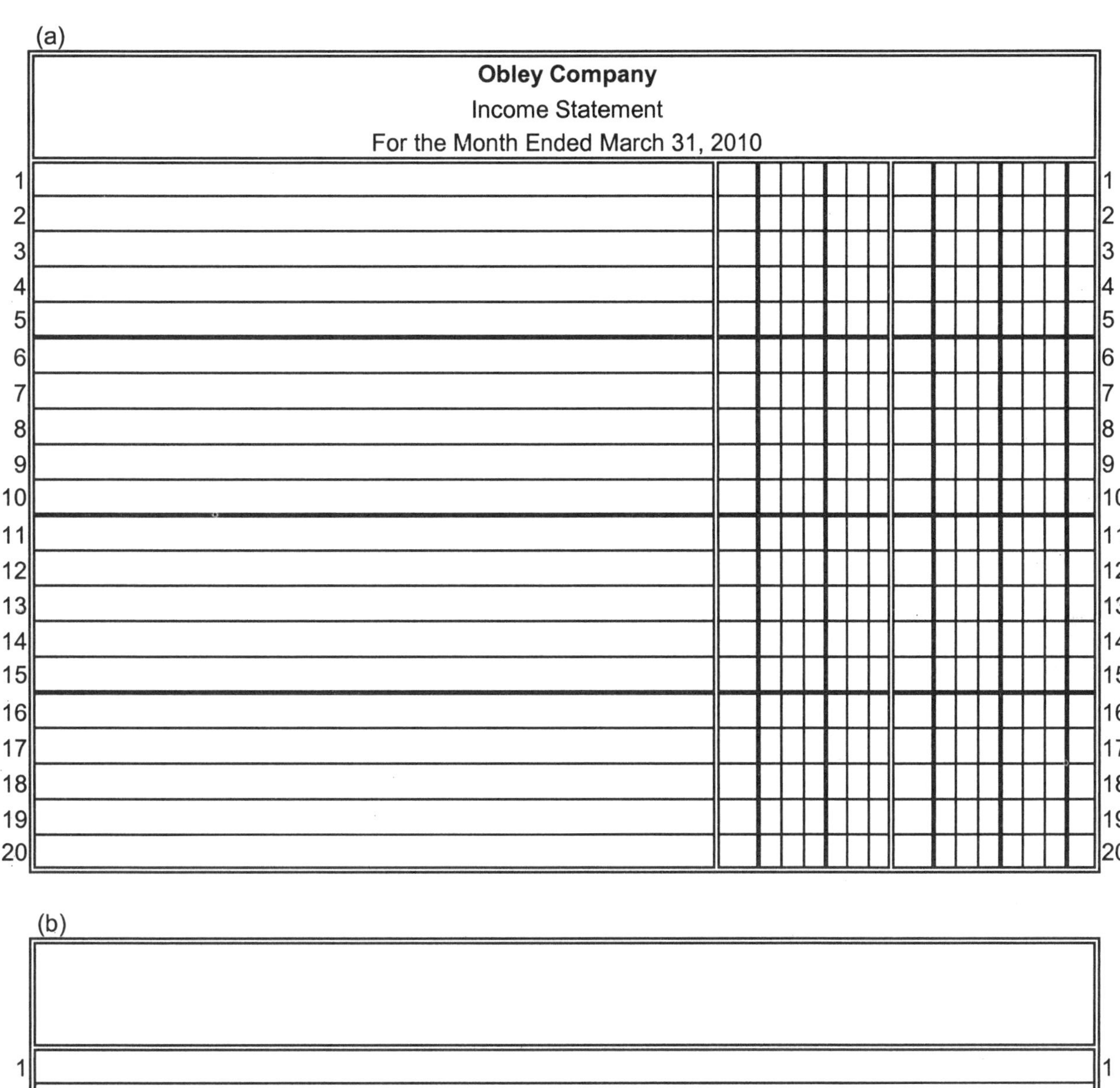

Obley Company
Income Statement
For the Month Ended March 31, 2010

(b)

Name | Exercise 5-10

Section

Date | Pele Company

(a)

Pele Company

Income Statement

For the Year Ended December 31, 2010

(b)

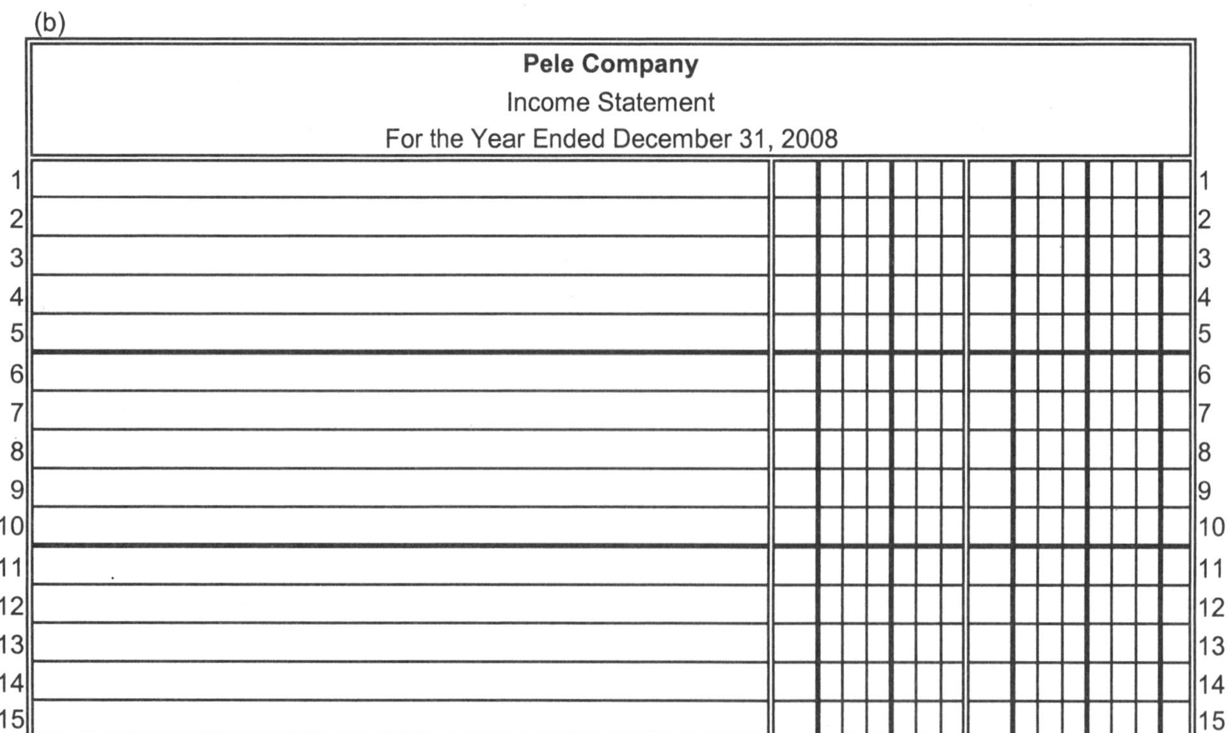

Pele Company

Income Statement

For the Year Ended December 31, 2008

Name

Section

Date

Exercises 5-11 and 5-13

E5-11

	Account Titles	Debit	Credit
1.			
2.			
3.			
4.			

E5-13

(a)	Nam Company	Mayo Company
Sales	$ 90000	$
Sales Returns		5000
Net Sales	84000	100000
Cost of Goods Sold	56000	
Gross Profit		41500
Operating Expenses	15000	
Net Income	$	$ 15000
(b) Gross profit rate		

Name Exercise 5-14

Section

Date Natural Cosmetics

		Natural Cosmetics	Mattar Grocery	Allied Wholesalers	
1	Sales	$ 90000	$	$ 144000	1
2	Sales returns and allowances		5000	12000	2
3	Net sales	81000	95000		3
4	Cost of goods sold	56000			4
5	Gross profit		38000	24000	5
6	Operating expenses	15000		18000	6
7	Income from operations				7
8	Other expenses and losses	4000	7000		8
9	Net income	$	$ 11000	$ 5000	9
10					10
11					11
12					12
13					13
14					14
15					15

Name

Section

Date

Exercises *5-15 and *5-17

***E5-15**

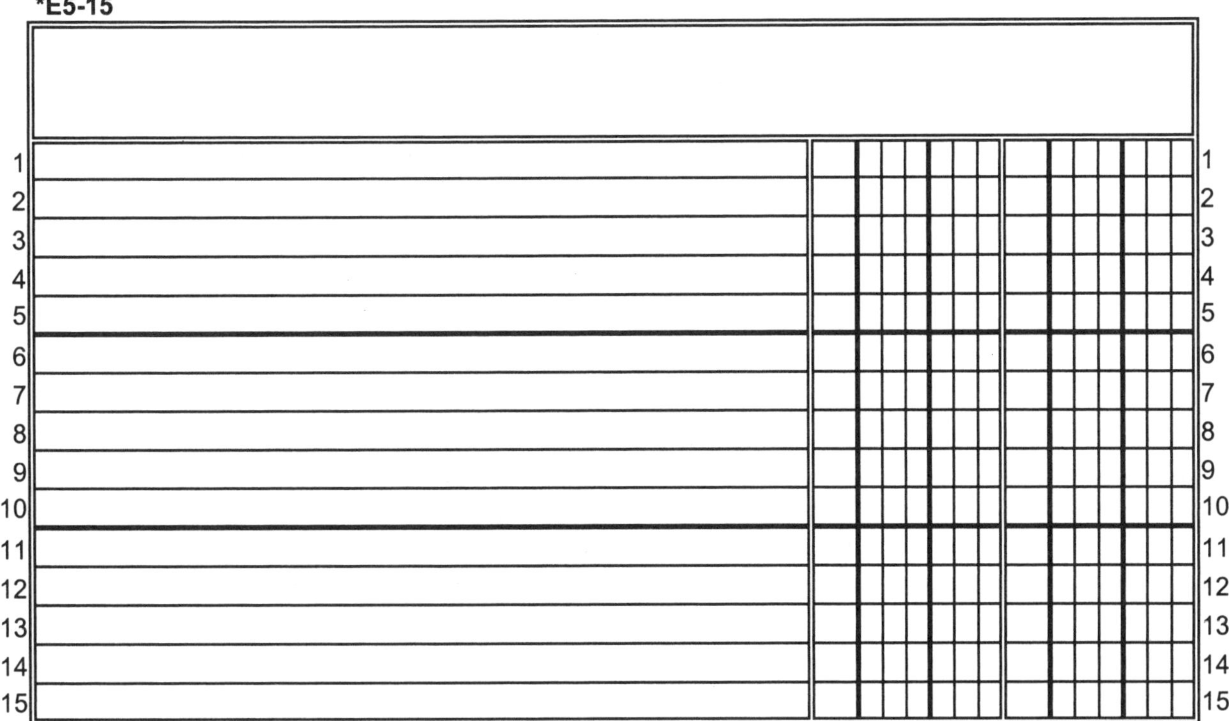

***E5-17**

	B	F	L	R
Beginning inventory	$ 150	$ 70	$ 1000	$
Purchases	1600	1080		43950
Purchase returns and allowances	40		290	
Net purchases		1030	6210	41090
Freight-in	110			2240
Cost of goods purchased		1280	7940	
Cost of goods available for sale	1820	1350		49530
Ending inventory	310		1450	6230
Cost of goods sold		1230	7490	43300

Name

Section

Date

Exercise 5-16

Rachael Ray Corporation

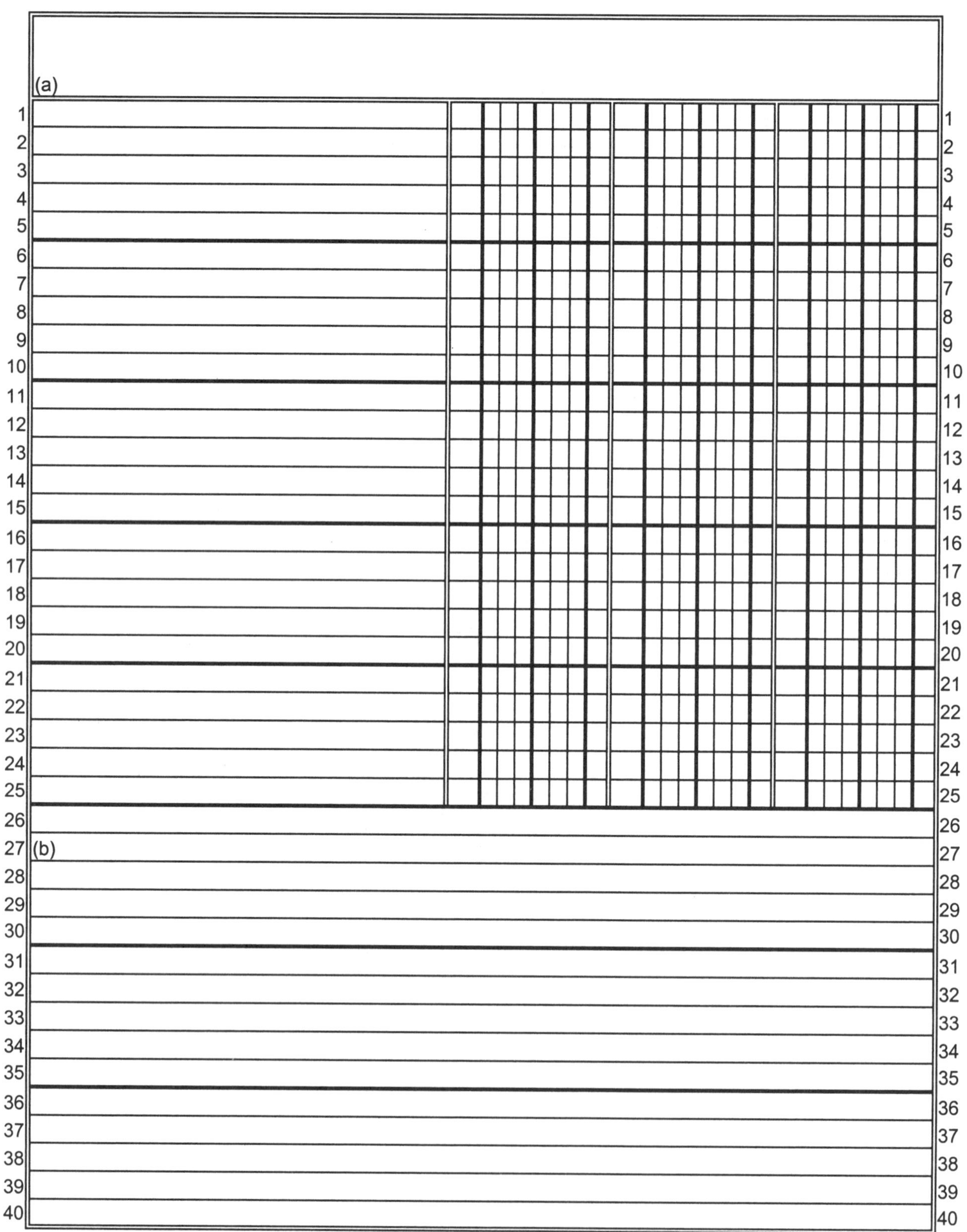

Name *Exercise 5-18

Section

Date Martinez Co.

Date	Account Titles	Debit	Credit
(a)			
Apr. 5			
6			
7			
8			
15			
(b)			
May 4			

Name *Exercise 5-19

Section

Date Chevalier Co.

Date	Account Titles	Debit	Credit
(a)			
Apr. 5			
6			
7			
8			
15			
(b)			
May 4			

Name

Section

Date

*Exercise 5-20

Carpenter Company

Carpenter Company
Worksheet (Partial)
For the Period Ended May 31, 2010

	Account Titles	Adjusted Trial Balance		Income Statement		Balance Sheet		
		Dr.	Cr.	Dr.	Cr.	Dr.	Cr.	
1	Cash	9000						1
2	Merchandise Inventory	76000						2
3	Sales		450000					3
4	Sales Returns and Allowances	10000						4
5	Sales Discounts	9000						5
6	Cost of Goods Sold	300000						6
7								7
8								8
9								9
10								10
11								11
12								12
13								13
14								14
15								15

Exercise 5-21

Green Company

See Appendix

Name | Problem 5-1A

Section

Date | Sansomite Co.

General Journal

Date	Account Titles	Debit	Credit
July 1			
3			
9			
12			
17			
18			
20			
21			

Name | Problem 5-1A Concluded

Section

Date | Sansomite Co.

General Journal

Date	Account Titles	Debit	Credit
July 22			
30			
31			

Name Problem 5-2A

Section

Date Olaf Distributing Company

(a) General Journal J1

Date	Account Titles	Ref.	Debit	Credit
Apr. 2				
4				
5				
6				
11				
13				
14				
16				
18				
20				
23				

(a) (Continued) J1

Date	Account Titles	Ref.	Debit	Credit
Apr. 26				
27				
29				
30				

(b)

Cash No. 101

Date	Explanation	Ref.	Debit	Credit	Balance
Apr. 1	Balance	√			9000

Accounts Receivable No. 112

Date	Explanation	Ref.	Debit	Credit	Balance

(b) (Continued)

Merchandise Inventory No. 120

Date	Explanation	Ref.	Debit	Credit	Balance

Accounts Payable No. 201

Date	Explanation	Ref.	Debit	Credit	Balance

M. Olaf, Capital No. 301

Date	Explanation	Ref.	Debit	Credit	Balance
Apr. 1	Balance	√			9000

Sales No. 401

Date	Explanation	Ref.	Debit	Credit	Balance

Sales Returns and Allowances No. 412

Date	Explanation	Ref.	Debit	Credit	Balance

Name
Section
Date

Problem 5-2A Concluded

Olaf Distributing Company

(b) (Continued)

Sales Discounts — No. 414

Date	Explanation	Ref.	Debit	Credit	Balance

Cost of Goods Sold — No. 505

Date	Explanation	Ref.	Debit	Credit	Balance

Freight-out — No. 644

Date	Explanation	Ref.	Debit	Credit	Balance

(c)

Olaf Distributing Company
Income Statement (Partial)
For the Month Ended April 30, 2010

1				1
2				2
3				3
4				4
5				5
6				6
7				7
8				8
9				9
10				10

Name Problem 5-3A

Section

Date Maine Department Store

(a)

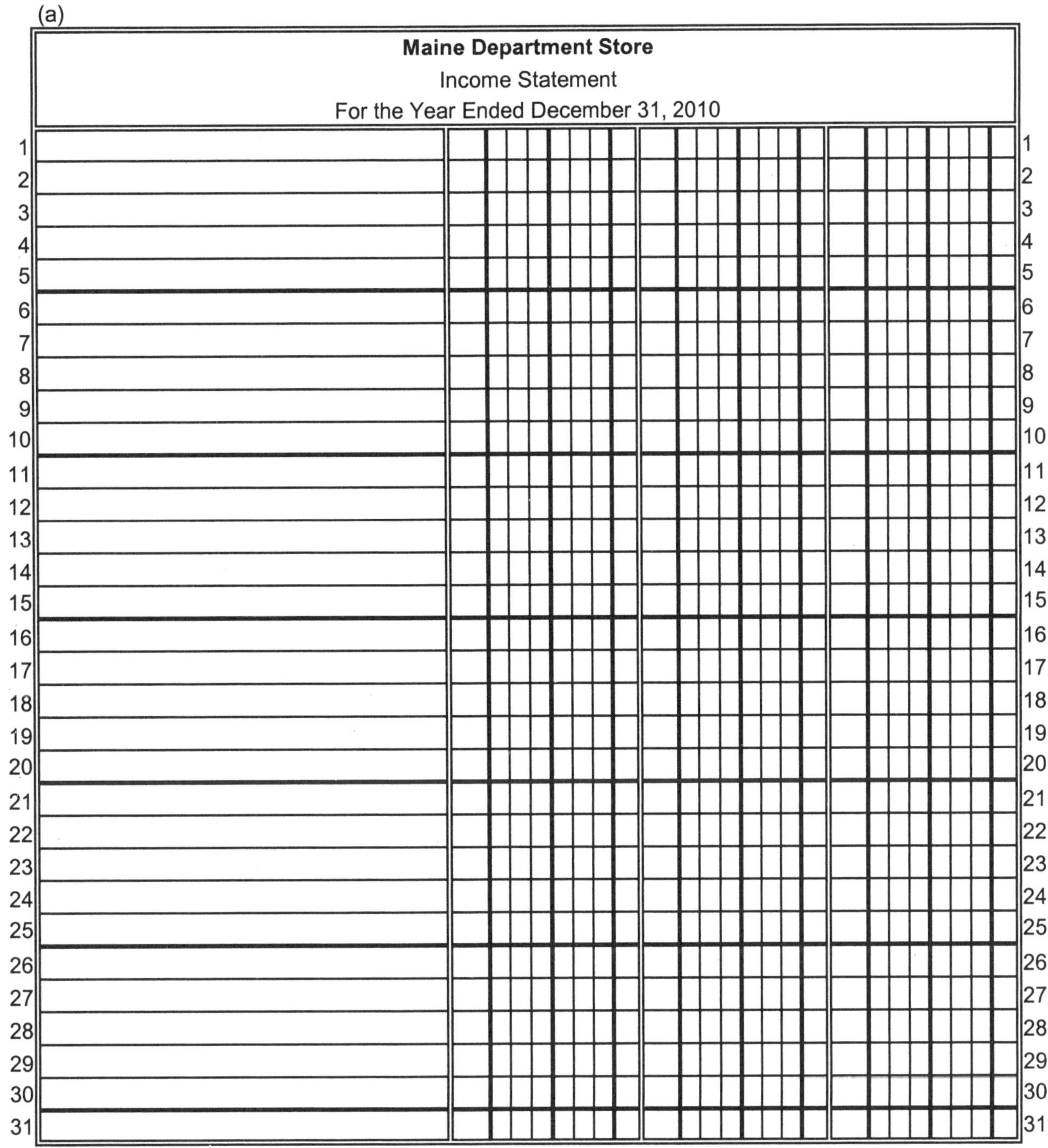

Maine Department Store

Income Statement

For the Year Ended December 31, 2010

Maine Department Store

Owner's Equity Statement

For the Year Ended December 31, 2010

Name

Section

Date

Problem 5-3A Continued

Maine Department Store

(a) (Continued)

Maine Department Store

Balance Sheet

December 31, 2010

Assets

Liabilities and Owner's Equity

(b) General Journal

Date	Account Titles	Debit	Credit
	Adjusting Entries		
Dec. 31			
31			
31			
31			
31			
31			
31			

Name

Section

Date

Problem 5-3A Concluded

Maine Department Store

(c) General Journal

Date	Account Titles	Debit	Credit
	Closing Entries		
Dec. 31			
31			
31			
31			

Name Problem 5-4A

Section

Date Hafner's Tennis Shop

(a) General Journal J1

Date	Account Titles	Ref.	Debit	Credit
Apr. 4				
6				
8				
10				
11				
13				
14				
15				
17				
18				

Name | Problem 5-4A Continued

Section

Date | Hafner's Tennis Shop

(a) (Continued) General Journal J1

Date	Account Titles	Ref.	Debit	Credit
Apr. 20				
21				
27				
30				

(b)

Cash No. 101

Date	Explanation	Ref.	Debit	Credit	Balance
Apr 1	Balance	√			2500

Accounts Receivable No. 112

Date	Explanation	Ref.	Debit	Credit	Balance

Merchandise Inventory No. 120

Date	Explanation	Ref.	Debit	Credit	Balance
Apr 1	Balance	√			1700

Accounts Payable No. 201

Date	Explanation	Ref.	Debit	Credit	Balance

(b) (Continued)

J. Hafner, Capital No. 301

Date	Explanation	Ref.	Debit	Credit	Balance
Apr 1	Balance	√			4200

Sales No. 401

Date	Explanation	Ref.	Debit	Credit	Balance

Sales Returns and Allowances No. 412

Date	Explanation	Ref.	Debit	Credit	Balance

Cost of Goods Sold No. 505

Date	Explanation	Ref.	Debit	Credit	Balance

(c)

Hafner's Tennis Shop
Trial Balance
April 30, 2010

		Debit	Credit	
1				1
2				2
3				3
4				4
5				5
6				6
7				7
8				8
9				9
10				10

Name *Problem 5-5A

Section

Date Gordman Department Store

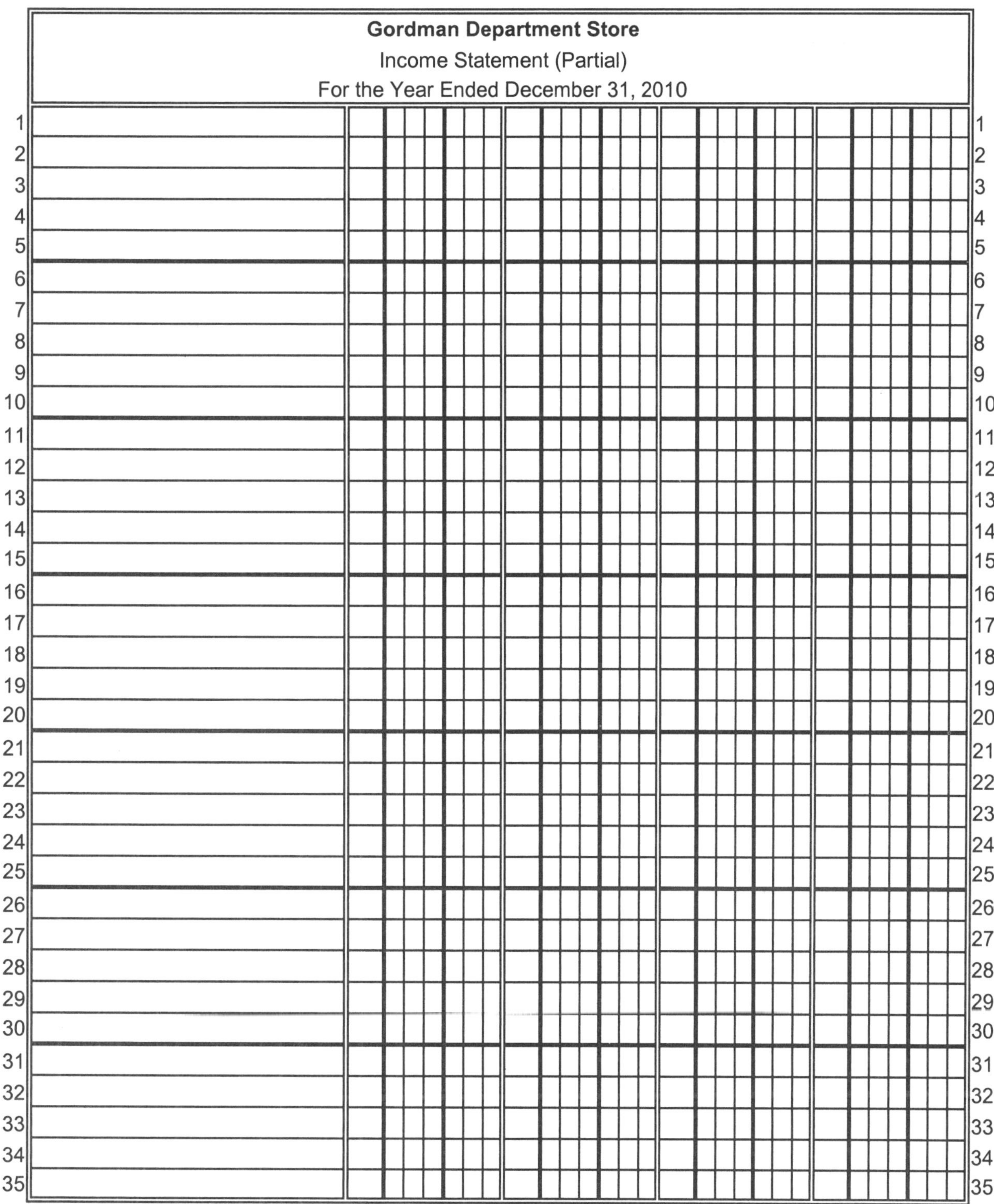

Gordman Department Store

Income Statement (Partial)

For the Year Ended December 31, 2010

Name *Problem 5-6A

Section

Date Kristen Montana

(a)	2008	2009	2010
Cost of goods sold:			
(b)			
Sales			
(c)			
Beginning accounts payable			
(d)			
Gross profit rate			

Name *Problem 5-7A

Section

Date Village Tennis Shop

(a)

General Journal

	Date	Account Titles	Debit	Credit	
1	Apr. 4				1
2					2
3					3
4	6				4
5					5
6					6
7	8				7
8					8
9					9
10	10				10
11					11
12					12
13	11				13
14					14
15					15
16	13				16
17					17
18					18
19					19
20	14				20
21					21
22					22
23	15				23
24					24
25					25
26	17				26
27					27
28					28
29	18				29
30					30

(a) (Continued) General Journal

Date	Account Titles	Debit	Credit
Apr. 20			
21			
27			
30			

(b)

Cash

4/1 Bal. 2,500	

Accounts Receivable

Merchandise Inventory

4/1/ Bal. 1,700	

Accounts Payable

Angie Wilbert, Capital

	4/1/ Bal. 4,200

Sales

Sales Returns and Allowances

Purchases

Purchase Returns and Allowances

Purchase Discount

Freight-in

(c)

Village Tennis Shop
Trial Balance
April 30, 2010

	Debit	Credit

Village Tennis Shop
Income Statement (Partial)
For the Month Ended April 30, 2010

(b) (Continued)

Terry Manning Fashion Center

Owner's Equity Statement

For the Year Ended November 30, 2010

Terry Manning Fashion Center

Balance Sheet

November 30, 2010

Assets

Liabilities and Owner's Equity

(c) General Journal

Date	Account Titles	Debit	Credit
	Adjusting Entries		
Nov. 30			
30			
30			
30			
30			

(d)

Date	Account Titles	Debit	Credit
	Closing Entries		
Nov. 30			
30			
30			
30			

(e)

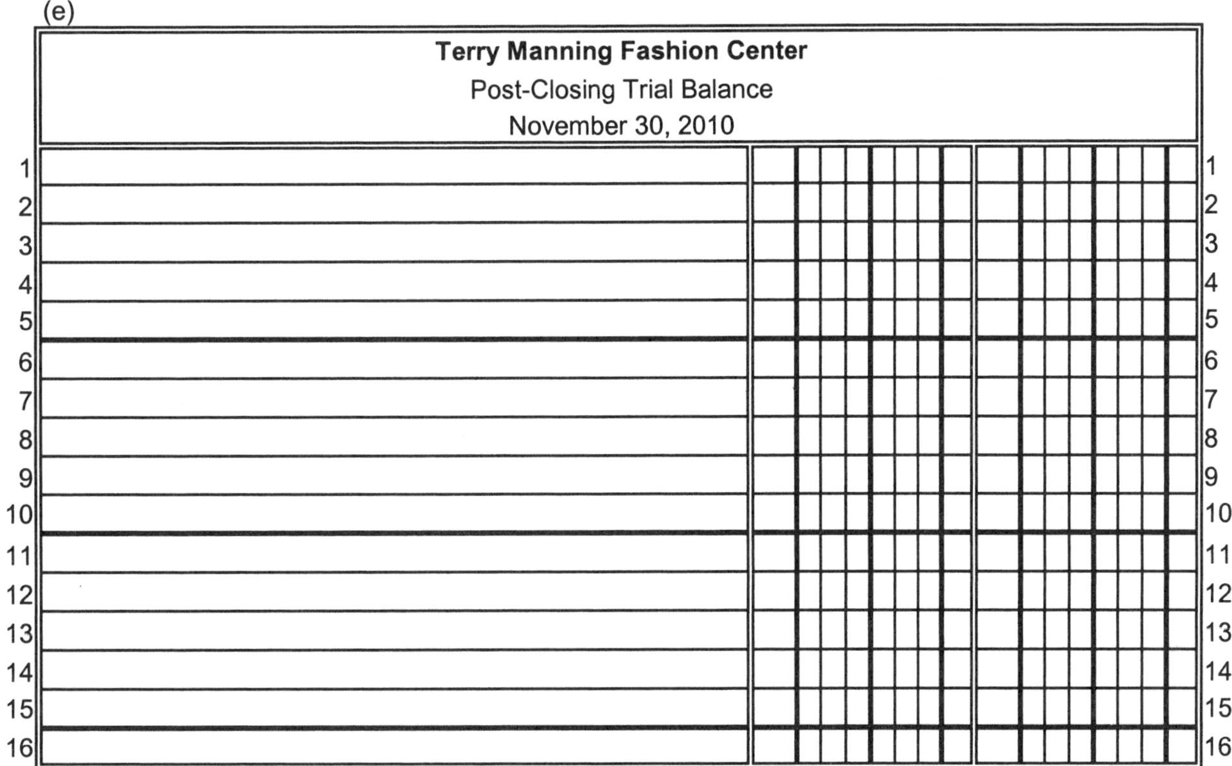

Terry Manning Fashion Center

Post-Closing Trial Balance

November 30, 2010

Name

Section

Date

Problem 5-1B

Paul's Book Warehouse

General Journal

Date	Account Titles	Debit	Credit
June 1			
3			
6			
9			
15			
17			
20			
24			
26			

Name Problem 5-1B Concluded

Section

Date Paul's Book Warehouse

General Journal

Date	Account Titles	Debit	Credit
June 28			
30			

Name

Section

Date

Problem 5-2B

Newman Hardware Store

(a)

General Journal

J1

Date	Account Titles	Ref.	Debit	Credit
May 1				
2				
5				
9				
10				
11				
12				
15				
17				
19				
24				

Name | Problem 5-2B Continued

Section

Date | Newman Hardware Store

(a) (Continued)

J1

Date	Account Titles	Ref.	Debit	Credit
May 25				
27				
29				
31				

(b)

Cash | No. 101

Date	Explanation	Ref.	Debit	Credit	Balance
May 1	Balance	√			10000

Accounts Receivable | No. 112

Date	Explanation	Ref.	Debit	Credit	Balance

(b) (Continued)

Merchandise Inventory No. 120

Date	Explanation	Ref.	Debit	Credit	Balance

Supplies No. 126

Date	Explanation	Ref.	Debit	Credit	Balance

Accounts Payable No. 201

Date	Explanation	Ref.	Debit	Credit	Balance

Newman, Capital No. 301

Date	Explanation	Ref.	Debit	Credit	Balance
May 1	Balance	√			10000

Sales No. 401

Date	Explanation	Ref.	Debit	Credit	Balance

Name | Problem 5-2B Concluded

Section

Date | Newman Hardware Store

(b) (Continued)

Sales Returns and Allowances — No. 412

Date	Explanation	Ref.	Debit	Credit	Balance

Sales Discounts — No. 414

Date	Explanation	Ref.	Debit	Credit	Balance

Cost of Goods Sold — No. 505

Date	Explanation	Ref.	Debit	Credit	Balance

(c)

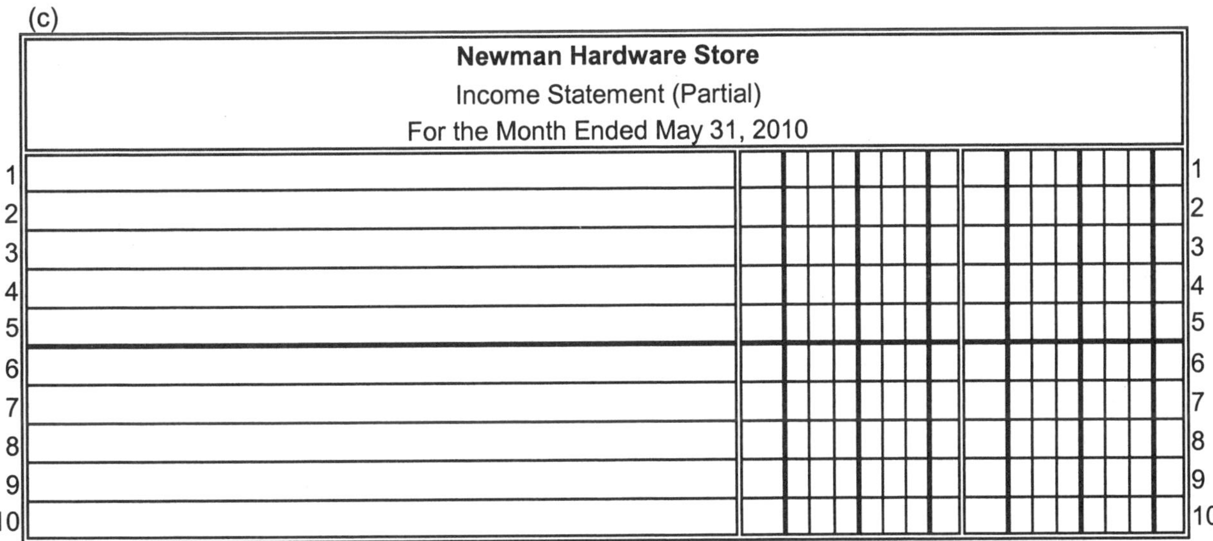

Newman Hardware Store

Income Statement (Partial)

For the Month Ended May 31, 2010

1				1
2				2
3				3
4				4
5				5
6				6
7				7
8				8
9				9
10				10

Name | Problem 5-3B

Section

Date | Tarp Department Store

(a)

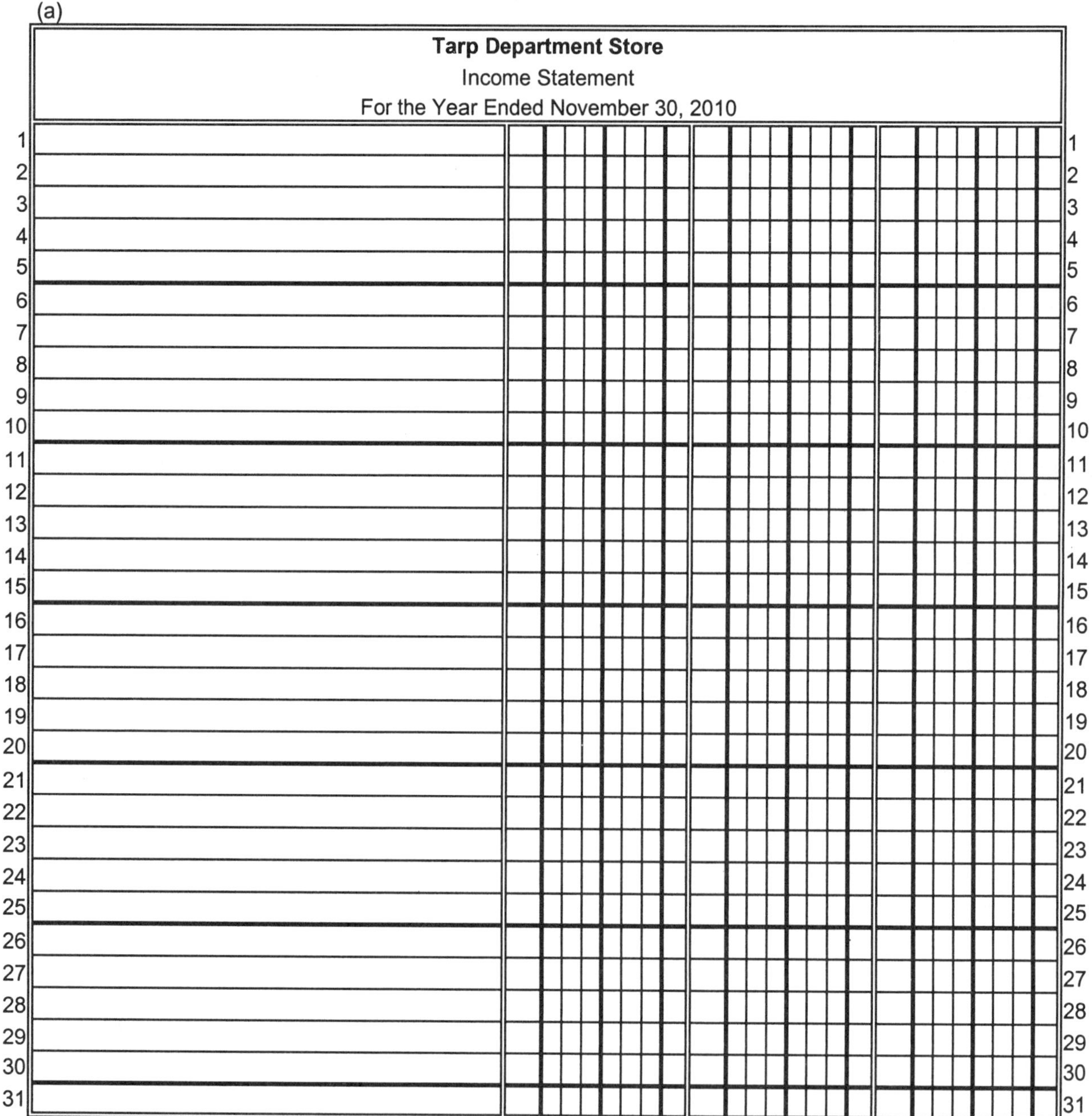

Tarp Department Store

Income Statement

For the Year Ended November 30, 2010

Tarp Department Store

Owner's Equity Statement

For the Year Ended November 30, 2010

Name

Section

Date

Problem 5-3B Continued

Tarp Department Store

(a) (Continued)

Tarp Department Store

Balance Sheet

November 30, 2010

Assets

Liabilities and Owner's Equity

Name

Section

Date

Problem 5-3B Continued

Tarp Department Store

(b) General Journal

Date	Account Titles	Debit	Credit
	Adjusting Entries		
Nov. 30			
30			
30			
30			
30			

Name Problem 5-3B Concluded

Section

Date Tarp Department Store

(c) General Journal

Date	Account Titles	Debit	Credit
	Closing Entries		
Nov. 30			
30			
30			
30			

Name | Problem 5-4B
Section
Date | Caleb's Discorama

(a) General Journal J1

Date	Account Titles	Ref.	Debit	Credit
Apr. 5				
7				
9				
10				
12				
14				
17				
20				
21				
27				
30				

(b)

Cash No. 101

Date	Explanation	Ref.	Debit	Credit	Balance
Apr 1	Balance	√			1800

Accounts Receivable No. 112

Date	Explanation	Ref.	Debit	Credit	Balance

Merchandise Inventory No. 120

Date	Explanation	Ref.	Debit	Credit	Balance
Apr 1	Balance	√			2500

Accounts Payable No. 201

Date	Explanation	Ref.	Debit	Credit	Balance

(b) (Continued)

C. Borke, Capital — No. 301

Date	Explanation	Ref.	Debit	Credit	Balance
Apr 1	Balance	√			4300

Sales — No. 401

Date	Explanation	Ref.	Debit	Credit	Balance

Sales Returns and Allowances — No. 412

Date	Explanation	Ref.	Debit	Credit	Balance

Cost of Goods Sold — No. 505

Date	Explanation	Ref.	Debit	Credit	Balance

(c)

Caleb's Discorama
Trial Balance
April 30, 2010

		Debit	Credit	
1				1
2				2
3				3
4				4
5				5
6				6
7				7
8				8
9				9
10				10

Name | Problem 5-5B

Section

Date | Duckworth Department Store

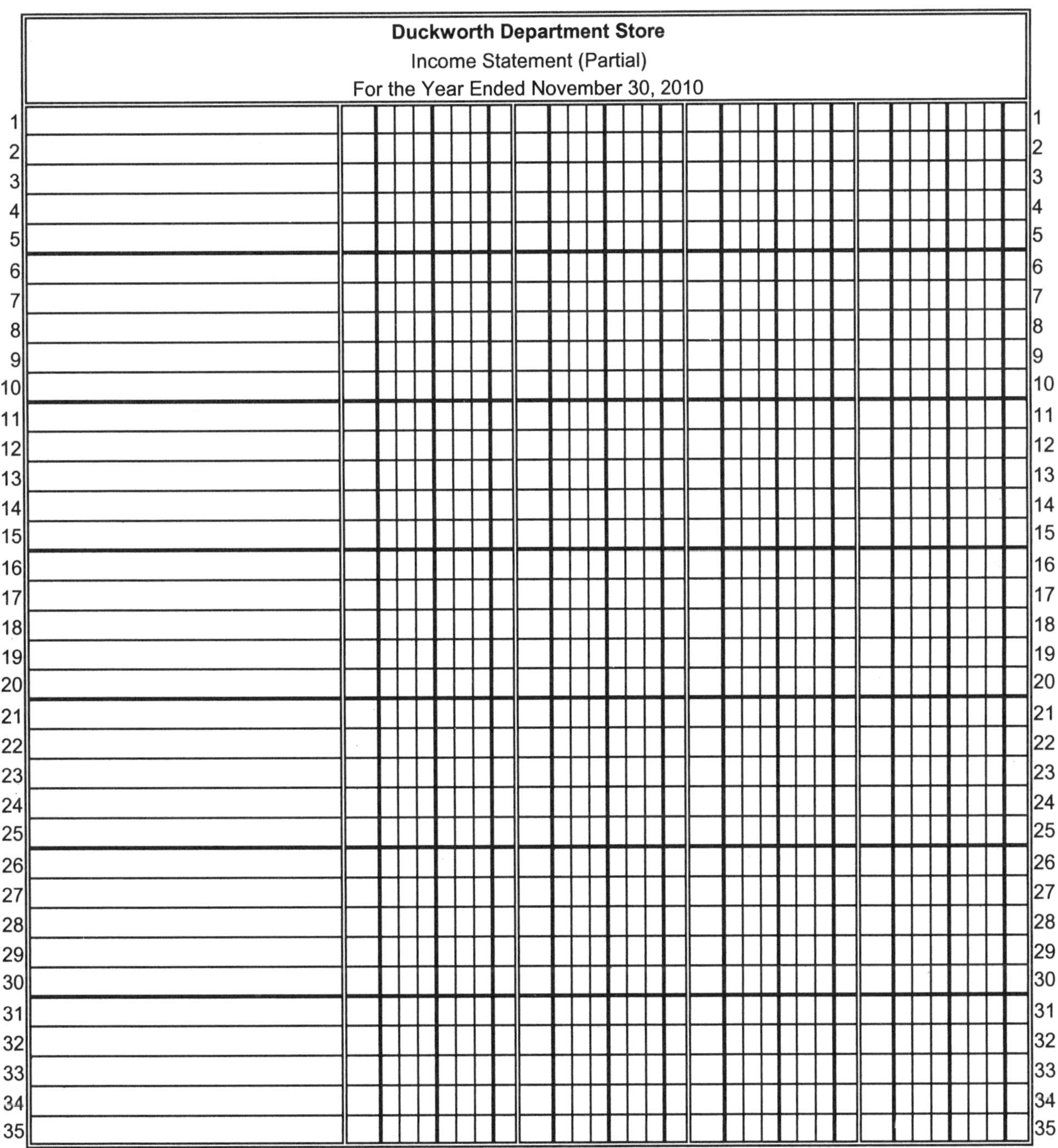

Duckworth Department Store

Income Statement (Partial)

For the Year Ended November 30, 2010

Name
Section
Date

Problem 5-6B

Letterman Inc.

(a)

	2007	2008	2009	2010
Income Statement Data				
Sales		$ 53300	$	$ 45200
Cost of goods sold			13800	14300
Gross profit		38300	33800	
Operating expenses		34900		28600
Net income		$	$ 2500	$
Balance Sheet Data				
Merchandise inventory	$ 7200		$ 8100	
Accounts payable	3200	3600	2500	
Additional Information				
Purchases of merchandise				
inventory on account		14200		13200
Cash payments to suppliers				13600

(b)

	2008	2009	2010
Gross profit rate			
Profit margin ratio			

Name *Problem 5-7B

Section

Date Five Pines Pro Shop

(a) General Journal

Date	Account Titles	Debit	Credit
Apr. 5			
7			
9			
10			
12			
14			
17			
20			
21			
27			
30			

(b)

Cash

4/1 Bal. 3,000	

Irene Tiger, Capital

	4/1 Bal. 7,000

Sales

Accounts Receivable

Sales Returns and Allowances

Merchandise Inventory

4/1 Bal. 4,000	

Purchases

Accounts Payable

Freight-in

Purchase Returns and Allowances

Purchase Discounts

(c)

Five Pines Pro Shop
Trial Balance
April 30, 2010

	Debit	Credit

(d)

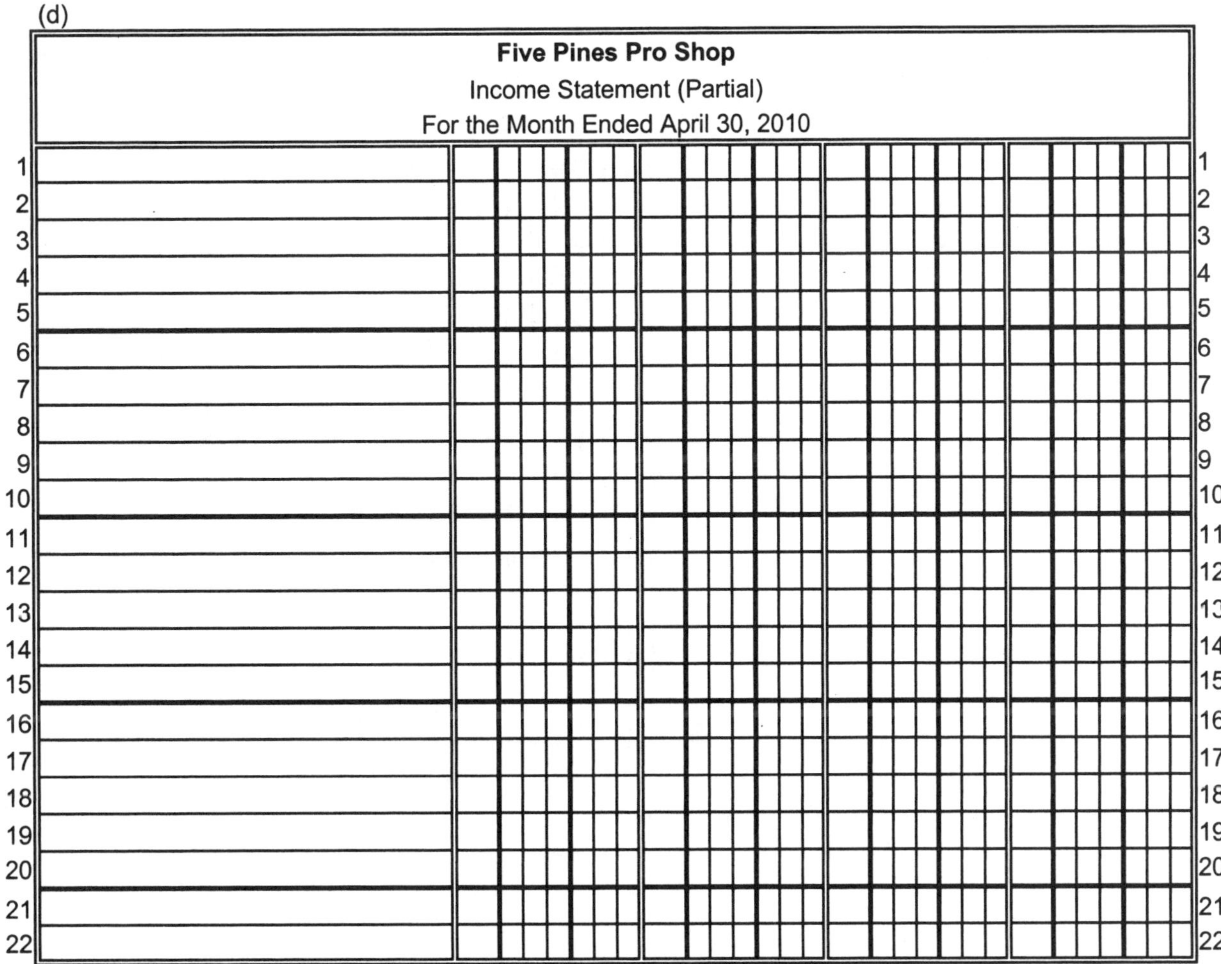

Five Pines Pro Shop
Income Statement (Partial)
For the Month Ended April 30, 2010

	2006		2007
(a) (1) Percentage change in sales:			
(2) Percentage change in net income:			

(b) Gross profit rate:	2005	2006	2007
(c) Percentage of net income to sales:			

Comment:

Name

Section

Date

	PepsiCo		Coca-Cola
(a)			
(1) 2007 Gross profit			
(2) 2007 Gross profit rate			
(3) 2007 Operating Income			
(4) Percentage change in operating income, 2006 to 2007			

(b)

(a) (1)

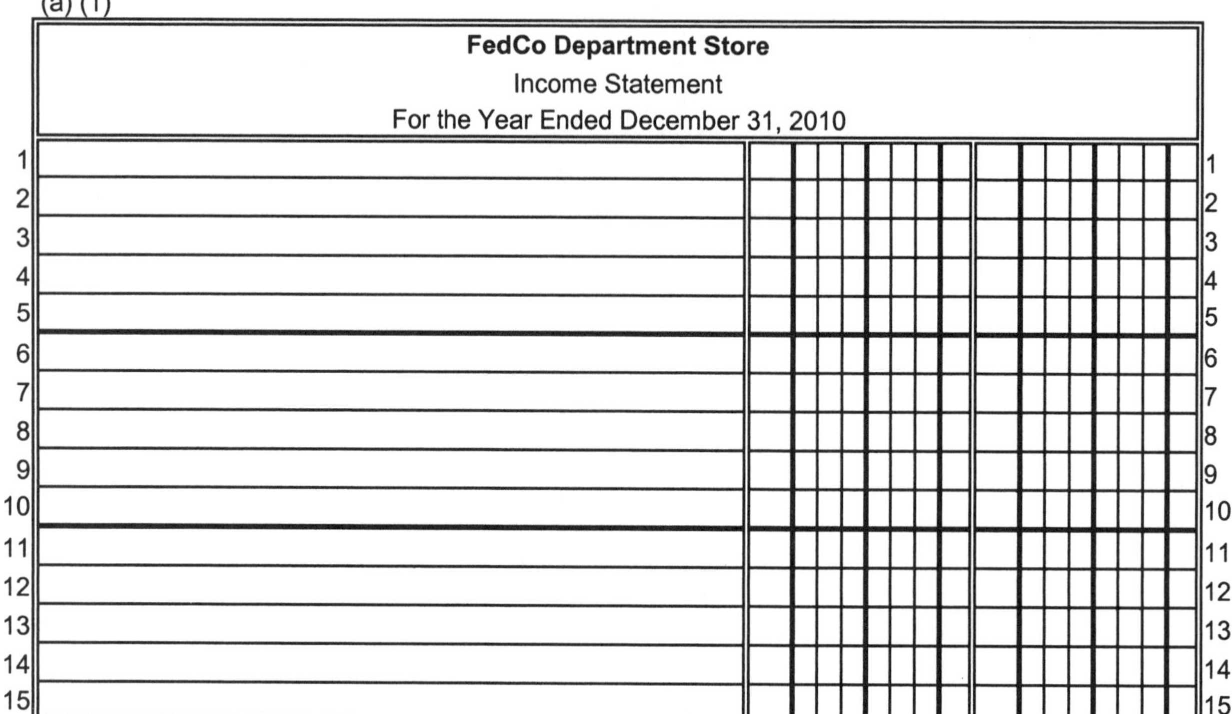
FedCo Department Store
Income Statement
For the Year Ended December 31, 2010

(2)

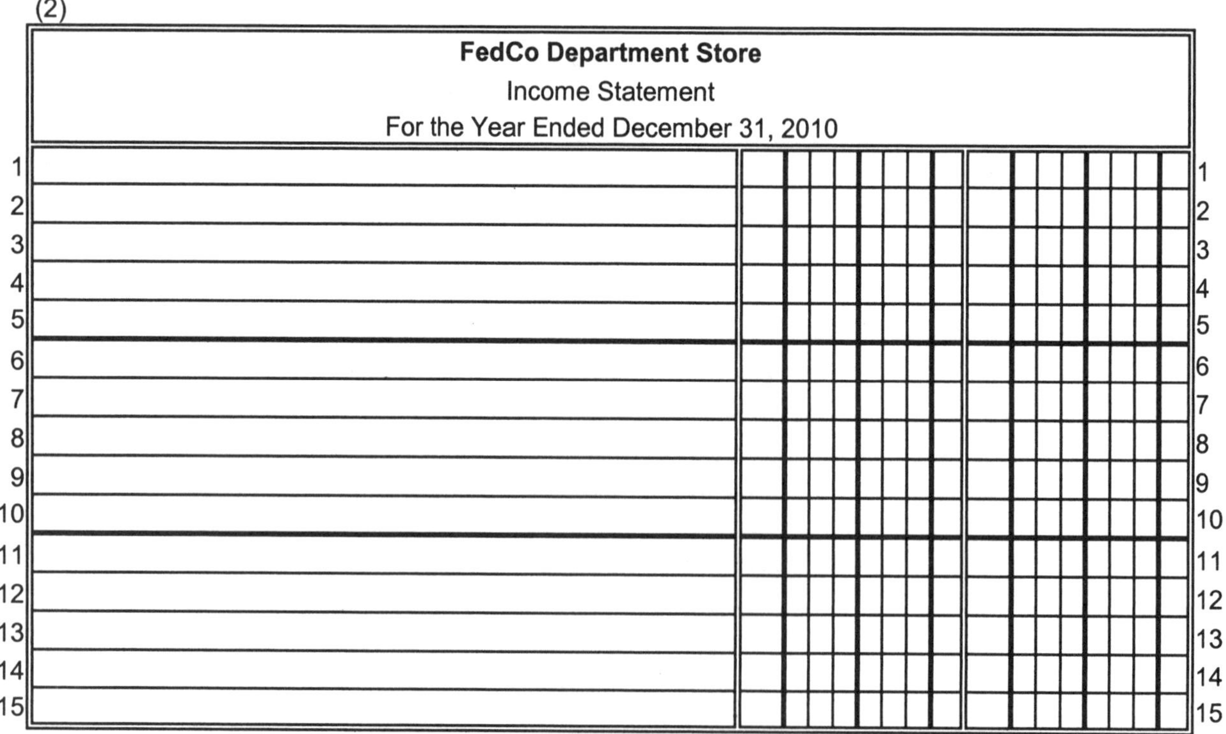
FedCo Department Store
Income Statement
For the Year Ended December 31, 2010

(b)

(c)

FedCo Department Store
Income Statement
For the Year Ended December 31, 2010

Name

Section

Date

BE6-1

(a)

(b)

(c)

(d)

BE6-2

BE6-3	(a) FIFO			(b) LIFO		
	Units	Unit Cost	Total	Units	Unit Cost	Total
Ending inventory				Ending inventory		

BE6-4	Units	Unit Cost	Total

Average cost per unit

Ending inventory

Name

Section

Date

BE6-5

(a)

(b)

(c)

(d)

BE6-6 Cost of goods sold under:	LIFO	FIFO
Purchases		
Cost of goods available for sale		
Less: Ending inventory		
Cost of goods sold		

BE6-7	Cost	Market	LCM
Inventory categories:			
Cameras			
Camcorders			
DVD players			
Total valuation			

BE6-8

Name

Section

Date

BE6-9

Inventory turnover:

Days in inventory:

***BE6-10** See next page

***BE6-11**

(1)

(2)

***BE6-12**	At Cost	At Retail

Cost-to-retail ratio:

Estimated cost of ending inventory:

Name

Section

Date

***BE6-10**

Product E2-D2

(1) FIFO Method

Date	Purchases	Cost of Goods Sold	Balance

(2) LIFO Method

Date	Purchases	Cost of Goods Sold	Balance

(3) Moving-Avergae

Date	Purchases	Cost of Goods Sold	Balance

Name

Section

Date

DO IT! 6-1

DO IT! 6-2

Cost of goods available for sale:

Ending inventory:

(a) FIFO:

(b) LIFO:

(c) Average-cost:

Name

Section

Date

DO IT! 6-3

(a) Inventory Item	Cost	Market	Lower of Cost or Market
Small	$ 64,000	$ 73,000	$
Medium	290,000	260,000	
Large	152,000	171,000	

(b)	2010	2011
Ending inventory		
Cost of goods sold		
Owner's equity		

DO IT! 6-4	2009	2010
Inventory turnover ratio		
Days in inventory		

Name | Exercises 6-1 and 6-2

Section

Date

E6-1

Ending Inventory - physical count	$	297000

E6-2

Ending inventory - as reported	$	740000

Name Exercise 6-3

Section

Date Bargain Electronics Ltd.

(a)

(b)

(c)

Name Exercise 6-4

Section

Date Boarders

(a)

FIFO

Proof:

	Date	Units	Unit Cost	Total Cost

LIFO

Proof:

	Date	Units	Unit Cost	Total Cost

(b)

Name | Exercise 6-5
Section
Date | Catlet Co.

FIFO

Proof:

	Date	Units	Unit Cost	Total Cost

LIFO

Proof:

	Date	Units	Unit Cost	Total Cost

Name Exercise 6-6

Section

Date Yount Company

(a) (1) FIFO

(2) LIFO

(b)

(c)

Name Exercise 6-7

Section

Date Jones Company

(a) (1) FIFO

(2) LIFO

(3) AVERAGE

(b)

(c)

(d)

Name

Section

Date

E6-8

Cost of Goods Available for Sale	÷	Total Units Avaialable for Sale	=	Weighted Average Unit Cost
(a)				
Ending inventory				
Cost of goods sold				
(b)				
(c)				

E6-9

	Cost	Market	Lower of Cost or Market	
Cameras				
Minolta				
Canon				
Total				
Light Meters				
Vivitar				
Kodak				
Total				
Total inventory				

E6-10

	Cost	Market	Lower of Cost or Market	
Cameras				
DVD players				
Ipods				
Total inventory				

Name

Section

Date

Exercise 6-12

Staley Watch Company

(a)	2010	2011

(b)

(c)

Name Exercise 6-11

Section

Date

		2010	2011		
1	Beginning inventory				1
2	Cost of goods purchased				2
3	Cost of goods available for sale				3
4	Corrected ending inventory				4
5	Cost of goods sold				5
6					6

Name

Section

Date

*Exercise 6-15

Klugman Appliance

(1)

FIFO

Date	Purchases	Cost of Goods Sold	Balance
Jan. 1			
8			
10			
15			

(2)

LIFO

Date	Purchases	Cost of Goods Sold	Balance
Jan. 1			
8			
10			
15			

(3)

AVERAGE-COST

Date	Purchases	Cost of Goods Sold	Balance
Jan. 1			
8			
10			
15			

Name

Section

Date

*Exercise 6-16

Yount Company

(a)

Cost of goods available for sale:

FIFO

Date	Purchases		Cost of goods sold		Balance	
June 1						
12						
15						
23						
27						

Ending inventory =

Cost of goods sold =

Name

Section

Date

*Exercise 6-16 Continued

Yount Company

(a) (Continued)

LIFO

Date	Purchases	Cost of goods sold	Balance
June 1			
12			
15			
23			
27			

Ending inventory = Cost of goods sold =

MOVING-AVERAGE

Date	Purchases	Cost of goods sold	Balance
June 1			
12			
15			
23			
27			

Ending inventory = Cost of goods sold =

(b)

(c)

Name

Section

Date

*Exercise 6-17

Boarders

(a)

FIFO

Date	Purchases	Cost of Goods Sold	Balance
9/1			
9/5			
9/12			
9/16			
9/19			
9/26			
9/29			

LIFO

Date	Purchases	Cost of Goods Sold	Balance
9/1			
9/5			
9/12			
9/16			
9/19			
9/26			
9/29			

Name

Section

Date

*Exercise 6-17 Concluded

Xpert

(a) (Continued)

MOVING-AVERAGE

Date	Purchases		Cost of Goods Sold		Balance	
9/1						
9/5						
9/12						
9/16						
9/19						
9/26						
9/29						

(b)

	Periodic		Perpetual
Ending inventory FIFO			
Ending inventory LIFO			

(c)

Name

Section

Date

*Exercise 6-18

Doc Gibbs Company

(a)

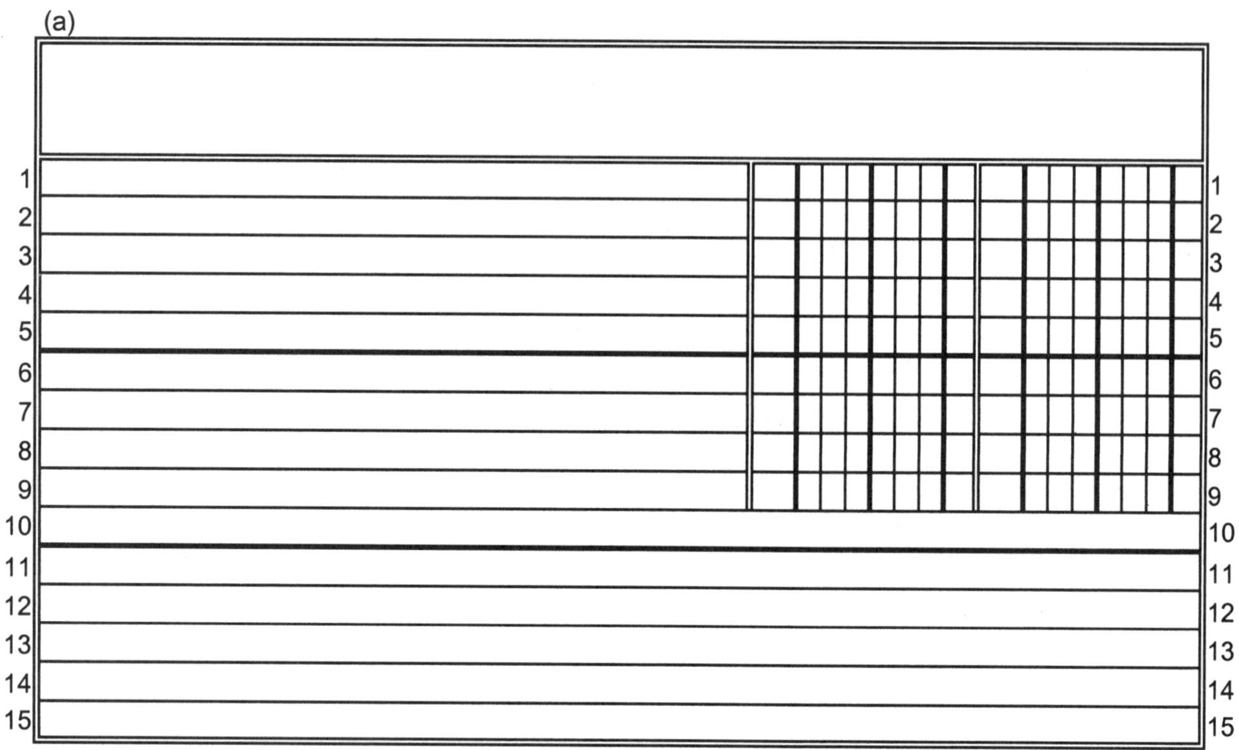

(b)

Name *Exercises 6-19 and 6-20

Section

Date

***E6-19**

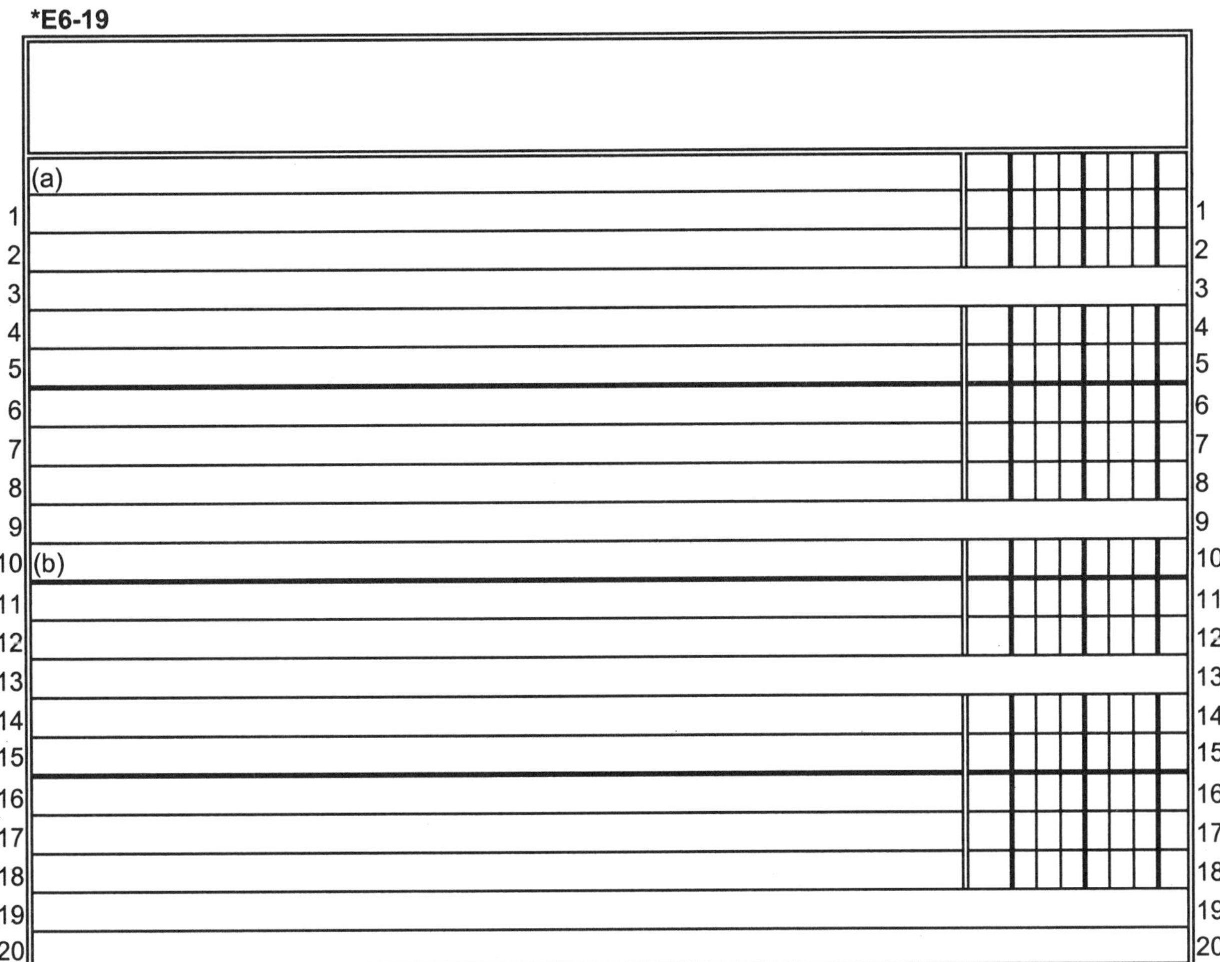

***E6-20**

	Women's Department		Men's Department	
	Cost	Retail	Cost	Retail
Beginning inventory				
Goods purchased				
Goods avail. for sale				
Net sales				
Ending inv. at retail				
Cost/retail ratio				
Estimated cost of ending inventory				

Name Problem 6-2A

Section

Date Glanville Distribution

(a)

COST OF GOODS AVAILABLE FOR SALE

Date	Explanation	Units	Unit Cost	Total Cost
March 1				
5				
13				
21				
26				

(b) **FIFO**

(1) Ending Inventory

Date		Units	Unit Cost	Total Cost

(2) Cost of Goods Sold

	Total Cost

Proof of Cost of Goods Sold

Date		Units	Unit Cost	Total Cost

(b) (Continued)

LIFO

(1) Date	Ending Inventory	Units	Unit Cost	Total Cost

(2) Cost of Goods Sold

Proof of Cost of Goods Sold

Date		Units	Unit Cost	Total Cost

Moving-Average

(1) Ending Inventory

Average Cost Per Unit	Units	Unit Cost	Total Cost

(2) Cost of Goods Sold

(c)

(1)

(2)

Name Problem 6-3A

Section

Date Eddings Company

(a)

COST OF GOODS AVAILABLE FOR SALE

Date	Explanation	Units	Unit Cost	Total Cost
2/1				
2/20				
5/5				
8/12				
12/8				

(b) **FIFO**

(1) Ending Inventory

Date		Units	Unit Cost	Total Cost

(2) Cost of Goods Sold

Proof of Cost of Goods Sold

Date		Units	Unit Cost	Total Cost

(b) (Continued)

LIFO

(1) Date	Ending Inventory	Units	Unit Cost	Total Cost

(2) Cost of Goods Sold

	Total Cost

Proof of Cost of Goods Sold

Date		Units	Unit Cost	Total Cost

Moving-Average

(1) Ending Inventory

Average Cost Per Unit	Units	Unit Cost	Total Cost

(2) Cost of Goods Sold

	Total Cost

(c)

(1)

(2)

Name

Section

Date

Problem 6-4A

Morales Co.

(a)

Morales Co.

Condensed Income Statements

For the Year Ended December 31, 2010

	FIFO	LIFO

(b)

(a)

Cost of Goods Available For Sale

Date	Explanation	Units	Unit Cost	Total Cost
Oct. 1				
9				
17				
25				

Ending Inventory in Units

Sales Revenue

Date		Units	Unit Price	Total Sales
Oct. 11				
22				
29				

(1) **LIFO**

(i) Ending Inventory

Date		Units	Unit Cost	Total Cost

(ii) Cost of Goods Sold

(iii) Gross Profit

(iv) Gross Profit Rate

(a) (Continued)

(2) **FIFO**

(i) Ending Inventory

Date		Units	Unit Cost	Total Cost

(ii) Cost of Goods Sold

(iii) Gross Profit

(iv) Gross Profit Rate

(3) **Moving-Average**

Weighted Average Cost Per Unit

(i) Ending Inventory

(ii) Cost of Goods Sold

(iii) Gross Profit

(a) (Continued)

Moving-Average

(iv) Gross Profit Rate

(b)

Name Problem 6-6A

Section

Date Bernelli Diamonds

(a)

Specific Identification

(1) To maximize gross profit

Sales Revenue

Date		Units	Unit Price	Sales Revenue
Mar. 5				
25				

Cost of Goods Sold

Date		Units	Unit Cost	Total Cost
Mar. 5				
25				

Sales Revenue	
Cost of Goods Sold	
Gross profit	

(2) To minimize gross profit

Sales Revenue

Date		Units	Unit Price	Sales Revenue
Mar. 5				
25				

Cost of Goods Sold

Date		Units	Unit Cost	Total Cost
Mar. 5				
25				

Sales Revenue	
Cost of Goods Sold	
Gross profit	

(b)

FIFO

Cost of Goods Available for Sale

Date		Units	Unit Cost	Total Cost
Mar. 1				
3				
10				

	Units	Unit Cost	Total Cost
Goods available for sale			
Units sold			
Ending inventory			

Goods available for sale	
Ending inventory	
Cost of goods sold	

Sales revenue	
Cost of goods sold	
Gross profit	

(c)

LIFO

Cost of Goods Available for Sale	
Ending inventory	
Cost of goods sold	

Sales revenue	
Cost of goods sold	
Gross profit	

(d)

Name Problem 6-7A

Section

Date Utley Inc.

(a)

Utley Inc.

Condensed Income Statement

For the Year Ended December 31, 2010

	FIFO	LIFO

(b)

Name | Problem 6-8A

Section

Date | Vasquez Ltd.

(a)

Cost of Goods Available for Sale

	Units	Unit Cost	Total Cost
Inventory			
Purchases:			
January 2			
January 9			
January 10 return			
Januarty 23			
Sales:			
January 6			
January 9 return			
January 10			
January 30			

Name

Section

Date

Problem 6-8A Continued

Vasquez Ltd.

(a) (Continued)

(1) Date	LIFO					
	Purchases		Cost of Goods Sold		Balance	
Jan. 1					(150 units @ $17)	2550
2						
6						
9						
9						
10						
10						
23						
30						

(i) Cost of goods sold =

(ii) Ending inventory =

(iii) Gross profit =

Name

Section

Date

Problem 6-8A Continued

Vasquez Ltd.

(a) (Continued)

(2) Date	FIFO Purchases		FIFO Cost of Goods Sold		FIFO Balance	
Jan. 1					(150 units @ $17)	2550
2						
6						
9						
9						
10						
10						
23						
30						

(i) Cost of goods sold =

(ii) Ending inventory =

(iii) Gross profit =

Name

Section

Date

Problem 6-8A Continued

Vasquez Ltd.

(a) (Continued)

(3) Date	Moving-Average					
	Purchases		Cost of Goods Sold		Balance	
Jan. 1					(150 units @ $17)	2550
2						
6						
9						
9						
10						
10						
23						
30						

(i) Cost of goods sold =

(ii) Ending inventory =

(iii) Gross profit =

(b)

	LIFO	FIFO	Moving-Average

Name

Section

Date

Problem 6-9A

Sandoval Appliance Mart

(a)

(1) Date	FIFO		
	Purchases	Cost of Goods Sold	Balance
May 1			
4			
8			
12			
15			
20			
25			

(2) Date	Moving-Average Cost		
	Purchases	Cost of Goods Sold	Balance
May 1			
4			
8			
12			
15			
20			
25			

Name

Section

Date

Problem 6-9A Concluded

Sandoval Appliance Mart

(a) (Continued)

(3) Date	LIFO					
	Purchases		Cost of Goods Sold		Balance	
May 1						
4						
8						
12						
15						
20						
25						

(b)

Name *Problem 6-10A

Section

Date Saffordville Company

(a)	February
Net sales	
Gross profit rate	

(b)

Net sales

Name *Problem 6-11A

Section

Date Neer Department Store

(a)	Sporting Goods		Jewelry and Cosmetics	
	Cost	Retail	Cost	Retail
Beginning inventory				
Purchases				
Purchase returns				
Purchase discounts				
Freight-in				
Goods available for sale				
Net sales				
Ending inventory at retail				

Cost-to-retail ratio:

Sporting goods:

Jewelry and cosmctics:

Estimated ending inventory at cost:

Sporting goods:

Jewelry and cosmetics:

(b) Sporting goods:

Jewelry and cosmetics:

Name | Problem 6-2B

Section

Date | Soul Patrol Distribution

(a)

COST OF GOODS AVAILABLE FOR SALE

Date	Explanation	Units	Unit Cost	Total Cost
Oct. 1				
3				
9				
19				
25				

(b) **FIFO**

(1) Ending Inventory

Date		Units	Unit Cost	Total Cost

(2) Cost of Goods Sold

Proof of Cost of Goods Sold

Date		Units	Unit Cost	Total Cost

Name Problem 6-2B Concluded

Section

Date Soul Patrol Distribution

(b) (Continued)

LIFO

(1) Ending Inventory

Date		Units	Unit Cost	Total Cost

(2) Cost of Goods Sold

Proof of Cost of Goods Sold

Date		Units	Unit Cost	Total Cost

Moving-Average

(1) Ending Inventory

Average Cost Per Unit	Units	Unit Cost	Total Cost

(2) Cost of Goods Sold

(c)

(1)

(2)

Name Problem 6-3B

Section

Date Lobster Company

(a)

COST OF GOODS AVAILABLE FOR SALE

Date	Explanation	Units	Unit Cost	Total Cost
1/1				
3/15				
7/20				
9/4				
12/2				

(b) **FIFO**

(1) Ending Inventory

Date		Units	Unit Cost	Total Cost

(2) Cost of Goods Sold

	Total Cost

Proof of Cost of Goods Sold

Date		Units	Unit Cost	Total Cost

(b) (Continued)

LIFO

(1) Date	Ending Inventory	Units	Unit Cost	Total Cost

(2) Cost of Goods Sold

Proof of Cost of Goods Sold

Date		Units	Unit Cost	Total Cost

Moving-Average

(1) Ending Inventory

Average Cost Per Unit	Units	Unit Cost	Total Cost

(2) Cost of Goods Sold

(c)

(1)

(2)

Name

Section

Date

Problem 6-4B

Moner Inc.

(a)

Moner Inc.

Condensed Income Statements

For the Year Ended December 31, 2010

	FIFO	LIFO

(b)

Name Problem 6-5B

Section

Date Web Inc.

(a)

Cost of Goods Available For Sale

Date	Explanation	Units	Unit Cost	Total Cost
June 1				
4				
18				
18				
28				

Ending Inventory in Units

Sales Revenue

Date		Units	Unit Price	Total Sales
June 10				
11				
25				

(1) **LIFO**

(i) Ending Inventory

Date		Units	Unit Cost	Total Cost

(ii) Cost of Goods Sold

(iii) Gross Profit

(iv) Gross Profit Rate

(a) (Continued)

(2) **FIFO**

(i) Ending Inventory

Date		Units	Unit Cost	Total Cost

(ii) Cost of Goods Sold

(iii) Gross Profit

(iv) Gross Profit Rate

(3) **Moving-Average**

Weighted Average Cost Per Unit

(i) Ending Inventory

(ii) Cost of Goods Sold

(iii) Gross Profit

(a) (Continued)

Moving-Average

(iv) Gross Profit Rate

(b)

Name | Problem 6-6B

Section

Date | Mondello Inc.

(a)

Mondello Inc.

Income Statement (Partial)

For the Year Ended December, 31, 2010

	Specific Identification	FIFO	LIFO

Specific identification ending inventory consists of:

	Units	Unit Cost	Total Cost

FIFO ending inventory consists of:

LIFO ending inventory consists of:

(b)

Name | Problem 6-7B

Section

Date | Clare Co.

(a)

Clare Co. Condensed Income Statement For the Year Ended December 31, 2010		
	FIFO	LIFO

(b)

Name

Section

Date

Problem 6-8B

Hector Inc.

(a)

Cost of Goods Available for Sale			
	Units	Unit Cost	Total Cost
Inventory			
Purchases:			
January 5			
January 15			
January 16 return			
January 25			
Sales:			
January 8			
January 10 return			
January 20			

Name
Section
Date

Problem 6-8B Continued

Hector Inc.

(a) (Continued)

(1) Date	LIFO Purchases		Cost of Goods Sold		Balance	
Jan. 1					(50 units @ $12)	600
5						
8						
10						
15						
16						
20						
25						

(i) Cost of goods sold =

(ii) Ending inventory =

(iii) Gross profit =

Name

Section

Date

Problem 6-8B Continued

Hector Inc.

(a) (Continued)

(2) Date	FIFO Purchases		Cost of Goods Sold		Balance	
Jan. 1					(50 units @ $12)	600
5						
8						
10						
15						
16						
20						
25						

(i) Cost of goods sold =

(ii) Ending inventory =

(iii) Gross profit =

Name

Section

Date

Problem 6-8B Continued

Hector Inc.

(a) (Continued)

(3) Date	**Moving-Average** Purchases		Cost of Goods Sold		Balance	
Jan. 1					(50 units @ $12)	600
5						
8						
10						
15						
16						
20						
25						

(i) Cost of goods sold =

(ii) Ending inventory =

(iii) Gross profit =

Name

Section

Date

Problem 6-8B Concluded

Hector Inc.

(b)

	LIFO	FIFO	Moving-Average

Name

Section

Date

*Problem 6-9B

Fontana Co.

(a)

(1) Date	FIFO		
	Purchases	Cost of Goods Sold	Balance
July 1			
6			
11			
14			
21			
27			

(2) Date	MOVING-AVERAGE		
	Purchases	Cost of Goods Sold	Balance
July 1			
6			
11			
14			
21			
27			

Name

Section

Date

Problem 6-9B Concluded

Fontana Co.

(a) (Continued)

	(3) Date	LIFO Purchases		LIFO Cost of Goods Sold		LIFO Balance		
1	July 1							1
2	6							2
3	11							3
4								4
5	14							5
6								6
7	21							7
8								8
9								9
10	27							10
11								11
12								12
13								13

(b)

1		1
2		2
3		3
4		4

Name *Problem 6-10B

Section

Date O'Reilly Company

(a)	November
Net sales	
Gross profit rate	
(b)	
Net sales	

Name

Section

Date

*Problem 6-11B

Fond du Lac Books

(a)	Hardcovers		Pperbacks	
	Cost	Retail	Cost	Retail
Beginning inventory				
Purchases				
Purchase returns				
Purchase discounts				
Freight-in				
Goods available for sale				
Net sales				
Ending inventory at retail				

Cost-to-retail ratio:

Hardcovers:

Paperbacks:

Estimated ending inventory at cost:

Hardcovers:

Paperbacks:

(b) Hardcovers:

Paperbacks:

	December 29, 2007	December 30, 2006
(a) Inventory (in millions)		

(b) Dollar change in inventories between 2006 and 2007:

Percent change in inventories between 2006 and 2007:

2007 inventory as a percent of current assets:

(c)

(d) PepsiCo (in millions)	2007	2006	2005
Cost of goods sold			

2007 cost of goods sold as a percent of sales:

Name Chapter 6 Comparative Analysis Problem

Section

Date PepsiCo, Inc. versus Coca-Cola Company

(a)	PepsiCo	Coca-Cola
(1) Inventory turnover:		
(2) Days in inventory:		

(b)

Name

Section

Date

(a) (1) Sales January 1 - March 31, 2010:

(2) Purchases January 1 - March 31, 2010:

*(b)	2010	2009
Net sales		
Gross profit rate		

Average gross profit rate

*(c) Sales

BE7-4

Accounts Receivable Subsidiary Ledger

Agler Co.

Date	Explanation	Ref.	Debit	Credit	Balance

Barto Co.

Date	Explanation	Ref.	Debit	Credit	Balance

Maris Co.

Date	Explanation	Ref.	Debit	Credit	Balance

General Ledger

Accounts Receivable

Date	Explanation	Ref.	Debit	Credit	Balance

Name

Section

Date

City Company

Subsidiary balances:

Eli Company

Teddy Company

U-2 Company

General ledger:

Accounts Payable

Name Exercise 7-3

Section

Date Montalvo Company

(a) & (b)

General Ledger

Accounts Receivable

Date	Explanation	Ref.	Debit	Credit	Balance
9/1	Balance	√			1 10960

Accounts Receivable Subsidiary Ledger

Bannister

Date	Explanation	Ref.	Debit	Credit	Balance
9/1	Balance	√			2060

Crampton

Date	Explanation	Ref.	Debit	Credit	Balance
9/1	Balance	√			4820

Iman

Date	Explanation	Ref.	Debit	Credit	Balance

Kingston

Date	Explanation	Ref.	Debit	Credit	Balance
9/1	Balance	√			2640

Ruiz

Date	Explanation	Ref.	Debit	Credit	Balance
9/1	Balance	√			1440

Name

Section

Date

E7-3 (c)

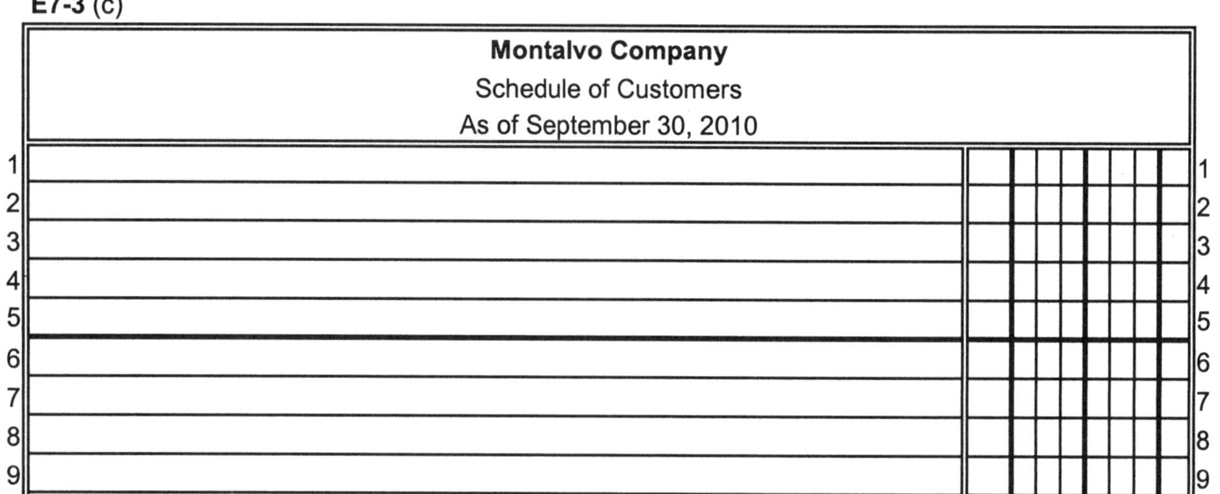

Montalvo Company

Schedule of Customers

As of September 30, 2010

E7-4

(a)

(b)

(c)

(d)

Name | Exercise 7-5
Section
Date | Nobo Uematsu Company

(a)

(b)

(c)

(d)

Name Exercise 7-6

Section

Date Montalvo Company

E-6 (a) & (b)

Montalvo Company

Sales Journal

S1

	Date	Account Debited	Invoice No.	Ref.	Accounts Receiv. Dr. Sales Cr.	COGS Dr. Merchandise Inventory Cr.	
1							1
2							2
3							3
4							4
5							5

Montalvo Company

Purchases Journal

P1

	Date	Account Credited	Terms	Ref	Merchandise Inventory (Dr.) Acc. Pay (Cr.)	
1						1
2						2
3						3
4						4
5						5

Name

Section

Date

Exercise 7-7

Pherigo Co.

#5 (a) & (b)

Pherigo Co.

Cash Receipts Journal

CR1

	Date	Account Credited	Ref.	Cash Dr.	Sales Discounts Dr.	Accounts Receivable Cr.	Sales Cr.	Other Accounts Cr.	COGS Dr. Merch Inv Cr.	
1										1
2										2
3										3
4										4
5										5

Pherigo Co.

Cash Payments Journal

CP1

	Date	Check Number	Account Debited	Ref	Other Accounts Dr.	Accounts Payable Dr.	Cash Cr.	
1								1
2								2
3								3
4								4

Name Exercise 7-9

Section

Date Velasquez Company

(a)

Date	Account Titles	Debit	Credit
Mar 2			
5			
7			

(b)

Name

Section

Date

E7-12 (a)

Purchases Journal

P1

Date	Account Credited	Ref.	Merchandise Inventory (Dr.) Acc. Pay. (Cr.)
July 3			
12			
14			
17			
20			
21			
29			

(b) General Journal

Date	Account Titles	Ref	Debit	Credit
July 1				
15				
18				
25				

E7-13

Name

Section

Date

Exercise 7-14

Matisyahu Company

(a) Accounts Payable

(b) Accounts Receivable

(c) Cash

(d) Inventory

(e) Sales

Name

Section

Date

Problem 7-1A

Grider Company

(a)

Cash Receipts Journal

CR1

	Date	Account Credited	Ref.	Cash Dr.	Sales Discounts Dr.	Accounts Receivable Cr.	Sales Cr.	Other Accounts Cr.	COGS Dr. Merch Inv Cr.	
1										1
2										2
3										3
4										4
5										5
6										6
7										7
8										8
9										9
10										10
11										11
12										12
13										13
14										14
15										15
16										16
17										17

(b)

General Ledger

Accounts Receivable — No. 112

Date	Explanation	Ref	Debit	Credit	Balance
Apr. 1	Balance	√			7450

Accounts Receivable Subsidiary Ledger

Ogden

Date	Explanation	Ref	Debit	Credit	Balance
Apr.1	Balance	√			1550

Chelsea

Date	Explanation	Ref	Debit	Credit	Balance
Apr. 1	Balance	√			1200

Eggleston Co.

Date	Explanation	Ref	Debit	Credit	Balance
Apr. 1	Balance	√			2900

Baez

Date	Explanation	Ref	Debit	Credit	Balance
Apr. 1	Balance	√			1800

(c)

1			1
2			2
3			3
4			4
5			5
6			6

Name

Section

Date

Problem 7-2A

Ming Company

(a)

Cash Payments Journal

CP1

	Date	Ck. No.	Account Debited	Ref.	Other Accounts Dr.	Accounts Payable Dr.	Merchandise Inventory Cr.	Cash Cr.	
1									1
2									2
3									3
4									4
5									5
6									6
7									7
8									8
9									9
10									10
11									11
12									12
13									13
14									14
15									15
16									16
17									17
18									18
19									19
20									20

(b)

General Ledger

Accounts Payable No. 201

Date	Explanation	Ref	Debit	Credit	Balance
Oct. 1	Balance	√			10700

Accounts Payable Subsidiary Ledger

Bovary Co.

Date	Explanation	Ref	Debit	Credit	Balance
Oct. 1	Balance	√			2700

Nyman Co.

Date	Explanation	Ref	Debit	Credit	Balance
Oct. 1	Balance	√			2500

Pyron Co.

Date	Explanation	Ref	Debit	Credit	Balance
Oct. 1	Balance	√			1800

Sims Company

Date	Explanation	Ref	Debit	Credit	Balance
Oct. 1	Balance	√			3700

(c)

1			1
2			2
3			3
4			4
5			5
6			6

Name

Section

Date

Problem 7-3A

Lopez Company

(a)

Purchases Journal

P1

Date	Account Credited (Debited)	Ref.	Other Accounts Cr.	Merchandise Inventory Dr.	Accounts Payable Dr.

Sales Journal

S1

Date	Account Debited	Ref.	Accounts Receiv. Dr. Sales Cr.	COGS Dr. Merchandise Inventory Cr.

(a) (Continued)

General Journal G1

	Date	Account Titles	Ref.	Debit	Credit	
1	July 8					1
2						2
3						3
4						4
5						5
6	22					6
7						7
8						8
9						9
10						10
11						11
12						12

(b)

General Ledger

Accounts Receivable No. 112

Date	Explanation	Ref.	Debit	Credit	Balance

Merchandise Inventory No. 120

Date	Explanation	Ref.	Debit	Credit	Balance

Supplies No. 126

Date	Explanation	Ref.	Debit	Credit	Balance

Equipment No. 157

Date	Explanation	Ref.	Debit	Credit	Balance

(b)(Continued)

Accounts Payable No. 201

Date	Explanation	Ref.	Debit	Credit	Balance

Sales No. 401

Date	Explanation	Ref.	Debit	Credit	Balance

Sales Returns and Allowances No. 412

Date	Explanation	Ref.	Debit	Credit	Balance

Cost of Goods Sold No. 505

Date	Explanation	Ref.	Debit	Credit	Balance

Advertising Expense No. 610

Date	Explanation	Ref.	Debit	Credit	Balance

(b)(Continued)

Accounts Receivable Subsidiary Ledger

Wayne Bros.

Date	Explanation	Ref.	Debit	Credit	Balance

Pinick Company

Date	Explanation	Ref.	Debit	Credit	Balance

Sager Company

Date	Explanation	Ref.	Debit	Credit	Balance

Haddad Company

Date	Explanation	Ref.	Debit	Credit	Balance

Name | Problem 7-3A Continued

Section

Date | Lopez Company

(b)(Continued)

Accounts Payable Subsidiary Ledger

Cress Supply

Date	Explanation	Ref.	Debit	Credit	Balance

Wayward Shipping

Date	Explanation	Ref.	Debit	Credit	Balance

Fritz Company

Date	Explanation	Ref.	Debit	Credit	Balance

Moon Company

Date	Explanation	Ref.	Debit	Credit	Balance

Lynda Advertisements

Date	Explanation	Ref.	Debit	Credit	Balance

Anton Company

Date	Explanation	Ref.	Debit	Credit	Balance

Name | Problem 7-3A Concluded
Section
Date | Lopez Company

(c)

Accounts receivable balance:

Subsidiary account balances:

Accounts payable balance:

Subsidiary account balances:

Name | Problem 7-4A
Section
Date | Boyden Company

(a), (b), & (c)

Sales Journal S1

	Date	Account Debited	Invoice No.	Ref.	Accounts Receivable Dr. Sales Cr.	COGS Dr. Merchandise Inventory Cr.	
1							1
2							2
3							3
4							4
5							5
6							6
7							7

Purchases Journal P1

	Date	Account Credited	Ref.	Merchandise Inventory (Dr.) Acc. Pay (Cr.)	
1					1
2					2
3					3
4					4
5					5
6					6
7					7
8					8

General Journal G1

	Date	Account Titles	Ref.	Debit	Credit	
1	Jan. 5					1
2						2
3						3
4	19					4
5						5
6						6

Name

Section

Date

Problem 7-4A Continued

Boyden Company

(a), (b), (c) (Continued)

Cash Receipts Journal

CR1

	Date	Account Credited	Ref.	Cash Dr.	Sales Discounts Dr.	Accounts Receivable Cr.	Sales Cr.	Other Accounts Cr.	COGS Dr. Merch Inv Cr.	
1										1
2										2
3										3
4										4
5										5
6										6
7										7
8										8
9										9
10										10
11										11
12										12
13										13
14										14
15										15

Name

Section

Date

Problem 7-4A Concluded

Boyden Company

(a), (b), (c) (Continued)

Cash Payments Journal

CP1

	Date	Account Debited	Ref.	Other Accounts Dr.	Accounts Payable Dr.	Merchandise Inventory Cr.	Cash Cr.	
1								1
2								2
3								3
4								4
5								5
6								6
7								7
8								8
9								9
10								10
11								11
12								12
13								13
14								14
15								15

Name Problem 7-5A

Section

Date Reyes Co.

(a), (d) & (g)

Cash No. 101

Date	Explanation	Ref.	Debit	Credit	Balance

Accounts Receivable No. 112

Date	Explanation	Ref.	Debit	Credit	Balance

Merchandise Inventory No. 120

Date	Explanation	Ref.	Debit	Credit	Balance

Store Supplies No. 127

Date	Explanation	Ref.	Debit	Credit	Balance

Prepaid Rent No. 131

Date	Explanation	Ref.	Debit	Credit	Balance

Accounts Payable No. 201

Date	Explanation	Ref.	Debit	Credit	Balance

Reyes, Capital No. 301

Date	Explanation	Ref.	Debit	Credit	Balance

(a), (d) & (g) (Continued)

Reyes, Drawing No. 306

Date	Explanation	Ref.	Debit	Credit	Balance

Sales No. 401

Date	Explanation	Ref.	Debit	Credit	Balance

Sales Discounts No. 414

Date	Explanation	Ref.	Debit	Credit	Balance

Cost of Goods Sold No. 505

Date	Explanation	Ref.	Debit	Credit	Balance

Supplies Expense No. 631

Date	Explanation	Ref.	Debit	Credit	Balance

Rent Expense No. 729

Date	Explanation	Ref.	Debit	Credit	Balance

(b), (c) & (d)

Sales Journal

S1

	Date	Account Debited	Ref.	Accounts Receivable Dr. Sales Cr.	COGS Dr. Merchandise Inventory Cr.	
1						1
2						2
3						3
4						4
5						5
6						6

Name

Section

Date

Problem 7-5A Continued

Reyes Co.

(b), (c) & (d) (Continued)

Cash Receipts Journal

CR1

	Date	Account Credited	Ref.	Cash Dr.	Sales Discounts Dr.	Accounts Receivable Cr.	Sales Cr.	Other Accounts Cr.	COGS Dr. Merch. Inv. Cr.	
1										1
2										2
3										3
4										4
5										5
6										6
7										7
8										8
9										9
10										10
11										11
12										12
13										13
14										14
15										15

Name | Problem 7-5A Continued
Section
Date | Reyes Co.

(c)

Accounts Receivable Subsidiary Ledger

Ewing Co.

Date	Explanation	Ref.	Debit	Credit	Balance

H. Prince

Date	Explanation	Ref.	Debit	Credit	Balance

W. Pitts

Date	Explanation	Ref.	Debit	Credit	Balance

S. Beauty

Date	Explanation	Ref.	Debit	Credit	Balance

Accounts Payable Subsidiary Ledger

C. Tabor

Date	Explanation	Ref.	Debit	Credit	Balance

A. Ernst

Date	Explanation	Ref.	Debit	Credit	Balance

M. Sneezy

Date	Explanation	Ref.	Debit	Credit	Balance

G. Clemens

Date	Explanation	Ref.	Debit	Credit	Balance

(c) (Continued)

J. Happy

Date	Explanation	Ref.	Debit	Credit	Balance

(e)

Reyes Co.
Trial Balance
July 31, 2010

	Debit	Credit

Name

Section

Date

Problem 7-5A Continued

Reyes Co.

(f)

Accounts payable balance:

Subsidiary accounts balance:

Accounts receivable balance:

Subsidiary accounts balance:

(g)

General Journal G1

Date	Account Titles	Ref.	Debit	Credit
July 31				
31				

(h)

Reyes Co.
Adjusted Trial Balance
July 31, 2010

		Debit	Credit	
1	Cash			1
2	Accounts Receivable			2
3	Merchandise Inventory			3
4	Store Supplies			4
5	Prepaid Rent			5
6	Accounts Payable			6
7	Reyes, Capital			7
8	Reyes, Drawing			8
9	Sales			9
10	Sales Discounts			10
11	Cost of Goods Sold			11
12	Supplies Expense			12
13	Rent Expense			13
14				14
15				15
16				16

Name Problem 7-6A

Section

Date Cortez Co.

(b) & (c)

Cash Receipts Journal

CR1

	Date	Account Credited	Ref.	Cash Dr.	Sales Discounts Dr.	Accounts Receivable Cr.	Sales Cr.	Other Accounts Cr.	COGS Dr. Merch Inv Cr.	
1										1
2										2
3										3
4										4
5										5
6										6

Cash Payments Journal

CP1

	Date	Account Debited	Ref.	Other Accounts Dr.	Accounts Payable Dr.	Merchandise Inventory Cr.	Cash Cr.	
1								1
2								2
3								3
4								4
5								5
6								6
7								7
8								8

Name | Problem 7-6A Continued

Section

Date | Cortez Co.

(b) & (c) (Continued)

Sales Journal

S1

	Date	Account Debited	Ref.	Accounts Receivable Dr. Sales Cr.	COGS Dr. Merchandise Inventory Cr.	
1						1
2						2
3						3
4						4
5						5

Purchases Journal

P1

	Date	Account Credited	Ref.	Merchandise Inventory Dr. Acc. Pay. Cr.	
1					1
2					2
3					3
4					4
5					5

General Journal

G1

	Date	Account Titles	Ref.	Debit	Credit	
1	Jan 14					1
2						2
3						3
4						4
5						5
6						6
7	20					7
8						8
9						9
10	30					10
11						11
12						12
13						13

Name Problem 7-6A Continued

Section

Date Cortez Co.

(a) and (c) *General Ledger*

Cash No. 101

Date	Explanation	Ref.	Debit	Credit	Balance
Jan. 1	Balance	√			41500

Accounts Receivable No. 112

Date	Explanation	Ref.	Debit	Credit	Balance
Jan. 1	Balance	√			15000

Notes Receivable No. 115

Date	Explanation	Ref.	Debit	Credit	Balance
Jan. 1	Balance	√			45000

Merchandise Inventory No. 120

Date	Explanation	Ref.	Debit	Credit	Balance
Jan. 1	Balance	√			23000

Equipment No. 157

Date	Explanation	Ref.	Debit	Credit	Balance
Jan. 1	Balance	√			6450

Accumulated Depreciation - Equipment No. 158

Date	Explanation	Ref.	Debit	Credit	Balance
Jan. 1	Balance	√			1500

(a) and (c) (Continued)

Notes Payable No. 200

Date	Explanation	Ref.	Debit	Credit	Balance

Accounts Payable No. 201

Date	Explanation	Ref.	Debit	Credit	Balance
Jan. 1	Balance	√			43000

B. Cortez, Capital No. 301

Date	Explanation	Ref.	Debit	Credit	Balance
Jan. 1	Balance	√			86450

Sales No. 401

Date	Explanation	Ref.	Debit	Credit	Balance

Sales Returns and Allowances No. 412

Date	Explanation	Ref.	Debit	Credit	Balance

Sales Discounts No. 414

Date	Explanation	Ref.	Debit	Credit	Balance

Cost of Goods Sold No. 505

Date	Explanation	Ref.	Debit	Credit	Balance

(a) and (c) (Continued)

Sales Salaries Expense — No. 726

Date	Explanation	Ref.	Debit	Credit	Balance

Office Salaries Expense — No. 727

Date	Explanation	Ref.	Debit	Credit	Balance

Rent Expense — No. 729

Date	Explanation	Ref.	Debit	Credit	Balance

Accounts Receivable Subsidiary Ledger

J. Anders

Date	Explanation	Ref.	Debit	Credit	Balance
Jan. 1	Balance	√			2500

F. Cone

Date	Explanation	Ref.	Debit	Credit	Balance
Jan. 1	Balance	√			7500

T. Dudley

Date	Explanation	Ref.	Debit	Credit	Balance
Jan. 1	Balance	√			5000

M. Rensing

Date	Explanation	Ref.	Debit	Credit	Balance

Name
Section
Date

Problem 7-6A Continued

Cortez Co.

(a) and (c) (Continued)

Accounts Payable Subsidiary Ledger

G. Marley

Date	Explanation	Ref.	Debit	Credit	Balance

J. Feeney

Date	Explanation	Ref.	Debit	Credit	Balance
Jan. 1	Balance	√			10000

D. Goodman

Date	Explanation	Ref.	Debit	Credit	Balance
Jan. 1	Balance	√			18000

K. Inwood

Date	Explanation	Ref.	Debit	Credit	Balance
Jan. 1	Balance	√			15000

E. Vietti

Date	Explanation	Ref.	Debit	Credit	Balance

(d)

Cortez Co.
Trial Balance
January 31, 2011

	Debit	Credit
Cash		
Accounts Receivable		
Notes Receivable		
Merchandise Inventory		
Equipment		
Accumulated Depreciation - Equipment		
Notes Payable		
Accounts Payable		
B. Cortez, Capital		
Sales		
Sales Returns and Allowances		
Sales Discounts		
Cost of Goods Sold		
Sales Salaries Expense		
Office Salaries Expense		
Rent Expense		

(e)

Accounts receivable subsidiary ledger:		
Account receivable control:		
Accounts payable subsidiary ledger:		
Accounts payable control:		

Name

Section

Date

Problem 7-1B

Kentucky Company

(a)

Cash Receipts Journal

CR1

	Date	Account Credited	Ref.	Cash Dr.	Sales Discounts Dr.	Accounts Receivable Cr.	Sales Cr.	Other Accounts Cr.	COGS Dr. Merch Inv Cr.	
1										1
2										2
3										3
4										4
5										5
6										6
7										7
8										8
9										9
10										10
11										11
12										12
13										13
14										14
15										15
16										16
17										17

(b)

General Ledger

Accounts Receivable No. 112

Date	Explanation	Ref	Debit	Credit	Balance
June 1	Balance	√			10700

Accounts Receivable Subsidiary Ledger

Moose & Son

Date	Explanation	Ref	Debit	Credit	Balance
June 1	Balance	√			3500

Chris Co.

Date	Explanation	Ref	Debit	Credit	Balance
June 1	Balance	√			2800

Cornell Bros.

Date	Explanation	Ref	Debit	Credit	Balance
June 1	Balance	√			2400

Marx Co.

Date	Explanation	Ref	Debit	Credit	Balance
June 1	Balance	√			2000

(c)

1		1
2		2
3		3

Name
Section
Date

Problem 7-2B

Starr Company

(a)

Cash Payments Journal

CP1

	Date	Ck. No.	Account Debited	Ref.	Other Accounts Dr.	Accounts Payable Dr.	Merchandise Inventory Cr.	Cash Cr.	
1									1
2									2
3									3
4									4
5									5
6									6
7									7
8									8
9									9
10									10
11									11
12									12
13									13
14									14
15									15
16									16
17									17
18									18
19									19
20									20

(b)

General Ledger

Accounts Payable No. 201

Date	Explanation	Ref	Debit	Credit	Balance
Nov. 1	Balance	√			8200

Accounts Payable Subsidiary Ledger

P. McCartney

Date	Explanation	Ref	Debit	Credit	Balance
Nov. 1	Balance	√			4000

J. Lennon

Date	Explanation	Ref	Debit	Credit	Balance
Nov. 1	Balance	√			2100

G. Harrison

Date	Explanation	Ref	Debit	Credit	Balance
Nov. 1	Balance	√			800

J. Lynne

Date	Explanation	Ref	Debit	Credit	Balance
Nov. 1	Balance	√			1300

Name Problem 7-2B Concluded

Section

Date Starr Company

(c)

Accounts payable balance:

Subsidiary account balances:

Name | Problem 7-3B

Section

Date | Dickinson Company

(a)

Purchases Journal

P1

	Date	Account Credited (Debited)	Ref.	Other Accounts Cr.	Merchandise Inventory Dr.	Accounts Payable Dr.
1						
2						
3						
4						
5						
6						
7						
8						
9						
10						
11						
12						
13						
14						
15						
16						
17						
18						

Sales Journal

S1

	Date	Account Debited	Ref.	Accounts Receiv. Dr. Sales Cr.	COGS Dr. Merchandise Inventory Cr.
1					
2					
3					
4					
5					
6					
7					
8					
9					
10					

(a) (Continued)

General Journal G1

Date	Account Titles	Ref.	Debit	Credit

(b)

General Ledger

Accounts Receivable No. 112

Date	Explanation	Ref.	Debit	Credit	Balance

Merchandise Inventory No. 120

Date	Explanation	Ref.	Debit	Credit	Balance

Supplies No. 126

Date	Explanation	Ref.	Debit	Credit	Balance

Equipment No. 157

Date	Explanation	Ref.	Debit	Credit	Balance

Name

Section

Date

Problem 7-3B Continued

Dickinson Company

(b) (Continued)

Accounts Payable — No. 201

Date	Explanation	Ref.	Debit	Credit	Balance

Sales — No. 401

Date	Explanation	Ref.	Debit	Credit	Balance

Sales Returns and Allowances — No. 412

Date	Explanation	Ref.	Debit	Credit	Balance

Cost of Goods Sold — No. 505

Date	Explanation	Ref.	Debit	Credit	Balance

Advertising Expense — No. 610

Date	Explanation	Ref.	Debit	Credit	Balance

(b)(Continued)

Accounts Receivable Subsidiary Ledger

May Company

Date	Explanation	Ref.	Debit	Credit	Balance

Coen Bros.

Date	Explanation	Ref.	Debit	Credit	Balance

Lucy Company

Date	Explanation	Ref.	Debit	Credit	Balance

Name | Problem 7-3B Continued
Section
Date | Dickinson Company

(b) (Continued) *Accounts Payable Subsidiary Ledger*

Fast Freight

Date	Explanation	Ref.	Debit	Credit	Balance

Older Company

Date	Explanation	Ref.	Debit	Credit	Balance

Michelle's Supplies

Date	Explanation	Ref.	Debit	Credit	Balance

Wolfe Company

Date	Explanation	Ref.	Debit	Credit	Balance

Zig Company

Date	Explanation	Ref.	Debit	Credit	Balance

Ole Advertising

Date	Explanation	Ref.	Debit	Credit	Balance

Name
Section
Date

Problem 7-3B Concluded

Dickinson Company

(c)

Accounts receivable balance:

Subsidiary account balances:

Accounts payable balance:

Subsidiary account balances:

Name Problem 7-4B

Section

Date Valente Company

(a), (b), & (c)

Sales Journal

S1

	Date	Account Debited	Invoice No.	Ref.	Accounts Receivable Dr. Sales Cr.	COGS Dr. Merchandise Inventory Cr.	
1							1
2							2
3							3
4							4
5							5
6							6
7							7

Purchases Journal

P1

	Date	Account Credited	Ref.	Merchandise Inventory (Dr.) Acc. Pay (Cr.)	
1					1
2					2
3					3
4					4
5					5
6					6
7					7
8					8

General Journal

G1

	Date	Account Titles	Ref.	Debit	Credit	
1	Oct 13					1
2						2
3						3
4	25					4
5						5
6						6

Name

Section

Date

Problem 7-4B Continued

Valente Company

(a), (b), (c) (Continued)

Cash Receipts Journal

CR1

	Date	Account Credited	Ref.	Cash Dr.	Sales Discounts Dr.	Accounts Receivable Cr.	Sales Cr.	Other Accounts Cr.	COGS Dr. Merch Inv Cr.	
1										1
2										2
3										3
4										4
5										5
6										6
7										7
8										8
9										9
10										10

Name

Section

Date

Problem 7-4B Concluded

Valente Company

(a), (b), (c) (Continued)

Cash Payments Journal

CP1

	Date	Account Debited	Ref.	Other Accounts Dr.	Accounts Payable Dr.	Merchandise Inventory Cr.	Cash Cr.	
1								1
2								2
3								3
4								4
5								5
6								6
7								7
8								8
9								9
10								10
11								11

Name
Section
Date

Problem 7-5B

Wicked Co.

(b)

Purchases Journal

P1

	Date	Account Credited	Ref.	Merchandise Inventory (Dr) Acc Pay (Cr)	
1					1
2					2
3					3
4					4
5					5
6					6
7					7

Cash Payments Journal

CP1

	Date	Account Debited	Ref.	Other Accounts Dr.	Accounts Payable Dr.	Merchandise Inventory Cr.	Cash Cr.	
1								1
2								2
3								3
4								4
5								5
6								6
7								7
8								8
9								9
10								10

(a), (d), & (g)

General Ledger

Cash No. 101

Date	Explanation	Ref.	Debit	Credit	Balance

Accounts Receivable No. 112

Date	Explanation	Ref.	Debit	Credit	Balance

Merchandise Inventory No. 120

Date	Explanation	Ref.	Debit	Credit	Balance

Supplies No. 126

Date	Explanation	Ref.	Debit	Credit	Balance

Equipment No. 157

Date	Explanation	Ref.	Debit	Credit	Balance

Accumulated Depreciation - Equipment No. 158

Date	Explanation	Ref.	Debit	Credit	Balance

(a), (d) and (g) (Continued)

Accounts Payable — No. 201

Date	Explanation	Ref.	Debit	Credit	Balance

B. Wicked, Capital — No. 301

Date	Explanation	Ref.	Debit	Credit	Balance

B. Wicked, Drawing — No. 306

Date	Explanation	Ref.	Debit	Credit	Balance

Sales — No. 401

Date	Explanation	Ref.	Debit	Credit	Balance

Sales Discounts — No. 414

Date	Explanation	Ref.	Debit	Credit	Balance

Cost of Goods Sold — No. 505

Date	Explanation	Ref.	Debit	Credit	Balance

Supplies Expense — No. 631

Date	Explanation	Ref.	Debit	Credit	Balance

Depreciation Expense — No. 711

Date	Explanation	Ref.	Debit	Credit	Balance

(c)

Accounts Receivable Subsidiary Ledger

C. Lion

Date	Explanation	Ref.	Debit	Credit	Balance

T. Mann

Date	Explanation	Ref.	Debit	Credit	Balance

S. Crow

Date	Explanation	Ref.	Debit	Credit	Balance

W. Oz

Date	Explanation	Ref.	Debit	Credit	Balance

Accounts Payable Subsidiary Ledger

Kansas Company

Date	Explanation	Ref.	Debit	Credit	Balance

J. Garland

Date	Explanation	Ref.	Debit	Credit	Balance

B. Lahr

Date	Explanation	Ref.	Debit	Credit	Balance

(c) (Continued)

D. Gale

Date	Explanation	Ref.	Debit	Credit	Balance

(e)

Wicked Co.
Trial Balance
February 28, 2010

	Debit	Credit
Cash		
Accounts Receivable		
Merchandise Inventory		
Supplies		
Equipment		
Accounts Payable		
B. Wicked, Capital		
B. Wicked, Drawing		
Sales		
Sales Discounts		
Cost of Goods Sold		

(f)

Accounts receivable control account:		
Accounts receivable subsidiary accounts:		
Accounts payable control account:		
Accounts payable subsidiary accounts:		

Name | Problem 7-5B Concluded

Section

Date | Wicked Co.

(g)

General Journal | G1

Date	Account Titles	Ref.	Debit	Credit
Feb 28				
28				

(h)

Wicked Co.
Adjusted Trial Balance
February 28, 2010

	Debit	Credit
Cash		
Accounts Receivable		
Merchandise Inventory		
Supplies		
Equipment		
Accumulated Depreciation - Equipment		
Accounts Payable		
B. Wicked, Capital		
B. Wicked, Drawing		
Sales		
Sales Discounts		
Cost of Goods Sold		
Supplies Expense		
Depreciation Expense		

Name

Section

Date

Packard Company

(a)

Sales Journal S1

	Date	Account Debited	Invoice No.	Ref.	Accounts Receiv. Dr. Sales Cr.	
1						1
2						2
3						3
4						4
5						5
6						6
7						7
8						8
9						9
10						10
11						11
12						12

Purchases Journal P1

	Date	Account Credited	Terms	Ref.	Purchases Dr. Acc. Pay Cr.	
1						1
2						2
3						3
4						4
5						5
6						6
7						7
8						8
9						9
10						10
11						11
12						12

Name

Section

Date

Comprehensive Problem: Chapters 3 to 7 Continued

Packard Company

(a) (Continued)

Cash Receipts Journal

CR1

	Date	Explanation	Account Credited	Ref.	Cash Dr.	Accounts Receivable Cr.	Sales Cr.	Other Accounts Cr.	
1									1
2									2
3									3
4									4
5									5
6									6
7									7
8									8
9									9
10									10
11									11
12									12
13									13
14									14
15									15

Name

Section

Date

Packard Company

(a) (Continued)

Cash Payments Journal

CR1

	Date	Explanation	Cash Cr.	Accounts Payable Dr.	Office Supplies Dr.	Accounts Debited	Ref.	Other Accounts Dr.	
1									1
2									2
3									3
4									4
5									5
6									6
7									7
8									8
9									9
10									10
11									11
12									12
13									13
14									14
15									15

Section

Date Packard Company

(e)

General Journal G1

Date	Account Titles	Ref	Debit	Credit

Name | Comprehensive Problem: Chapters 3 to 7

Section

Date | Packard Company

(a) and (e)

General Journal G1

Date	Account Titles	Ref	Debit	Credit

(b) and (e)

General Ledger

Cash No. 101

Date	Explanation	Ref.	Debit	Credit	Balance
Jan. 1	Balance	√			33750

Accounts Receivable No. 112

Date	Explanation	Ref.	Debit	Credit	Balance
Jan. 1	Balance	√			13000

Notes Receivable No. 115

Date	Explanation	Ref.	Debit	Credit	Balance
Jan. 1	Balance	√			39000

Merchandise Inventory No. 120

Date	Explanation	Ref.	Debit	Credit	Balance
Jan. 1	Balance	√			20000

Office Supplies No. 125

Date	Explanation	Ref.	Debit	Credit	Balance
Jan. 1	Balance	√			1000

Prepaid Insurance No. 130

Date	Explanation	Ref.	Debit	Credit	Balance
Jan. 1	Balance	√			2000

(b) and (e) (Continued)

Equipment — No. 157

Date	Explanation	Ref.	Debit	Credit	Balance
Jan. 1	Balance	√			6450

Accumulated Depreciation - Equipment — No. 158

Date	Explanation	Ref.	Debit	Credit	Balance
Jan. 1	Balance	√			1500

Notes Payable — No. 200

Date	Explanation	Ref.	Debit	Credit	Balance
	Balance				

Accounts Payable — No. 201

Date	Explanation	Ref.	Debit	Credit	Balance
Jan. 1	Balance	√			35000

Interest Payable — No. 230

Date	Explanation	Ref.	Debit	Credit	Balance

I. Packard, Capital — No. 301

Date	Explanation	Ref.	Debit	Credit	Balance
Jan. 1	Balance	√			78700

I. Packard, Drawing — No. 306

Date	Explanation	Ref.	Debit	Credit	Balance

(b) and (e) (Continued)

Income Summary No. 350

Date	Explanation	Ref.	Debit	Credit	Balance

Sales No. 401

Date	Explanation	Ref.	Debit	Credit	Balance

Sales Returns and Allowances No. 412

Date	Explanation	Ref.	Debit	Credit	Balance

Purchases No. 510

Date	Explanation	Ref.	Debit	Credit	Balance

Purchase Returns and Allowances No. 512

Date	Explanation	Ref.	Debit	Credit	Balance

Freight-in No. 516

Date	Explanation	Ref.	Debit	Credit	Balance

Sales Salaries Expense No. 627

Date	Explanation	Ref.	Debit	Credit	Balance

(b) and (e) (Continued)

Depreciation Expense No. 711

Date	Explanation	Ref.	Debit	Credit	Balance

Interest Expense No. 718

Date	Explanation	Ref.	Debit	Credit	Balance

Insurance Expense No. 722

Date	Explanation	Ref.	Debit	Credit	Balance

Office Salaries Expense No. 727

Date	Explanation	Ref.	Debit	Credit	Balance

Office Supplies Expense No. 728

Date	Explanation	Ref.	Debit	Credit	Balance

Rent Expense No. 729

Date	Explanation	Ref.	Debit	Credit	Balance

(b) (Continued)

Accounts Receivable Subsidiary Ledger

R. Draves

Date	Explanation	Ref.	Debit	Credit	Balance
Jan. 1	Balance	√			1500

J. Fine

Date	Explanation	Ref.	Debit	Credit	Balance

B. Hachinski

Date	Explanation	Ref.	Debit	Credit	Balance
Jan. 1	Balance	√			7500

S. Ingles

Date	Explanation	Ref.	Debit	Credit	Balance
Jan. 1	Balance	√			4000

B. Remy

Date	Explanation	Ref.	Debit	Credit	Balance

(b) (Continued)

Accounts Payable Subsidiary Ledger

D. Laux

Date	Explanation	Ref.	Debit	Credit	Balance

S. Kosko

Date	Explanation	Ref.	Debit	Credit	Balance
Jan. 1	Balance	√			9000

R. Mikush

Date	Explanation	Ref.	Debit	Credit	Balance
Jan. 1	Balance	√			15000

D. Moreno

Date	Explanation	Ref.	Debit	Credit	Balance
Jan. 1	Balance	√			11000

S. Yost

Date	Explanation	Ref.	Debit	Credit	Balance

Comprehensive Problem: Chapters 3 to 7

Packard Company

See Appendix

(d)

Packard Company

Income Statement

For the Month Ended January 31, 2010

(d) (Continued)

Packard Company
Statement of Owner's Equity
For the Month Ended January 31, 2010

Packard Company
Balance Sheet
January 31, 2010

Assets

Liabilities and Owner's Equity

(f)

Packard Company
Post-Closing Trial Balance
January 31, 2010

	Debit	Credit
Cash		
Notes Receivable		
Accounts Receivable		
Merchandise Inventory		
Office Supplies		
Prepaid Insurance		
Equipment		
Accumulated Depreciation - Equipment		
Notes Payable		
Accounts Payable		
Interest Payable		
I. Packard, Capital		

Accounts Receivable balance:		
Subsidiary account balances:		
Accounts Payable balance:		
Subsidiary account balances:		

Name Chapter 7 Financial Reporting Problem

Section

Date Bluma Co.

Sales Journal

S1

	Date	Account Debited	Invoice No.	Ref.	Accounts Receiv. Dr. Sales Cr.	COGS Dr. Merchandise Inventory Cr.	
1							1
2							2
3							3
4							4
5							5
6							6
7							7
8							8
9							9
10							10
11							11
12							12

Purchases Journal

P1

	Date	Account Credited	Terms	Ref.	Merchandise Inventory (Dr.) Acc. Pay (Cr.)	
1						1
2						2
3						3
4						4
5						5
6						6
7						7
8						8
9						9
10						10
11						11
12						12

Name
Section
Date

Bluma Co.

(a) (Continued)

Cash Receipts Journal

CR1

	Date	Account Credited	Ref.	Cash Dr.	Sales Discounts Dr.	Accounts Receivable Cr.	Sales Cr.	Other Accounts Cr.	COGS Dr. Inventory Cr.	
1										1
2										2
3										3
4										4
5										5
6										6
7										7
8										8
9										9
10										10
11										11
12										12
13										13
14										14
15										15

Name

Section

Date

Bluma Co.

(a) (Continued)

Cash Payments Journal

CP1

	Date	Account Debited	Ref.	Other Accounts Dr.	Accounts Payable Dr.	Office Supplies Dr.	Merchandise Inventory Cr.	Cash Cr.	
1									1
2									2
3									3
4									4
5									5
6									6
7									7
8									8
9									9
10									10
11									11
12									12
13									13
14									14
15									15

(a) (Continued) and (e)

General Journal G1

	Date	Account Titles	Ref	Debit	Credit	
1						1
2						2
3						3
4						4
5						5
6						6
7						7
8						8
9						9
10						10
11						11
12						12
13						13
14						14
15						15
16						16
17						17
18						18
19						19
20						20
21						21
22						22
23						23
24						24
25						25
26						26
27						27
28						28
29						29
30						30
31						31
32						32
33						33
34						34
35						35
36						36
37						37
38						38
39						39
40						40

(e) (Continued)

General Journal G1

Date	Account Titles	Ref	Debit	Credit

(b) and (e)

General Ledger

Cash — No. 101

Date	Explanation	Ref.	Debit	Credit	Balance
Jan. 1	Balance	√			35750

Accounts Receivable — No. 112

Date	Explanation	Ref.	Debit	Credit	Balance
Jan. 1	Balance	√			13000

Notes Receivable — No. 115

Date	Explanation	Ref.	Debit	Credit	Balance
Jan. 1	Balance	√			39000

Merchandise Inventory — No. 120

Date	Explanation	Ref.	Debit	Credit	Balance
Jan. 1	Balance	√			18000

Office Supplies — No. 125

Date	Explanation	Ref.	Debit	Credit	Balance
Jan. 1	Balance	√			1000

Prepaid Insurance — No. 130

Date	Explanation	Ref.	Debit	Credit	Balance
Jan. 1	Balance	√			2000

(b) and (e) (Continued)

Equipment No. 157

Date	Explanation	Ref.	Debit	Credit	Balance
Jan. 1	Balance	√			6450

Accumulated Depreciation - Equipment No. 158

Date	Explanation	Ref.	Debit	Credit	Balance
Jan. 1	Balance	√			1500

Notes Payable No. 200

Date	Explanation	Ref.	Debit	Credit	Balance

Accounts Payable No. 201

Date	Explanation	Ref.	Debit	Credit	Balance
Jan. 1	Balance	√			35000

Interest Payable No. 230

Date	Explanation	Ref.	Debit	Credit	Balance

M.Bluma, Capital No. 301

Date	Explanation	Ref.	Debit	Credit	Balance
Jan. 1	Balance	√			78700

M. Bluma, Drawing No. 306

Date	Explanation	Ref.	Debit	Credit	Balance

(b) and (e) (Continued)

Income Summary No. 350

Date	Explanation	Ref.	Debit	Credit	Balance

Sales No. 401

Date	Explanation	Ref.	Debit	Credit	Balance

Sales Returns and Allowances No. 412

Date	Explanation	Ref.	Debit	Credit	Balance

Sales Discounts No. 414

Date	Explanation	Ref.	Debit	Credit	Balance

Cost of Goods Sold No. 505

Date	Explanation	Ref.	Debit	Credit	Balance

Sales Salaries Expense No. 627

Date	Explanation	Ref.	Debit	Credit	Balance

Depreciation Expense No. 711

Date	Explanation	Ref.	Debit	Credit	Balance

(b) and (e) (Continued)

Interest Expense — No. 718

Date	Explanation	Ref.	Debit	Credit	Balance

Insurance Expense — No. 722

Date	Explanation	Ref.	Debit	Credit	Balance

Office Salaries Expense — No. 727

Date	Explanation	Ref.	Debit	Credit	Balance

Office Supplies Expense — No. 728

Date	Explanation	Ref.	Debit	Credit	Balance

Rent Expense — No. 729

Date	Explanation	Ref.	Debit	Credit	Balance

(b) (Continued)

Accounts Receivable Subsidiary Ledger

R. Dvorak

Date	Explanation	Ref.	Debit	Credit	Balance
Jan. 1	Balance	√			1500

J. Forbes

Date	Explanation	Ref.	Debit	Credit	Balance

B. Garcia

Date	Explanation	Ref.	Debit	Credit	Balance
Jan. 1	Balance	√			7500

S. LaDew

Date	Explanation	Ref.	Debit	Credit	Balance
Jan. 1	Balance	√			4000

B. Richey

Date	Explanation	Ref.	Debit	Credit	Balance

(b) (Continued)

Accounts Payable Subsidiary Ledger

D. Lynch

Date	Explanation	Ref.	Debit	Credit	Balance

S. Hoyt

Date	Explanation	Ref.	Debit	Credit	Balance
Jan. 1	Balance	√			9000

R. Moses

Date	Explanation	Ref.	Debit	Credit	Balance
Jan. 1	Balance	√			15000

D. Omara

Date	Explanation	Ref.	Debit	Credit	Balance
Jan. 1	Balance	√			11000

S. Vogel

Date	Explanation	Ref.	Debit	Credit	Balance

Chapter 7 Financial Reporting Problem

Bluma Co.

See Appendix

Name

Section

Date

Bluma Co.

(d)

Bluma Co.

Income Statement

For the Month Ended January 31, 2010

(d) (Continued)

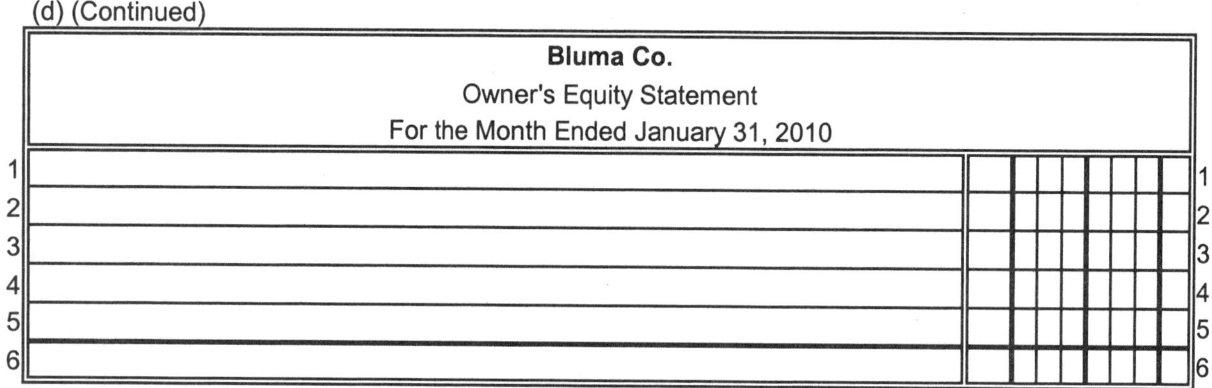

Bluma Co.

Balance Sheet

January 31, 2010

Assets

Liabilities and Owner's Equity

Name

Section

Date

Bluma Co.

(f)

Bluma Co.

Post-Closing Trial Balance

January 31, 2010

	Debit	Credit
Cash		
Notes Receivable		
Accounts Receivable		
Merchandise Inventory		
Office Supplies		
Prepaid Insurance		
Equipment		
Accumulated Depreciation - Equipment		
Notes Payable		
Accounts Payable		
Interest Payable		
M. Bluma, Capital		

Accounts Receivable balance:		
Subsidiary account balances:		
Accounts Payable balance:		
Subsidiary account balances:		

Name

Section

Date

BE8-6

	Account Titles	Debit	Credit
(a)			
(b)			

BE 8-7	Account Titles	Debit	Credit

BE 8-9

Date	Account Titles	Debit	Credit

BE 8-13

BE 8-14

Name

Section

Date

Chapter 8 DO IT! 8-3

Mengke Company

	Date	Account Titles	Debit	Credit	
1	Aug. 1				1
2					2
3					3
4					4
5	30				5
6					6
7					7
8					8
9					9
10					10
11					11
12					12
13					13
14					14
15					15
16					16
17					17
18					18
19					19
20					20
21					21

Name Exercise 8-7

Section

Date James Hughes Company

Date	Account Titles	Debit	Credit
May 1			
June 1			
July 1			
July 10			

Name

Section

Name

E8-8

Date	Account Titles	Debit	Credit
Mar. 1			
15			
20			

E8-9 (a)

Anna Pelo

Bank Reconciliation

January 31

(b)

Date	Account Titles	Debit	Credit

Name | Exercises 8-10 and 8-11

Section

Name

E8-10

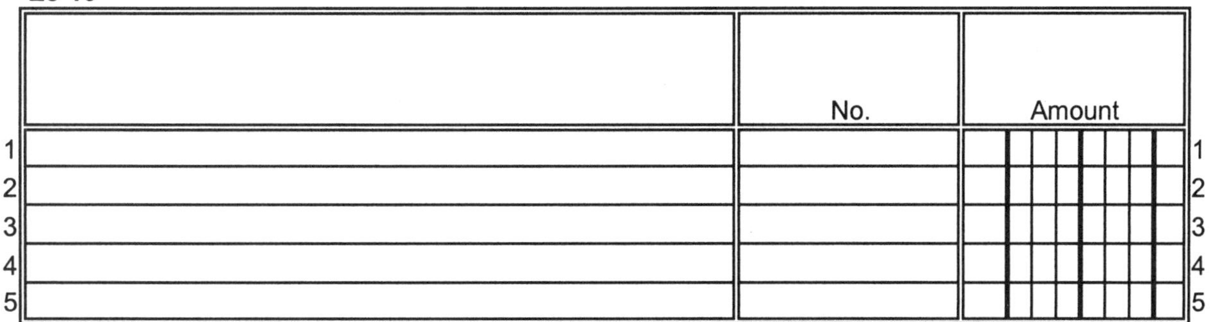

E8-11 (a)

	Family Video Company Bank Reconciliation July 31		
1			1
2			2
3			3
4			4
5			5
6			6
7			7
8			8
9			9
10			10
11			11
12			12
13			13
14			14
15			15
16			16

(b)

	Date	Account Titles	Debit	Credit	
1	July 31				1
2					2
3					3
4					4
5					5
6	31				6
7					7
8					8
9					9
10					10

Name	Exercise 8-12
Section	
Date	Robertson Company

(a)

Robertson Company
Bank Reconciliation
September 30

1				1
2				2
3				3
4				4
5				5
6				6
7				7
8				8
9				9
10				10
11				11
12				12
13				13
14				14
15				15
16				16
17				17
18				18
19				19
20				20

(b)

	Date	Account Titles	Debit	Credit	
1	Sept. 30				1
2					2
3					3
4					4
5					5
6	30				6
7					7
8					8
9	30				9
10					10
11					11
12	30				12
13					13
14					14
15					15

Name | Exercise 8-13
Section
Date | Givens Company

(a) Deposits in transit:

(b) Outstanding checks:

(c) Deposits in transit:

(d) Outstanding checks:

Name Exercise 8-14

Section

Date Lipkus Company

(a)

(b)

(c)

Name Problem 8-2A

Section

Date Winningham Company

(a) General Journal

Date	Account Titles	Debit	Credit
July 1			
15			
31			
Aug. 15			
16			
31			

(b)

Petty Cash

Date	Explanation	Ref.	Debit	Credit	Balance

(c)

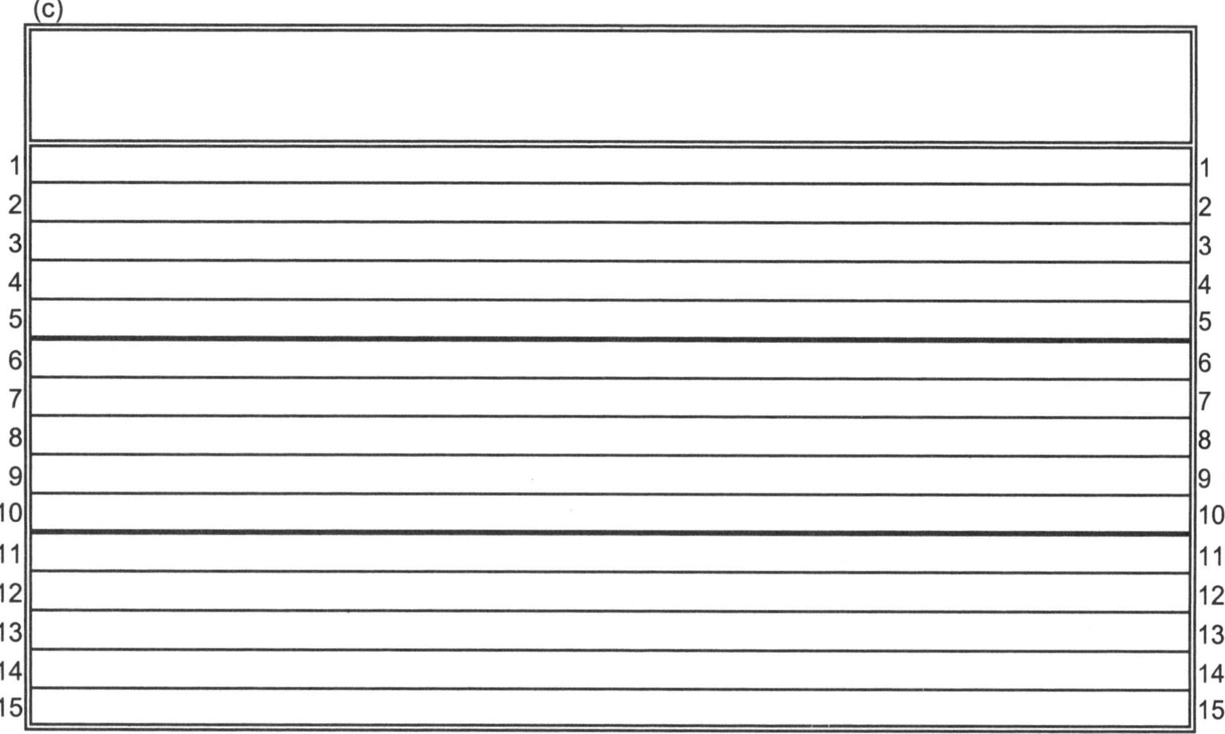

Name

Section

Date

Problem 8-3A

James Logan Company

(a)

James Logan Company

Bank Reconciliation

July 2, 1905

(b) General Journal

Date	Account Titles	Debit	Credit
May 31			
31			
31			
31			
31			

Name

Section

Date

Problem 8-4A

Backhaus Company

(a)

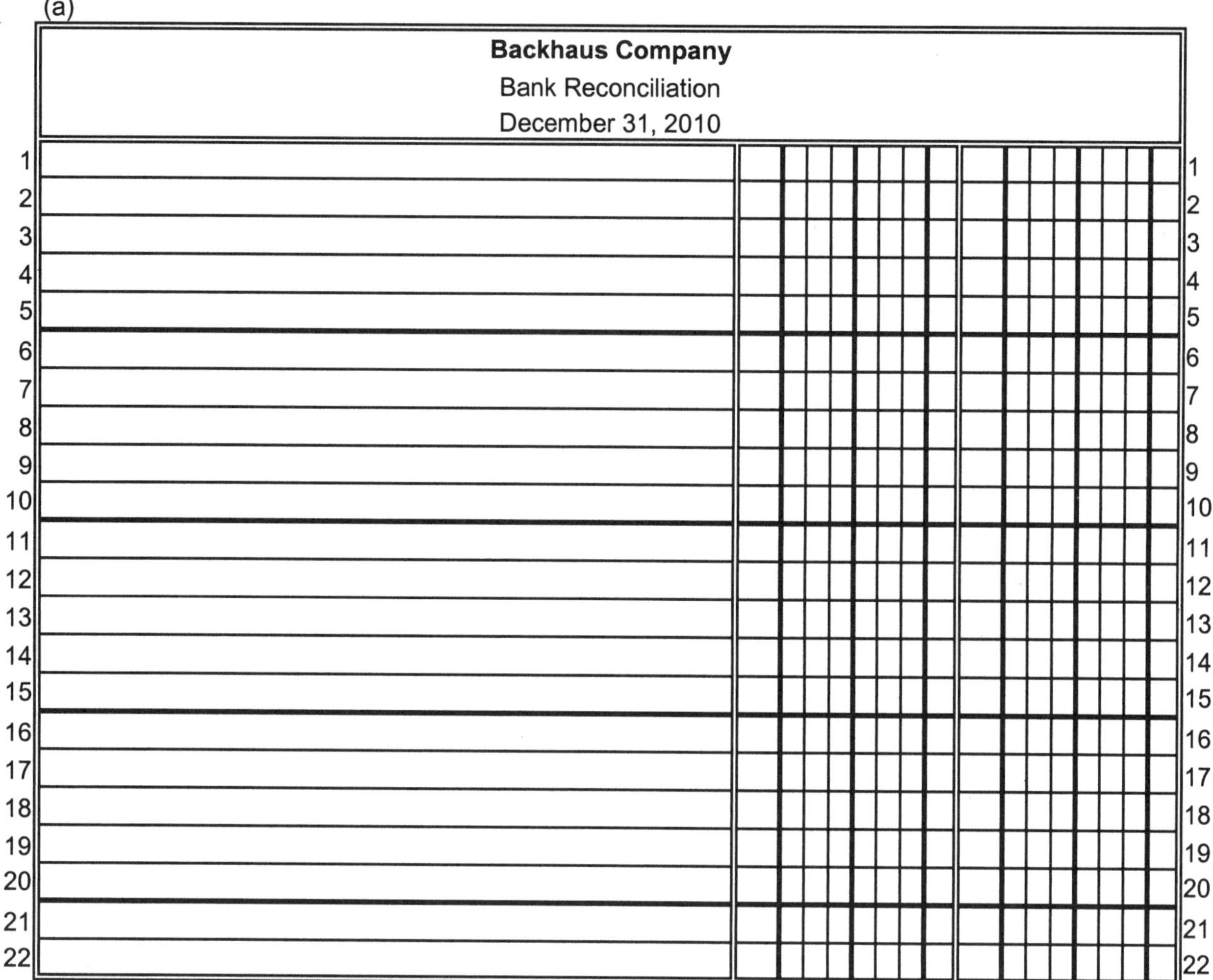

Backhaus Company

Bank Reconciliation

December 31, 2010

(b)

General Journal

Date	Account Titles	Debit	Credit
Dec. 31			
31			
31			
31			

(a)

Haverman Company
Bank Reconciliation
July 31, 2010

Computations

Name

Section

Date

Problem 8-5A Concluded

Haverman Company

(b)

General Journal

	Date	Account Titles	Debit	Credit	
1	July 31				1
2					2
3					3
4					4
5	31				5
6					6
7					7
8	31				8
9					9
10					10
11					11
12					12
13					13
14					14
15					15
16					16
17					17
18					18
19					19
20					20

Name | Problem 8-2B
Section
Date | Loganberry Company

(a)

General Journal

Date	Account Titles	Debit	Credit
July 1			
15			
31			
Aug. 15			
16			
31			

Name | Problem 8-2B Concluded
Section
Date | Loganberry Company

(b)

Petty Cash

Date	Explanation	Ref.	Debit	Credit	Balance

(c)

Name

Section

Date

Problem 8-3B

Wolverine Genetics Company

(a)

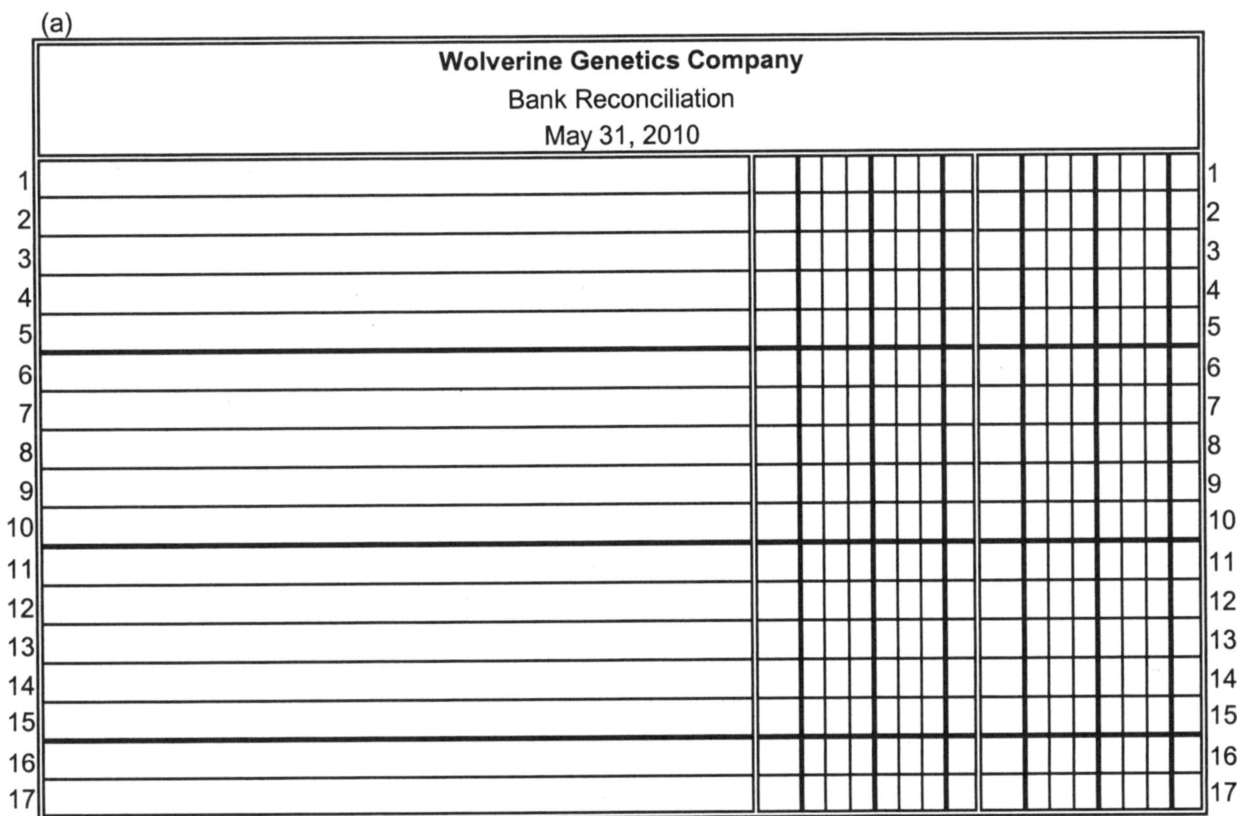

Wolverine Genetics Company

Bank Reconciliation

May 31, 2010

(b)

General Journal

Date	Account Titles	Debit	Credit
May 31			
31			
31			
31			
31			

Name

Section

Date

Problem 8-4B

Chapin Company

(a)

Chapin Company

Bank Reconciliation

November 30, 2010

(b)

General Journal

Date	Account Titles	Debit	Credit
Nov. 30			
30			
30			
30			

Name Problem 8-5B

Section

Date Bummer Company

Bummer Company

Bank Reconciliation

August 31, 2010

Computations

Name　　　　　　　　　　　　　　　　　　　　　　　　Problem 8-5B Concluded

Section

Date　　　　　　　　　　　　　　　　　　　　　　　　Bummer Company

(b)

General Journal

	Date	Account Titles	Debit	Credit	
1	Aug. 31				1
2					2
3					3
4					4
5	31				5
6					6
7					7
8	31				8
9					9
10					10
11	31				11
12					12
13					13
14					14
15					15
16					16
17					17
18					18
19					19
20					20

Name Problem 8-6B

Section

Date Gazarra Company

(a)

Gazarra Company

Bank Reconciliation

October 31, 2010

(b)

(c)

Name

Section

Date

PepsiCo, Inc. versus Coca-Cola Company

(a) (In millions)	PepsiCo	Coca-Cola
(1) Cash and cash equivalents at year-end 2007		
(2) Increase/decrease in cash and cash equivalents from 2006 to 2007		
(3) Cash provided by operating activities during year ended Dec. 31, 2007		

(b)

Name

Section

Date

BE9-1

(a)

(b)

(c)

BE9-2	Account Titles	Debit	Credit
(a)			
(b)			
(c)			

BE9-3	Account Titles	Debit	Credit
(a)			

(b) Current assets:

BE9-4	Account Titles	Debit	Credit
(a)			

(b)	(1) Before Write-Off	(2) After Write-Off

Name

Section

Date

BE9-5	Account Titles	Debit	Credit
BE9-6			
BE9-7			
(a)			
(b)			

BE9-8	Account Titles	Debit	Credit
(a)			
(b)			

BE9-9		Interest	Maturity Date
(a)			
(b)			
(c)			

BE9-10	Date of Note	Maturity Date	Annual Interest Rate	Total Interest
(a)	April 1		9%	
(b)	July 2			$ 600
(c)	March 7		10%	

Name

Section

Date

BE9-11

Date	Account Titles	Debit	Credit
Jan. 10			
Feb. 9			

BE9-12

Accounts receivable turnover ratio:

Average collection period for accounts receivable:

Name

Section

Date

DO IT! 9-1

	Account Titles	Debit	Credit

DO IT! 9-2

	Account Titles	Debit	Credit

DO IT! 9-3

(a)

(b)	Account Titles	Debit	Credit

DO IT! 9-4

(a) Accounts receivable turnover =

(b) Average collection period in days =

Name

Section

Date

E9-1

Date	Account Titles	Debit	Credit
March 1			
3			
9			
15			
31			
E9-2			
(a)			
Jan. 6			
16			
(b)			
Jan. 10			
Feb. 12			
Mar. 10			

Name

Section

Date

E9-3

Date	Account Titles	Debit	Credit
(a)			
Dec. 31			
(b) (1)			
Dec. 31			
(2)			
Dec. 31			
(c) (1)			
Dec. 31			
(2)			
Dec. 31			

E9-4

(a)

Accounts Receivable	Amount	%	Estimated Uncollectible
1 - 30 days			
30 - 60 days			
60 - 90 days			
Over 90 days			

(b)

Date	Account Titles	Debit	Credit
Mar. 31			

Name

Section

Date

E9-5

Date	Account Titles	Debit	Credit

E9-6

Date	Account Titles	Debit	Credit
2010			
Dec. 31			
2011			
May 11			
2011			
Jun. 12			

Name

Section

Date

E9-7

Date	Account Titles	Debit	Credit
(a)			
Mar. 3			
(b)			
May 10			
E9-8			
(a)			
Apr. 2			
May 3			
Jun. 1			
(b)			
July 4			

Name

Section

Date

E9-9

Date	Account Titles	Debit	Credit
(a)			
Jan. 15			
20			
Feb 10			
15			

(b)

E9-10

Date	Account Titles	Debit	Credit
(a)	2010		
Nov. 1			
Dec. 11			
16			
31			
	Calculation of interest:		
(b)	2011		
Nov. 1			

Name

Section

Date

E9-11

Date	Account Titles	Debit	Credit
	2010		
May 1			
Dec. 31			
31			
	2011		
May 1			
E9-12			
4/1/10			
7/1/10			
12/31/10			
4/1/11			
4/1/11			

Section

Date

E9-13

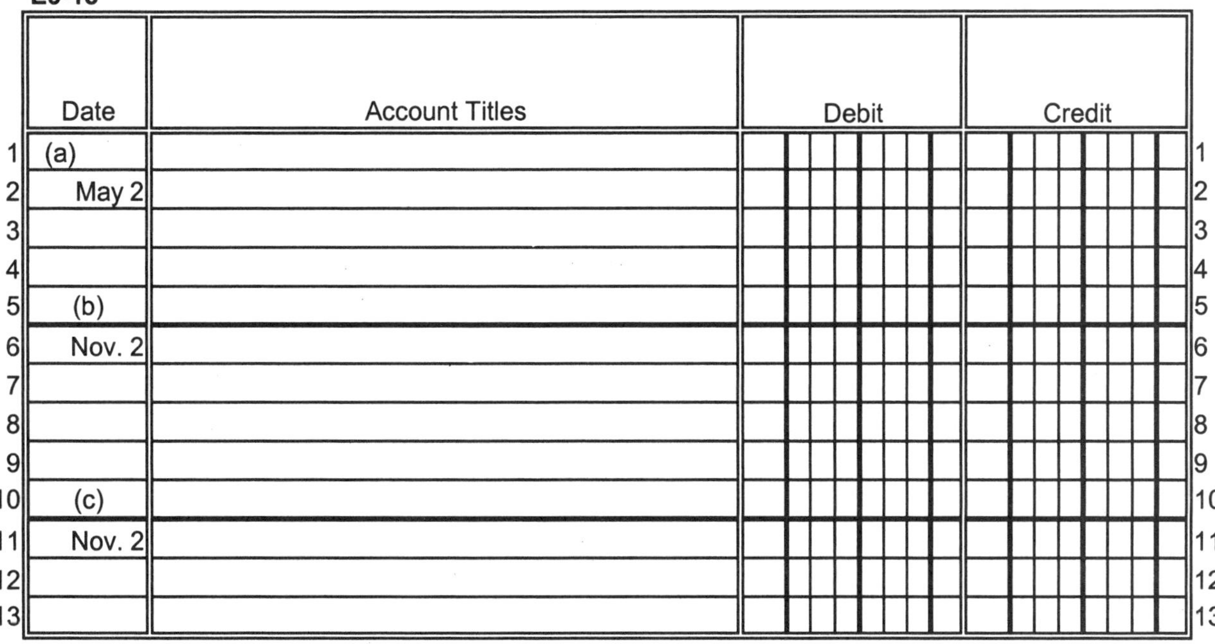

Date	Account Titles	Debit	Credit
(a)			
May 2			
(b)			
Nov. 2			
(c)			
Nov. 2			

E9-14

(a)

(b) Accounts receivable turnover ratio =

(c) Average collection period in days =

Name | Problem 9-1A

Section

Date | Leis Co.

	Account Titles	Debit	Credit
1.			
2.			
3.			
4.			
5.			

(b)

Accounts Receivable

Bal. 960,000	

Allowance for Doubtful Accounts

	Bal. 80,000

(c)

Date	Account Titles	Debit	Credit

(d)

Accounts receivable turnover ratio =

Name　　　　　　　　　　　　　　　　　　　　　　　　　　　　　　　　Problem 9-3A

Section

Date　　　　　　　　　　　　　　　　　　　　　　　　　　　　　　　　Zillmann Company

(a), (b), and (c)　　　　　　General Journal

Date	Account Titles	Debit	Credit
(a)			
Dec. 31			
(b)	(1) 2011		
Mar. 31			
	(2)		
May 31			
31			
(c)	2011		
Dec. 31			

(a) & (b)

Bad Debt Expense

Date	Explanation	Ref.	Debit	Credit	Balance

Allowance for Doubtful Accounts

Date	Explanation	Ref.	Debit	Credit	Balance
2010					
Dec. 31	Balance	√			12000

Name

Section

Date

Problem 9-4A

Wall Inc.

(a)

		Total	Number of Days Outstanding					
			0 - 30	31 - 60	61 - 90	91 - 120	Over 120	
1	Accounts receivable	$ 375000	$ 220000	$ 90000	$ 40000	$ 10000	$ 15000	1
2								2
3	% uncollectible		1%	4%	5%	8%	10%	3
4								4
5	Estimated Bad Debts							5

Date	Account Titles	Debit	Credit
(b)			
(c)			
(d)			

(e)

Name Problem 9-5A

Section

Date Worcester Company

(a)

Date	Account Titles	Debit	Credit
(b) (1)			
Dec. 31			
(2)			
Dec. 31			
(c) (1)			
Dec. 31			
(2)			
Dec. 31			
(d)			
(e)			

(f)

Name Problem 9-6A

Section

Date Mendosa Company

(a)

General Journal

Date	Account Titles	Debit	Credit
Oct. 7			
12			
15			
15			
24			
31			

Name
Section
Date

Problem 9-6A Concluded

Mendosa Company

(b)

Notes Receivable

	Date	Explanation	Ref.	Debit	Credit	Balance
1	Oct 1	Balance	√			33000
2						
3						
4						

Accounts Receivable

	Date	Explanation	Ref.	Debit	Credit	Balance
1						
2						
3						
4						

Interest Receivable

	Date	Explanation	Ref.	Debit	Credit	Balance
1	Oct 1	Balance	√			170
2						
3						
4						
5						

(c)

	Assets		
2	Current Assets		
3			
4			
5			
6			
7			
8			

Name

Section

Date

Problem 9-7A

Kloppenberg Company

General Journal

Date	Account Titles	Debit	Credit
Jan. 5			
20			
Feb. 18			
Apr. 20			
30			
May 25			
Aug. 18			
25			
Sept. 1			

Name Problem 9-1B

Section

Date Dill Imports

		Account Titles	Debit	Credit	
1	1.				1
2					2
3					3
4	2.				4
5					5
6					6
7	3.				7
8					8
9					9
10	4.				10
11					11
12					12
13	5.				13
14					14
15					15
16					16
17					17
18					18
19					19
20					20

(b)

Accounts Receivable	
Bal. 250,000	

Allowance for Doubtful Accounts	
	Bal. 15,000

(c)

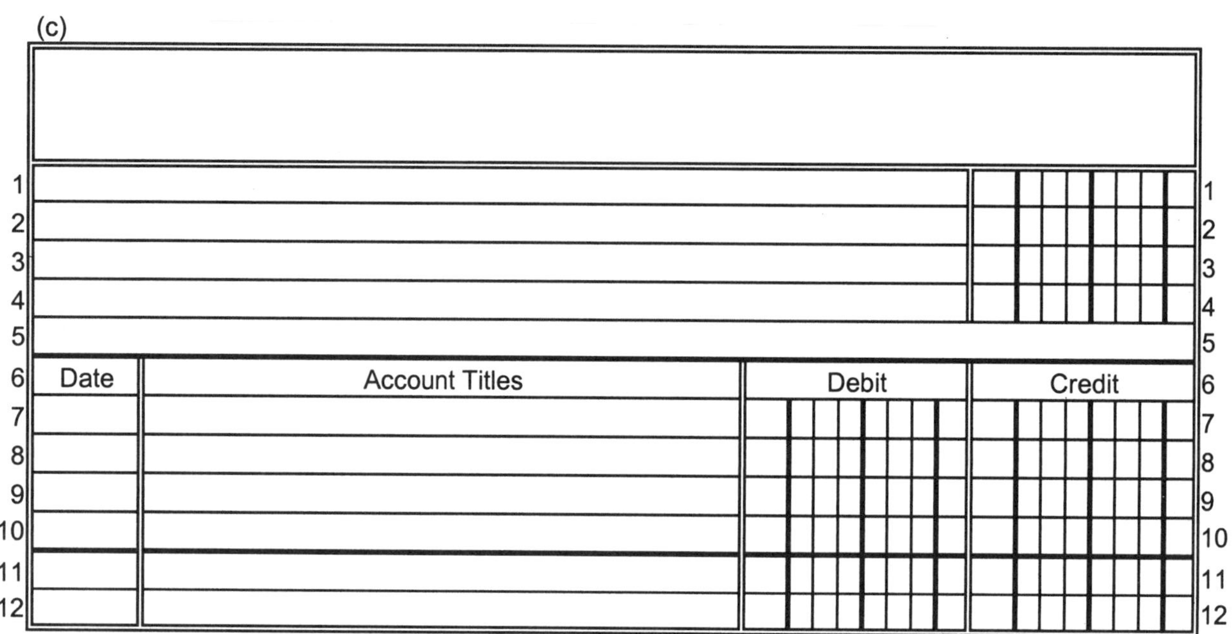

Date	Account Titles	Debit	Credit

(d)

Accounts Receivable turnover ratio =

Name | Problem 9-3B

Section

Date | Jafar Company

(a), (b), and (c)

General Journal

Date	Account Titles	Debit	Credit
(a)			
Dec. 31			
(b)	(1) 2011		
Mar. 1			
	(2)		
May 1			
1			
(c)	2011		
Dec. 31			

(a) & (b)

Bad Debt Expense

Date	Explanation	Ref.	Debit	Credit	Balance

Allowance for Doubtful Accounts

Date	Explanation	Ref.	Debit	Credit	Balance
2010					
Dec. 31	Balance	√			16000

Name

Section

Date

Problem 9-4B

Aging Accounts Receivable

(a)

			Number of Days Outstanding					
		Total	0 - 30	31 - 60	61 - 90	91 - 120	Over 120	
1	Accounts receivable	$ 375,000	$ 220,000	$ 90,000	$ 40,000	$ 10,000	$ 15,000	1
2								2
3	% uncollectible		1%	4%	5%	8%	10%	3
4								4
5	Estimated Bad Debts							5

	Date	Account Titles	Debit	Credit	
1	(b)				1
2					2
3					3
4	(c)				4
5					5
6					6
7	(d)				7
8					8
9					9
10					10
11					11
12					12
13					13
14					14
15					15

(e)

1		1
2		2
3		3
4		4
5		5

Name

Section

Date

Problem 9-5B

Liquid Snake Company

General Journal

Date	Account Titles	Debit	Credit
(a) (1)			
Dec. 31			
(2)			
Dec. 31			
(b) (1)			
Dec. 31			
(2)			
Dec. 31			
(c)			
(d)			
(e)			
(1)			
(2)			

Name | Problem 9-6B

Section

Date | Marty Co.

(a) General Journal

Date	Account Titles	Debit	Credit
July 5			
14			
14			
15			
25			
31			

(b)

Notes Receivable

Date	Explanation	Ref.	Debit	Credit	Balance
July 1	Balance	√			57000

Accounts Receivable

Date	Explanation	Ref.	Debit	Credit	Balance

Interest Receivable

Date	Explanation	Ref.	Debit	Credit	Balance
July 1	Balance	√			420

(c)

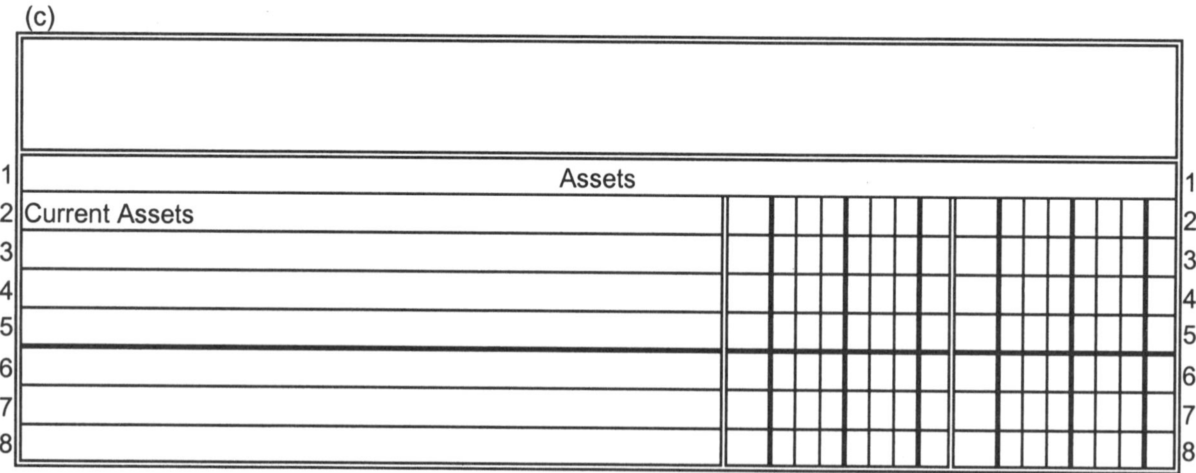

Assets		
Current Assets		

Name | Problem 9-7B

Section

Date | Furball Company

General Journal

Date	Account Titles	Debit	Credit
Jan. 5			
Feb. 2			
12			
26			
Apr. 5			
12			
June 2			
July 5			
15			
Oct. 15			

Name

Section

Date

(a)

SEK Company
Accounts Receivable Aging Schedule
May 31, 2010

	Proportion of Total %	Amount in Category	Probability of Non-Collection %	Estimated Uncollectible Amount
Not yet due				
Less than 30 days past due				
30 to 60 days past due				
61 to 120 days past due				
121 to 180 days past due				
Over 180 days past due				
Totals				

(b)

SEK Company
Analysis of Allowance for Doubtful Accounts
May 31, 2010

Account Titles	Debit	Credit

Name

Section

Date

SEK Company

(c)

1. Steps to Improve the Accounts Receivable Situation	2. Risks and Costs Involved

(a)	2010	2009	2008
Net credit sales			
Credit and collection expenses			
Collection agency fees			
Salary of accounts receivable clerk			
Uncollectible accounts			
Billing and mailing costs			
Credit investigation fees			
Total			
Total expenses as a percentage of net credit sales			
(b) Average accounts receivable			
Investment earnings			
Total credit and collection expenses per above			
Add: Investment earnings			
Net credit and collection expenses			
Net expenses as a percentage of net credit sales			

(c)

Name

Section

Date

BE10-1

BE10-2

BE10-3

BE10-4

BE10-5

Year	Book Value	X	Rate	=	Depreciation
1					
2					

BE10-6

Depreciation cost per unit:

Year	
1	
2	

Name

Section

Date

BE10-7

BE10-8

Account Titles	Debit	Credit
1.		
2.		

BE10-9

Account Titles	Debit	Credit
(a)		
(b)		

Calculations:

Name

Section

Date

BE10-10

Account Titles	Debit	Credit
(a)		
(b)		

Calculations:

BE10-11

(a) Depletion cost per unit =

Depletion expense =

Account Titles	Debit	Credit
(b)		

BE10-12 Account Titles	Debit	Credit
(a)		
(b)		

Name

Section

Date

BE10-13

Spain Company
Balance Sheet (Partial)
December 31, 2010

BE10-14

*BE10-15 Account Titles	Debit	Credit

Calculations:

Name

Section

Date

*BE10-16 Account Titles	Debit	Credit

Calculations:

Name

Section

Date

DO IT! 10-1

Cost of truck:

Other costs:

DO IT! 10-2

Depreciation expense =

	Account Titles	Debit	Credit

DO IT! 10-3

Account Titles	Debit	Credit
(a)		
(b)		

Name

Section

Date

E10-3

(a) Cost of land:

(b)

E10-4

1.

2.

3.

4.

5.

6.

7.

8.

9.

10.

Name

Section

Date

E10-5

(a) Depreciation cost per unit =

(b)

Year	Computation: Units of Activity	X	Computation: Depreciation Cost/Unit	=	Annual Depreciation Expense	End of Year Accumulated Depreciation	Book Value
2010							
2011							
2012							
2013							

E10-6

(a) Straight-line method:

(b) Units-of-activity method:

(c) Declining-balance method:

Name Exercise 10-7

Section

Date Brainiac Company

(a)

(1) 2010:

2011:

(2) Calculation of depreciation cost per unit:

2010:

2011:

(3) 2010:

2011:

(b)	Account Tiles	Debit	Credit
(1)			

(2) Balance sheet presentation:

Name

Section

Date

E10-8

	Building	Warehouse
(a)		

(b)

Date	Account Titles	Debit	Credit
Dec. 31			

E10-9

Date	Account Titles	Debit	Credit
Jan. 1			
June 30			
30			
Dec. 31			
31			

Name Exercise 10-10

Section

Date Beka Company

	Account Titles	Debit	Credit
(a)			
(b)			
(c)			
(d)			

Name

Section

Date

E10-11

Date	Account Titles	Debit	Credit
(a)			
Dec. 31			

Calculations

(b)

E10-12

Date	Account Titles	Debit	Credit
Dec. 31			

E10-13

Date	Account Titles	Debit	Credit
1/2/10			
4/1/10			
7/1/10			
9/1/10			
12/31/10			

Ending balances:

Patent	
Goodwill	
Franchise	
R&D expense	

Name

Section

Date

E10-14

Asset turnover ratio

***E10-15**

Account Titles	Debit	Credit
(a)		

Calculations:

(b) Account Titles	Debit	Credit

Calculations:

Name

Section

Date

*Exercise 10-16

Coran's Delivery Company

Date	Account Titles	Debit	Credit
(a)			

Calculations:

(b)	Account Titles	Debit	Credit

Calculations:

Name Problem 10-1A

Section

Date Diaz Company

Item	Land	Building	Other Accounts: Amount	Other Accounts: Account Titles
1.				
2.				
3.				
4.				
5.				
6.				
7.				
8.				
9.				
10.				

Name Problem 10-2A

Section

Date Juresic Transportation

	Year	Computation	Cumulative, 12/31
(a)		BUS 1	
	2008		
	2009		
	2010		
		BUS 2	
	2008		
	2009		
	2010		
		BUS 3	
	2009		
	2010		

	Year	Depreciation Computation	Expense
(b)		BUS 2	
	(1) 2008		
	(2) 2009		

Name Problem 10-3A

Section

Date Pele Company

Total cost of machinery:

(a) (1)

Account Titles	Debit	Credit

(2) Annual depreciation:

Account Titles	Debit	Credit

(b) (1)

(2)

	Year	Book Value at Beginning of Year	DDB Rate	Annual Depreciation Expense	Accumulated Depreciation
	2010				
	2011				
	2012				
	2013				

(b) (Continued) and (c)

(b) (3) Depreciation cost per unit:

Year	Computation	Depreciation Expense
2010		
2011		
2012		
2013		

(c)

Name

Section

Date

Problem 10-4A

Lehman Company

Year		Depreciation Expense	Accumulated Depreciation
2008			
2009			
2010			
2011			
2012			
2013			
2014			

Supporting calculations:

Name Problem 10-5A

Section

Date Jimenez Company

(a) General Journal

Date	Account Titles	Debit	Credit
Apr. 1			
May 1			
1			

Calculations:

Date	Account Titles	Debit	Credit
June 1			
July 1			
Dec. 31			
31			

Calculations:

(b) General Journal

Date	Account Titles	Debit	Credit
Dec. 31			
31			

Calculations:

(c)

Jimenez Company
Partial Balance Sheet
December 31, 2011

Name Problem 10-5A Concluded

Section

Date Jimenez Company

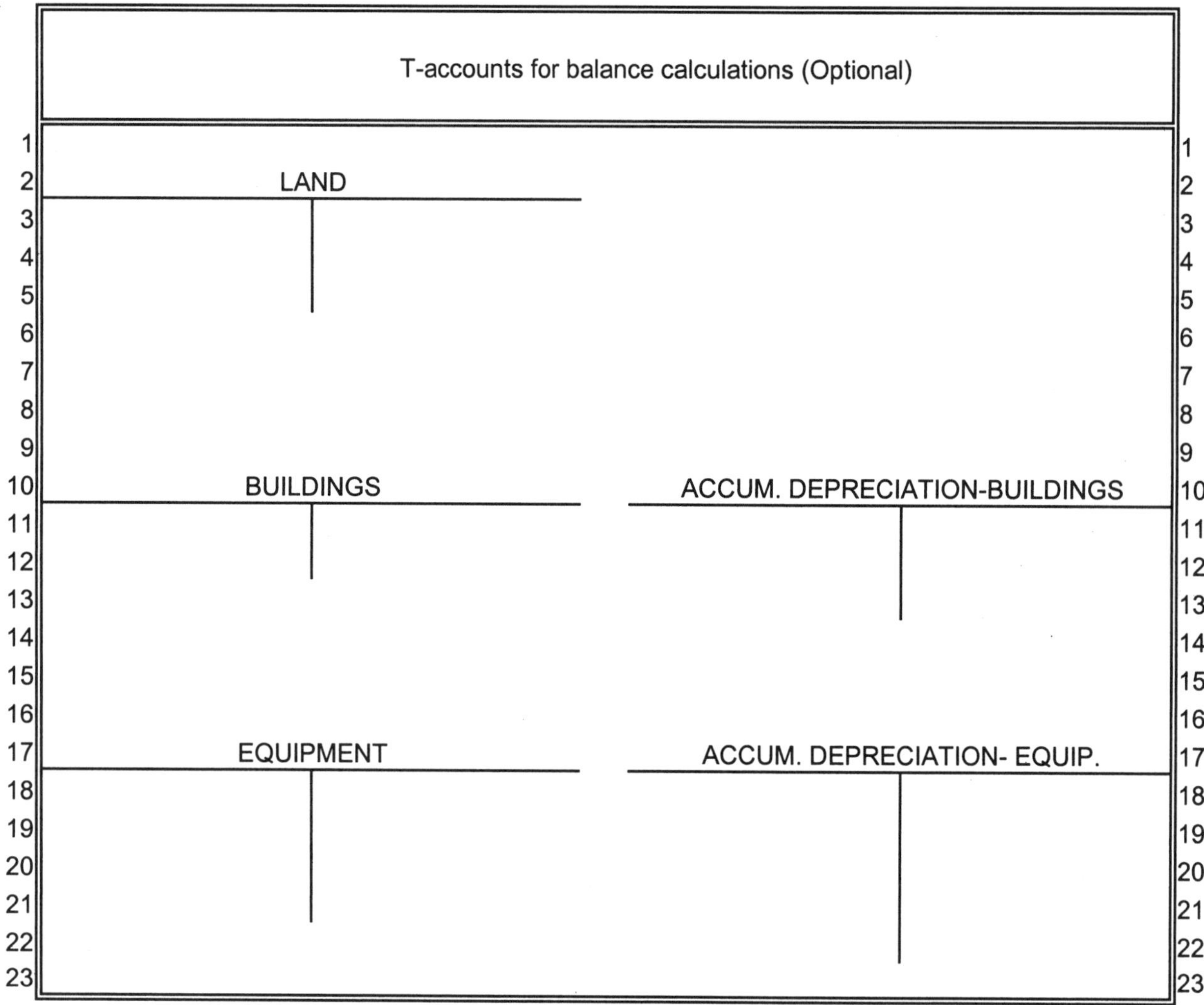

Name | Problem 10-6A

Section

Date | Puckett Co.

	Account Titles	Debit	Credit
(a)			
(b)			
(c)			

Name | Problem 10-7A

Section

Date | Redeker Company

General Journal

Date	Account Titles	Debit	Credit
(a)			
Jan. 2			
Jan. -			
June			
Sept. 1			
Oct. 1			
(b)			
Dec. 31			
31			

(c) Intangible Assets:

Name Problem 10-8A

Section

Date Thorne Company

General Journal

	Account Titles	Debit	Credit
1.			
2.			

Name

Section

Date

Problem 10-1B

Dewey Company

Item	Land	Building	Other Accounts	
			Amount	Account Titles
1.				
2.				
3.				
4.				
5.				
6.				
7.				
8.				
9.				
10.				

Name | Problem 10-2B

Section

Date | Pablo Company

	Year	Computation	Cumulative, 12/31
(a)		MACHINE 1	
	2007		
	2008		
	2009		
	2010		
		MACHINE 2	
	2008		
	2009		
	2010		
		MACHINE 3	
	2010		

(b)	Year	Depreciation Computation	Expense
		MACHINE 2	
	(1) 2008		
	(2) 2009		

Name

Section

Date

Problem 10-3B

Arlo Company

Total cost of machinery:

(a) (1)

Account Titles	Debit	Credit

(2) Annual depreciation:

Account Titles	Debit	Credit

(b) (1)

(2)

Year	Book Value at Beginning of Year	DDB Rate	Annual Depreciation Expense	Accumulated Depreciation
2010				
2011				
2012				
2013				

Name | Problem 10-3B Concluded
Section
Date | Arlo Company

(b) (Continued) and (c)

(b) (3) Depreciation cost per unit:

	Year	Computation	Depreciation Expense
	2010		
	2011		
	2012		
	2013		

(c)

Name

Section

Date

Problem 10-4B

Anfernee Company

Year		Depreciation Expense	Accumulated Depreciation
2008			
2009			
2010			
2011			
2012			
2013			
2014			

Supporting calculations:

Name
Section
Date

Problem 10-5B

Starkey Company

(a)

General Journal

Date	Account Titles	Debit	Credit
Apr. 1			
May 1			
1			

Calculations:

Date	Account Titles	Debit	Credit
June 1			
July 1			
Dec. 31			
31			

Calculations:

Name

Section

Date

Problem 10-5B Continued

Starkey Company

(b)

General Journal

Date	Account Titles	Debit	Credit
Dec. 31			
31			

Calculations:

(c)

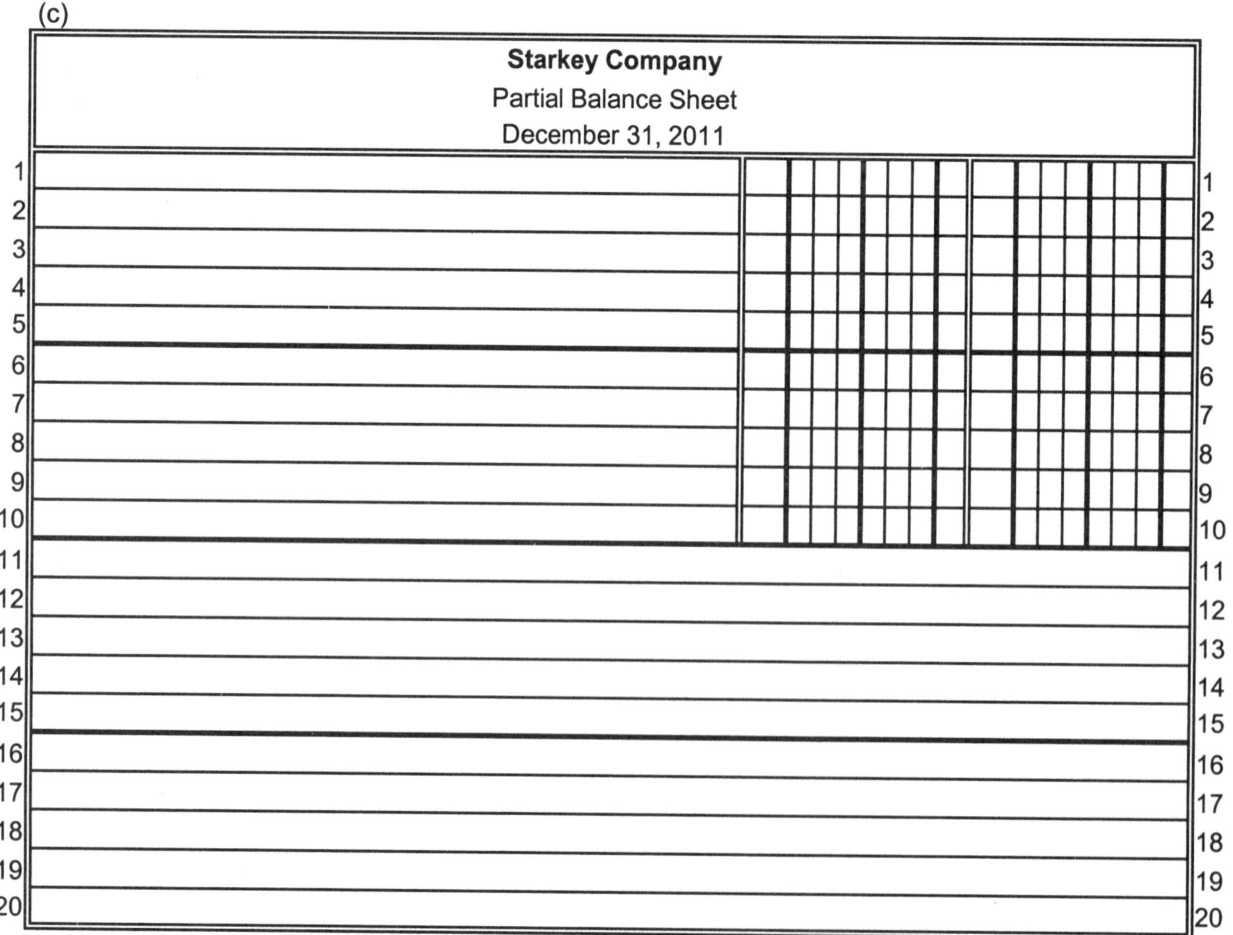

Starkey Company

Partial Balance Sheet

December 31, 2011

Name Problem 10-5B Concluded

Section

Date Starkey Company

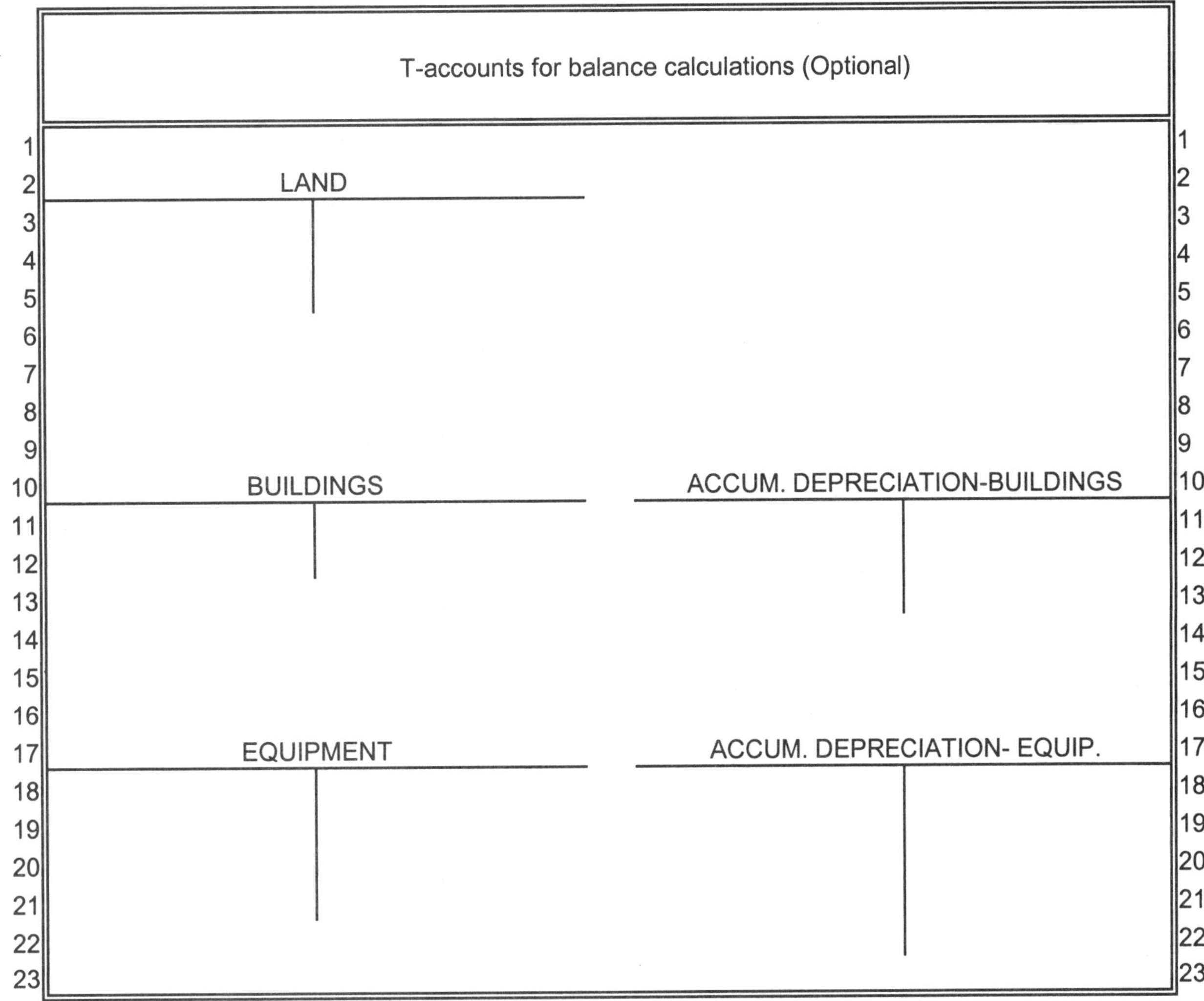

Name

Section

Date

Problem 10-6B

Bobby's

	Account Titles	Debit	Credit
(a)			
(b)			
(c)			

Name Problem 10-7B

Section

Date Time Company

General Journal

Date	Account Titles	Debit	Credit
(a)			
Jan. 2			
Jan -			
June			
Sept. 1			
Oct. 1			
(b)			
Dec. 31			
31			

(c) Intangible Assets:

(d)

Name Problem 10-8B

Section

Date Wasp Company

General Journal

	Account Titles	Debit	Credit
1.			
2.			

(a)

	Account Titles	Debit	Credit
1.			
2.			
3.			
4.			
5.			
6.			
7.			
8.			
9.			
10.			

Name

Section

Date

Winterschid Company

(a) (Continued)

	Account Titles	Debit	Credit
11.			
12.			
13.			

Section

Date

(b)

Winterschid Company
Trial Balance
December 31, 2010

		Debits	Credits	
1	Cash			1
2	Accounts Receivable			2
3	Notes Receivable			3
4	Interest Receivable			4
5	Merchandise Inventory			5
6	Prepaid Insurance			6
7	Land			7
8	Building			8
9	Equipment			9
10	Patent			10
11	Allowance for Doubtful Accounts			11
12	Accumulated Depreciation - Building			12
13	Accumulated Depreciation - Equipment			13
14	Accounts Payable			14
15	Salaries Payable			15
16	Unearned Rent			16
17	Notes Payable (short-term)			17
18	Interest Payable			18
19	Notes Payable (long-term)			19
20	Winterschid, Capital			20
21	Winterschid, Drawing			21
22	Sales			22
23	Interest Revenue			23
24	Rent Revenue			24
25	Gain on Disposal			25
26	Bad Debts Expense			26
27	Cost of Goods Sold			27
28	Depreciation Expense - Building			28
29	Depreciation Expense - Equipment			29
30	Insurance Expense			30
31	Interest Expense			31
32	Other Operating Expense			32
33	Amortization Expense - Patents			33
34	Salaries Expense			34
35	Totals			35
36				36
37				37
38				38
39				39

Name

Section

Date

(c)

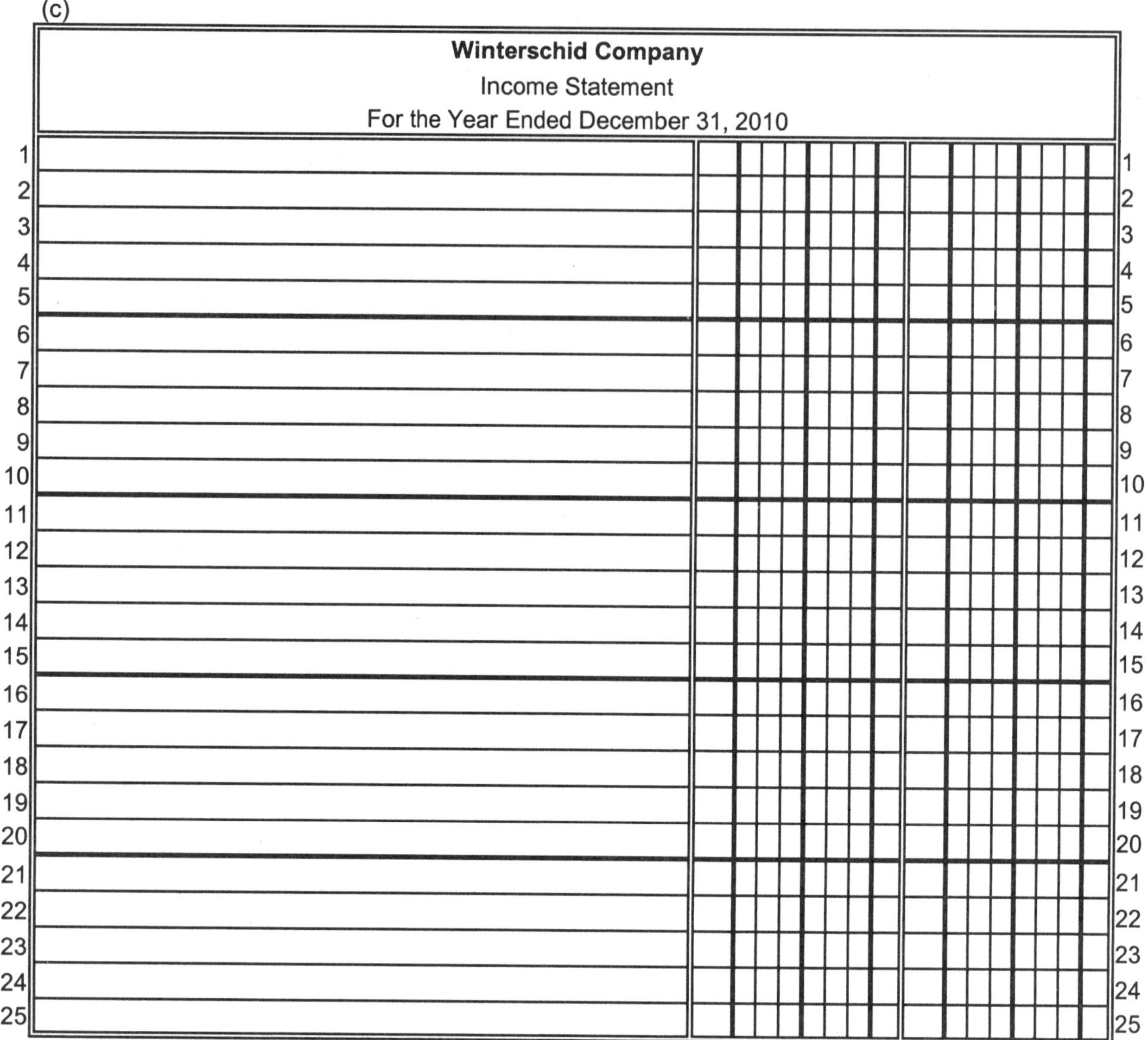

Winterschid Company

Income Statement

For the Year Ended December 31, 2010

Winterschid Company

Owner's Equity Statement

For the Year Ended December 31, 2010

(d)

Winterschid Company
Balance Sheet
December 31, 2010

Assets

Liabilities and Owner's Equity

(a) Reimer Company- Straight-line method

Lingo Company- Double-declining-balance method

Year	Asset	Computation	Annual Depreciation	Accumulated Depreciation
2008	Building			
	Equipment			
2009	Building			
	Equipment			
2010	Building			
	Equipment			

(b) Year	Reimer Company Net Income	Lingo Co. Net Inc. as Adjusted	Computations for Lingo Company
2008			
2009			
2010			
Total			

(c)

Name

Section

Date

Buster Container Company

(a)

(b)

(c)

	Old Estimates

	Revised Estimates

Name

Section

Date

BE11-1

(a)

(b)

(c)

(d)

BE11-2

Date	Account Titles	Debit	Credit
July 1			
Dec 31			

BE11-3

Date	Account Titles	Debit	Credit
Mar. 16			

Name

Section

Date

BE11-4

Date	Account Titles	Debit	Credit

BE11-5

(a)

(b)

BE11-6

Date	Account Titles	Debit	Credit
Dec. 31			

BE11-7

Gross earnings:

Name
Section
Date

BE11-8

Date	Account Titles	Debit	Credit
Jan. 15			
15			

BE11-9

Date	Account Titles	Debit	Credit
Jan. 31			

BE11-10

(a)
(b)
(c)
(d)

***BE11-11**

Date	Account Titles	Debit	Credit
Jan. 31			

Name

Section

Date

DO IT! 11-1

1.

2.

3.

DO IT! 11-1

(a) Current liabilities:

(b) Working capital:

Current ratio:

DO IT! 11-3

(a) Net pay:

Name

Section

Date

DO IT! 11-3 (Continued)

	Account Titles	Debit	Credit
(b)			

DO IT! 11-4

	Account Titles	Debit	Credit

Name

Section

Date

Exercise 11-1

Rob Judson Company

Date	Account Titles	Debit	Credit
	July 1, 2010		
	November 1, 2010		
	December 31, 2010		
	February 1, 2011		
	April 1, 2011		

Name

Section

Date

E11-2

Date	Account Titles	Debit	Credit
(a)			
June 1			
(b)			
June 30			
(c)			
Dec. 1			

(d)

E11-3

Date	Account Titles	Debit	Credit
	Warkentinne Company		
Apr. 10			
	Rivera Company		
15			

Name

Section

Date

E11-4

Date	Account Titles	Debit	Credit
(a)			
Nov. 30			
(b)			
Dec. 31			
(c)			
Mar. 31			

E11-5

(a) Estimated warrranties outstanding:

Month	Estimate	Units Defective	Outstanding
November			
December			
Total			

Date	Account Titles	Debit	Credit
(b)			
(c)			

Name

Section

Date

E11-6

(a)

(b)

(c)

E11-7 (a)

Jewett Online Company

Partial Balance Sheet

(b)

Name

Section

Date

E11-10

(a)

(1) Regular

Overtime

Gross earnings

(2) FICA taxes

(3) Federal income taxes

(4) State income taxes

(5) Net pay

(b)

Date	Account Titles	Debit	Credit

E11-11

C. Ogle

D. Delgado

L. Jeter

T. Spivey

Name | Exercise 11-12

Section

Date | Alvamar Company

(a)

Alvamar Company Payroll Register For the Week Ending January 31					
		Earnings			
Employee	Total Hours	Regular	Overtime	Gross Pay
M. Hashmi				
E. Benson				
K. Kern				
Totals				

(a) Continued

Alvamar Company Payroll Register (continued) For the Week Ending January 31					
	Deductions				
	FICA Taxes	Federal Income Taxes	Health Insurance	Total	Net Pay
Hashmi					
Benson					
Kern					
Totals					

(b)

Date	Account Titles	Debit	Credit
Jan 31			
31			

Name

Section

Date

E11-13

(a)

Gross earnings:	$ 8,900	State income taxes	
Regular		Union dues	100
Overtime		Total deductions	
Total		Net pay	$ 7,660
Deductions:		Accounts debited:	
FICA taxes	800	Warehouse wages	
Federal income taxes	1,140	Store wages	4,000

(b)

Date	Account Titles	Debit	Credit
Feb 28			
28			

E11-14

(a)

(b)

Date	Account Titles	Debit	Credit

Name   *Exercises 11-15 and 11-16

Section

Date

***E11-15**

Date	Account Titles	Debit	Credit
Mar. 31			
31			

***E11-16**

Date	Account Titles	Debit	Credit
1.			
2.			
3.			

Name Problem 11-1A

Section

Date Mane Company

Date	Account Titles	Debit	Credit
(a)			
Jan 5			
12			
14			
20			
21			
25			
(b) (1)			
Jan 31			
(2)			
31			

(c)

Mane Company

Balance Sheet (Partial)

January 31, 2010

Current liabilities:		

Name

Section

Date

Problem 11-2A

Winsky Company

(a)

Date	Account Titles	Debit	Credit
Jan 2			
Feb 1			
Mar 31			
Apr 1			
July 1			
Sept 30			
Oct 1			
Dec 1			
Dec 31			

(c)

Winsky Company

Balance Sheet (Partial)

December 31

Current liabilities:		

(b)

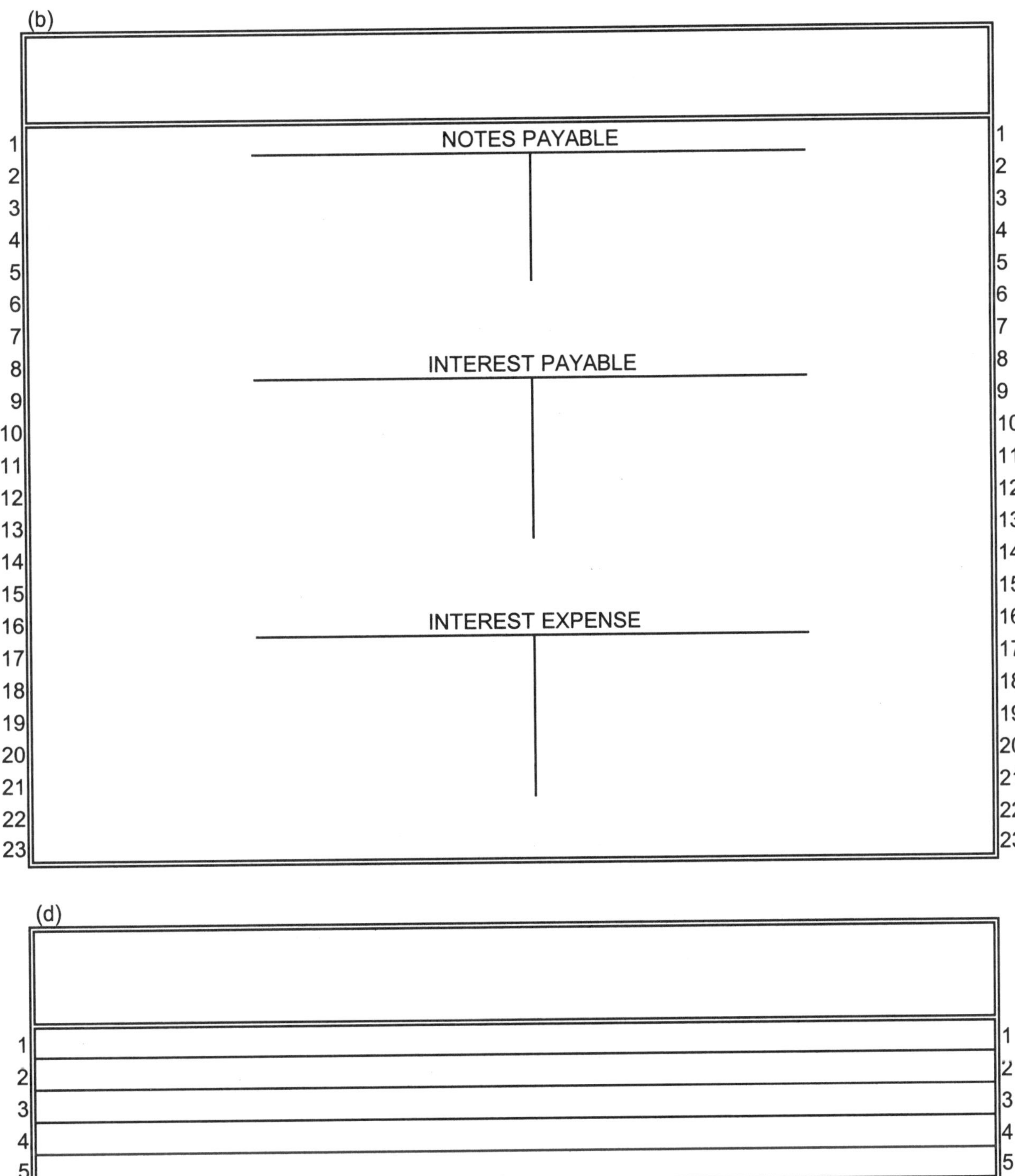

(d)

Name

Section

Date

Problem 11-3A

Del Hardware

(a)

Del Hardware

Payroll Register

For the Week Ended March 15, 2010

		Earnings		
Employee	Hours	Regular	Over-time	Gross Pay
Joe Devena	40			
Mary Keener	42			
Andy Dye	44			
Kim Shen	46			
Totals				

Deductions				
FICA Taxes	Fed. Inc. Tax	State Inc. Tax	United Fund	Total
			$ 5	
			5	
	60		8	
	61		5	

Net Pay	Store Wages Exp.	Office Wages Exp.

Name
Section
Date

Problem 11-3A Concluded

Del Hardware

Date	Account Titles	Debit	Credit
(b)			
Mar 15			
15			
(c)			
Mar 16			
(d)			
Mar 31			

Name

Section

Date

Problem 11-4A

Armitage Company

Date	Account Titles	Debit	Credit
(a)			
Jan 10			
12			
15			
17			
20			
31			
31			
(b) 1.			
Jan 31			
*2.			
31			

Date	Account Titles	Debit	Credit
(a)			
(b)			

(c)

Employee	Wages, Tips, Other Compensation	Federal Income Tax Withheld	State Income Tax Withheld	FICA Wages	FICA Tax Withheld
J.Eckman	$ 59,000	$ 28,500			
S. Bishop	26,000	10,200			

Name

Section

Date

Problem 11-1B

Software Company

Date	Account Titles	Debit	Credit
(a)			
Jan 1			
5			
12			
14			
20			
25			
(b) (1)			
Jan 31			
(2)			
31			

Name Problem 11-1B Concluded

Section

Date Software Company

(c)

Software Company

Balance Sheet (Partial)

January 31, 2010

Current liabilities:		

Name

Section

Date

Problem 11-2B

Donn Company

(a)

Date	Account Titles	Debit	Credit
Jan 2			
Feb 1			
Mar 31			
Apr 1			
July 1			
Sept 30			
Oct 1			
Dec 1			
Dec 31			

(c)

Donn Company

Balance Sheet (Partial)

December 31

Current liabilities:		

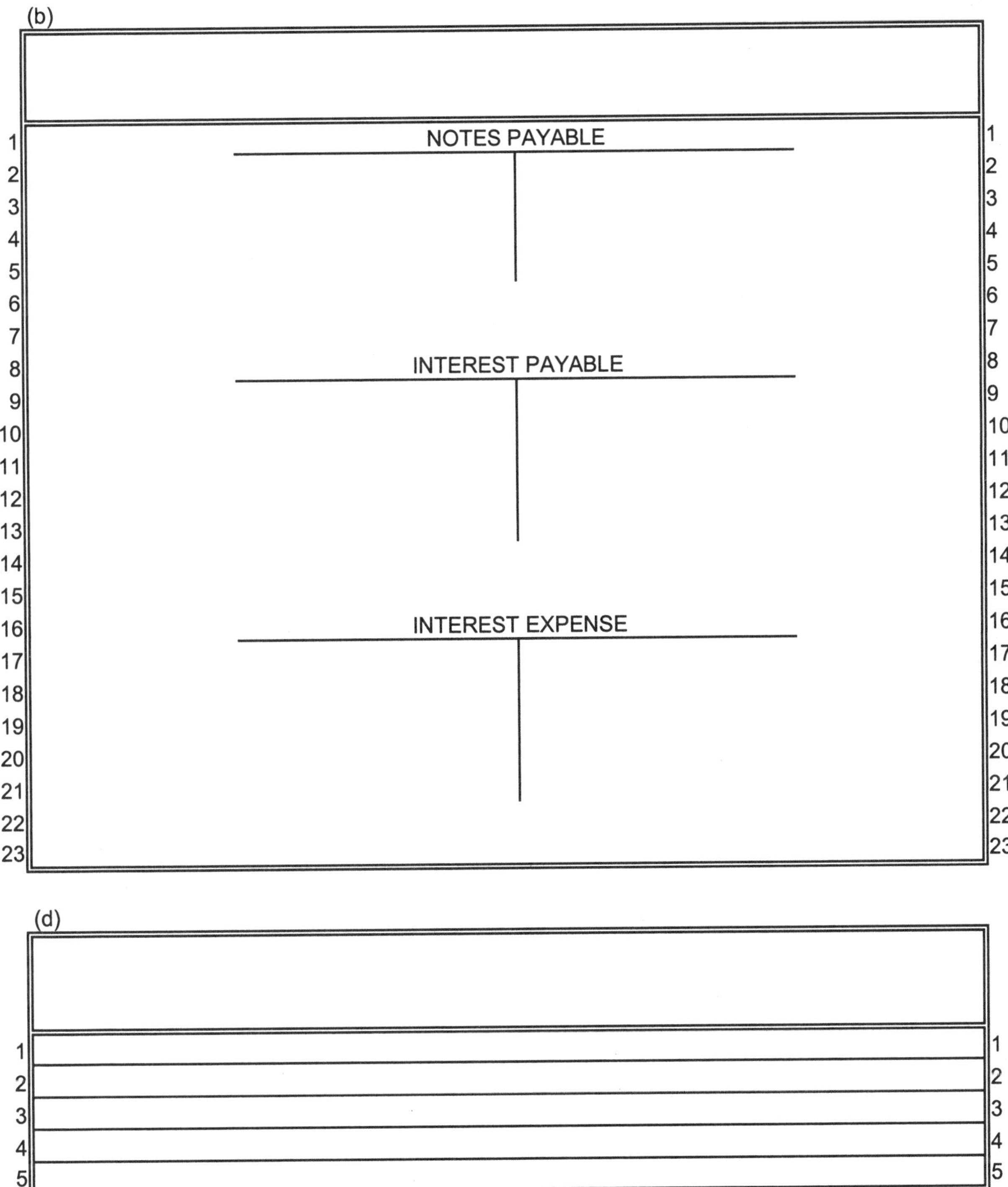
(b)
NOTES PAYABLE
INTEREST PAYABLE
INTEREST EXPENSE
(d)

Name Problem 11-3B

Section

Date John's Drug Store

(a)

John's Drug Store
Payroll Register
For the Week Ended February 15, 2010

	Employee	Hours	Earnings: Regular	Earnings: Over-time	Earnings: Gross Pay	
1	J. Uddin	39				1
2						2
3	B. Conway	42				3
4						4
5	S. Becker	44				5
6						6
7	L. Blum	46				7
8						8
9	Totals					9

	Deductions: FICA Taxes	Deductions: Fed. Inc. Tax	Deductions: State Inc. Tax	Deductions: United Fund	Deductions: Total	
1		34		$ 0		1
2						2
3		20		10 00		3
4						4
5		51		5 00		5
6						6
7		36		5 00		7
8						8
9						9

	Net Pay	Store Wages Exp.	Office Wages Exp.	
1				1
2				2
3				3
4				4
5				5
6				6
7				7
8				8
9				9

Name Problem 11-3B Concluded

Section

Date John's Drug Store

Date	Account Titles	Debit	Credit
(b)			
Feb 15			
15			
(c)			
Feb 16			
(d)			
Feb 28			

Name

Section

Date

Problem 11-4B

Pettibone Company

Date	Account Titles	Debit	Credit
(a)			
Jan 10			
12			
15			
17			
20			
31			
31			
(b) 1.			
Jan 31			
*2.			
31			

Name Problem 11-5B

Section

Date Ullman Company

Date	Account Titles	Debit	Credit
(a)			
(b)			

(c)

Employee	Wages, Tips, Other Compensation	Federal Income Tax Withheld	State Income Tax Withheld	FICA Wages	FICA Tax Withheld
R. Lowski	$ 50000	$ 18300			
K. Monez	24000	4800			

Name

Section

Date

(a)

Metcalfe Services Inc.

Month	Number of Employees	Days Worked	Daily Rate	Cost
January - March				
April - May				
June - October				
November - December				
Total Cost				

Payroll Costs for Kensingtown's Permanent Employees

(b)

(a)

(b)

(c)

(d)

(e)

(f)

(g) Total taxes:

Name

Section

Date

BE12-1	Debit	Credit

BE12-2

	Debit	Credit

BE12-3

Calculation of net income division:

	Debit	Credit

BE12-4	Division of Net Income			
	Espino	Sears	Utech	Total

Name

Section

Date

BE12-5

	Division of Net Income		
	Joe	Sam	Total

BE12-6

Account Titles	Debit	Credit

***BE12-7**

Account Titles	Debit	Credit

***BE12-8**

Account Titles	Debit	Credit

***BE12-9**

Account Titles	Debit	Credit

***BE12-10**

Account Titles	Debit	Credit

Name

Section

Date

DO IT! 12-2

	Division of Net Income		
	S. Wiborg	G. Murphy	Total

	Account Titles	Debit	Credit

DO IT! 12-4

	Account Titles	Debit	Credit

Name

Section

Date

Clash Company

Schedule of Cash Payments

	Item	Cash	Non-cash Assets	Liabilities	M. Jones, Capital	J. Strummer, Capital	P. Simonon, Capital	
1	Balances before liquidation	15000	90000	40000	20000	32000	13000	1
2	Sale of noncash assets and							2
3	allocation of gain							3
4	New balances							4
5	Pay liabilities							5
6	New balances							6
7	Cash distribution to partners							7
8	Final balances							8
9								9
10								10
11								11
12								12
13								13
14								14
15								15
16								16
17								17
18								18
19								19
20								20

Name

Section

Date

E12-1

1.

2.

3.

4.

5.

6.

7.

8.

9.

E12-2

Account Titles	Debit	Credit
(a)		

(b)

Name

Section

Date

E12-3

	Date	Account Titles	Debit	Credit	
1	Jan 1				1
2					2
3					3
4					4
5					5
6					6
7					7

E12-6 (a)

Starrite Co.
Partners' Capital Statement
For the Year Ended December 31, 2010

		G. Stark	J. Nyland	Total	
2					2
3					3
4					4
5					5
6					6
7					7
8					8

(b)

Starrite Co.
Partial Balance Sheet
December 31, 2010

1	Owner's Equity			1
2				2
3				3
4				4
5				5
6				6

Name Exercise 12-4

Section

Date F. Calvert and G. Powers

(a)

	F. Calvert	G. Powers	Total
(1) Net income is $50,000:			
(2) Net income is $36,000:			

(b)

	Debit	Credit
(1) Net income is $50,000:		
(2) Net income is $36,000:		

Name | Exercise 12-5

Section

Date | O. Guillen and K. Williams

Account Titles	Debit	Credit
(a)		
(b)		
(c)		
(d)		

Name Exercise 12-7

Section

Date The Stooges Partnership

The Stooges Partnership

Balance Sheet

December 31, 2010

Assets

Liabilities and Owner's Equity

Name ______________________ Exercise 12-8

Section ______________________

Date ______________________ The Best Company

The Best Company
Schedule of Cash Payments

	Item	Cash	Non-cash Assets	Liabilities	Rodriquez Capital	Escobedo Capital	
1							1
2							2
3							3
4							4
5							5
6							6
7							7
8							8
9							9
10							10
11							11
12							12
13							13
14							14
15							15
16							16
17							17
18							18
19							19
20							20

Name Exercises 12-9 and 12-10

Section

Date

E12-9

		Account Titles	Debit	Credit	
1	(a)				1
2					2
3					3
4					4
5	(b)				5
6					6
7					7
8					8
9	(c)				9
10					10
11					11
12	(d)				12
13					13
14					14
15					15

E12-10

		Account Titles	Debit	Credit	
1	(a) (1)				1
2					2
3					3
4					4
5	(2)				5
6					6
7					7
8					8
9	(b) (1)				9
10					10
11					11
12					12
13	(2)				13
14					14
15					15
16					16
17					17
18					18
19					19
20					20

Name

Section

Date

*Exercises 12-11 and 12-13

***E12-11**

		Account Titles	Debit	Credit	
1	(a)				1
2					2
3					3
4	(b)				4
5					5
6					6
7	(c)				7
8					8
9					9
10					10

***E12-13**

		Account Titles	Debit	Credit	
1	(a)				1
2					2
3					3
4					4
5					5
6	(b)				6
7					7
8					8
9					9
10	(c)				10
11					11
12					12
13					13
14					14
15					15

Name *Exercise 12-12

Section

Date G. Olde and R. Young

	Account Titles	Debit	Credit
(a)			

Calculation of Twener's capital account and bonus to old partners:

	Account Titles	Debit	Credit
(b)			

Calculation of Twener's capital account and bonus to new partner:

Name *Exercise 12-14

Section

Date H. Barrajas, T. Dingler, and R. Fisk

	Account Titles	Debit	Credit
(a)			

Calculation of bonus to retiring partner and allocation of bonus to remaining partners:

	Debit	Credit

(b)	Account Titles	Debit	Credit

Calculation of bonus to remaining partners and allocation of bonus:

	Debit	Credit

Name *Exercise 12-15

Section

Date Carson, Letterman, and O'Brien

	Account Titles	Debit	Credit
(a)			
(b)			

Name

Section

Date

Problem 12-1A

Pasa Company

(a)

Date	Account Titles	Debit	Credit
Jan 1			
1			

(b)

Date	Account Titles	Debit	Credit
Jan 1			
1			

(c)

Pasa Company
Balance Sheet
January 1, 2010

Assets

Liabilities and Owners' Equity

Name   Problem 12-2A

Section

Date   CNU Company

(a)

	Account Titles	Debit	Credit
(1)			
(2)			

Calculation to support net income distribution for (a)(2) above:

(3)			

Calculations to support net income distribution for (a)(3) above:

Name Problem 12-2A Concluded

Section

Date CNU Company

(b)

CNU Company

Division of Net Income

		Reese Caplin	Phyllis Newell	Betty Uhrich	Total	
1						1
2						2
3						3
4						4
5						5
6						6
7						7
8						8
9						9
10						10
11						11
12						12
13						13
14						14
15						15
16						16
17						17
18						18
19						19
20						20

(c)

CNU Company

Partners' Capital Statement

For the Year Ended December 31, 2010

		Reese Caplin	Phyllis Newell	Betty Uhrich	Total	
1						1
2						2
3						3
4						4
5						5
6						6
7						7
8						8
9						9
10						10

Name | Problem 12-3A
Section
Date | New Yorker Company

(a)

	Account Titles	Debit	Credit
(1)			

(2)	Account Titles	Debit	Credit
(3)			
(4)			
(5)			

(b)

Cash			
Bal	27,500		

M. Mantle, Capital			
		Bal.	33,000

W. Mays, Capital			
		Bal	21,000

D. Snider, Capital			
		Bal.	3,000

(c)

Account Titles	Debit	Credit
(1)		
(2)		

Name

Section

Date

*Problem 12-4A

SKG Company

(a)

	Account Titles	Debit	Credit
(1)			
(2)			
(3)			

Calculations of bonus paid by new partner and distribution to old partners:

	Account Titles	Debit	Credit
(4)			

Calculation of bonus to new partner:

Name *Problem 12-4A Concluded

Section

Date SKG Company

(b)

(1)

(2)

Name *Problem 12-5A

Section

Date FAD Company

(a)

		Account Titles	Debit	Credit	
1	(1)				1
2					2
3					3
4					4
5	(2)				5
6					6
7					7
8	(3)				8
9					9
10					10
11					11
12	Calculation of bonus to Durham in (a)(3) above:				12
13					13
14					14
15					15
16					16
17	(4)				17
18					18
19					19
20					20
21	Calculation of bonus to old partners in (a)(4) above:				21
22					22
23					23
24					24
25					25
26	(b) (1)				26
27					27
28					28
29					29
30					30
31					31
32					32
33					33
34	(2)				34
35					35
36					36
37					37
38					38
39					39
40					40

Name Problem 12-1B

Section

Date John-Calvin Company

(a)

	Date	Account Titles	Debit	Credit	
1	Jan 1				1
2					2
3					3
4					4
5					5
6					6
7					7
8					8
9					9
10					10
11	1				11
12					12
13					13
14					14
15					15
16					16
17					17
18					18
19					19
20					20

(b)

	Date	Account Titles	Debit	Credit	
1	Jan 1				1
2					2
3					3
4					4
5					5
6	1				6
7					7
8					8
9					9
10					10

(c)

John-Calvin Company
Balance Sheet
January 1, 2010

Assets

Liabilities and Owners' Equity

Name | Problem 12-2B

Section

Date | KAT Company

(a)

	Account Titles	Debit	Credit
(1)			
(2)			

Calculation to support net income distribution for (a)(2) above:

(3)			

Calculation to support net income distribution for (a)(3) above:

(b)

KAT Company
Division of Net Income

	H. Krik	N. Andres	S. Thabo	Total

(c)

KAT Company
Partners' Capital Statement
For the Year Ended December 31, 2010

	H. Krik	N. Andres	S. Thabo	Total

Name

Section

Date

Problem 12-3B

Apache Company

Apache Company
Schedule of Cash Payments

Item	Cash	Non-cash Assets	Liabilities	Scottie, Capital	Spock, Capital	Kirk, Capital

Name

Section

Date

Problem 12-3B Continued

Apache Company

(b)

	Account Titles	Debit	Credit
(1)			
(2)			
(3)			
(4)			

(c)

Cash

4/30 Bal	30,000		

Spock, Capital

		4/30 Bal	13,650

Scottie, Capital

		4/30 Bal	28,000

Kirk, Capital

		4/30 Bal	5,850

Name *Problem 12-4B

Section

Date BAB Company

(a)

	Account Titles	Debit	Credit
(1)			
(2)			
(3)			

Calculation of bonus paid to new partner:

(4)			

Calculation of bonus paid by new partner and distribution to old partners:

Name *Problem 12-4B Concluded

Section

Date BAB Company

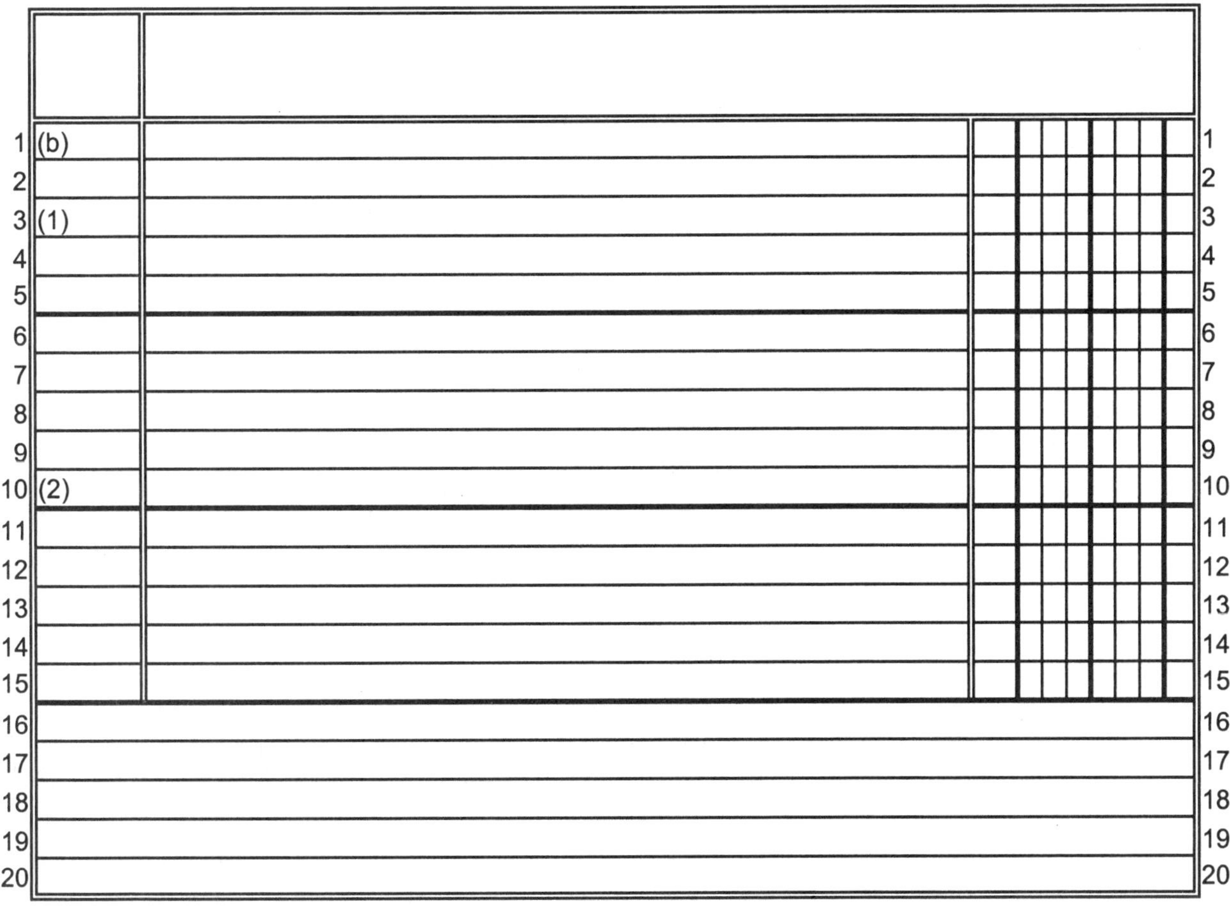

(b)

(1)

(2)

Name | *Problem 12-5B
Section
Date | Canasta Company

(a)

	Account Titles	Debit	Credit
(1)			
(2)			
(3)			

Calculation of bonus to Spade in (a)(3) above:

(4)			

Calculation of bonus to old partners in (a)(4) above:

(b) (1)		
(2)		

Name

Section

Date

BE13-1

Advantages	Disadvantages

BE13-2

Date	Account Titles	Debit	Credit
Dec. 31			

BE13-3

Date	Account Titles	Debit	Credit
May 10			

BE13-4

Date	Account Titles	Debit	Credit
June 1			

BE13-5

Date	Account Titles	Debit	Credit

BE13-6

Date	Account Titles	Debit	Credit
July 1			
Sept. 1			

Name

Section

Date

BE13-7

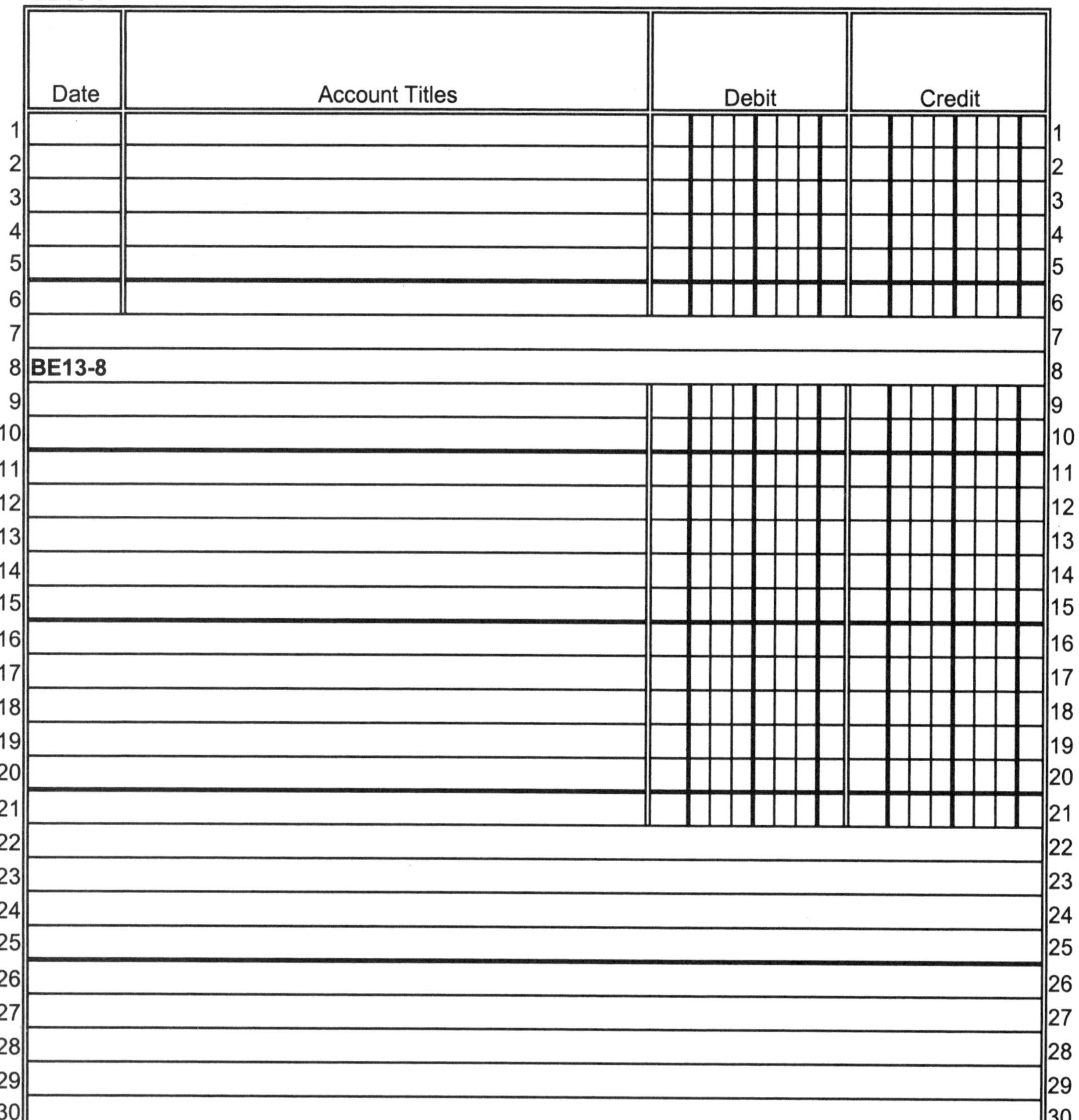

Date	Account Titles	Debit	Credit

BE13-8

Name

Section

Date

DO IT! 13-1

1.
2.
3.
4.
5.

DO IT!13-2

	Account Titles	Debit	Credit
(a)			

(b)

DO IT!13-3

	Account Titles	Debit	Credit
Apr. 1			
Apr. 19			

DO IT! 13-4

	Account Titles	Debit	Credit
Aug. 1			
Dec. 1			

Name Chapter 13 DO IT! 13-5

Section

Date Connolly Corporation

Connolly Corporation

Balance Sheet (Partial)

Name

Section

Date

E13-3

Date	Account Titles	Debit	Credit
(a)			
Jan. 10			
July 1			
(b)			
Jan. 10			
July 1			
E13-4			
(a)			
(b)			
(c)			
(d)			
(e)			

Name

Section

Date

E13-5

Date	Account Titles	Debit	Credit
Mar. 2			
June 12			
July 11			
Nov. 28			
E13-6			
(1)			
(2)			

Name

Section

Date

E13-7

Date	Account Titles	Debit	Credit
(a)			
Mar. 1			
July 1			
Sept. 1			
(b)			
Sept. 1			
E13-8			

Name — Exercise 13-9

Section

Date — Polzin Corporation

(a)

General Journal

Date	Account Titles	Debit	Credit
Feb. 1			
July 1			

(b)

Preferred Stock

Date	Explanation	Ref.	Debit	Credit	Balance

Paid-in Capital in Excess of Par Value-Preferred Stock

Date	Explanation	Ref.	Debit	Credit	Balance

(c)

Name

Section

Date

E13-10

Date	Account Titles	Debit	Credit
(a)			

Date	Account Titles	Credit
(b)		
(c)		

E13-11

Date	Account Titles	Debit	Credit
May 2			
10			
15			
31			

Name

Section

Date

Exercise 13-12

Freeze Corporation

Freeze Corporation

Partial Balance Sheet

December 31, 2010

Name | Exercise 13-14

Section

Date | Aluminum Company of America

Aluminum Company of America

Balance Sheet (Partial)

Stockholders' equity (in millions of dollars)

Name
Section
Date

Problem 13-1A

Franco Corporation

(a) General Journal J5

Date	Account Titles	Debit	Credit
Jan. 10			
Mar. 1			
Apr. 1			
May 1			
Aug. 1			
Sept. 1			
Nov. 1			

Name Problem 13-1A Continued

Section

Date Franco Corporation

(b)

Preferred Stock

Date	Explanation	Ref.	Debit	Credit	Balance

Common Stock

Date	Explanation	Ref.	Debit	Credit	Balance

Paid-in Capital in Excess of Par Value - Preferred Stock

Date	Explanation	Ref.	Debit	Credit	Balance

Paid-in Capital in Excess of Stated Value-Common Stock

Date	Explanation	Ref.	Debit	Credit	Balance

Name

Section

Date

Problem 13-1A Concluded

Franco Corporation

(c)

Franco Corporation

Balance Sheet (Partial)

December 31, 2010

Stockholders' equity		

Name

Section

Date

Problem 13-2A

Jacobsen Corporation

(a)

General Journal

J12

Date	Account Titles	Debit	Credit
Mar. 1			
June 1			
Sept. 1			
Dec. 1			
31			

(b)

Paid-in Capital from Treasury Stock

Date	Explanation	Ref.	Debit	Credit	Balance

Treasury Stock

Date	Explanation	Ref.	Debit	Credit	Balance

(b) (Continued)

Retained Earnings

Date	Explanation	Ref.	Debit	Credit	Balance
Jan. 1	Balance	√			10000

(c)

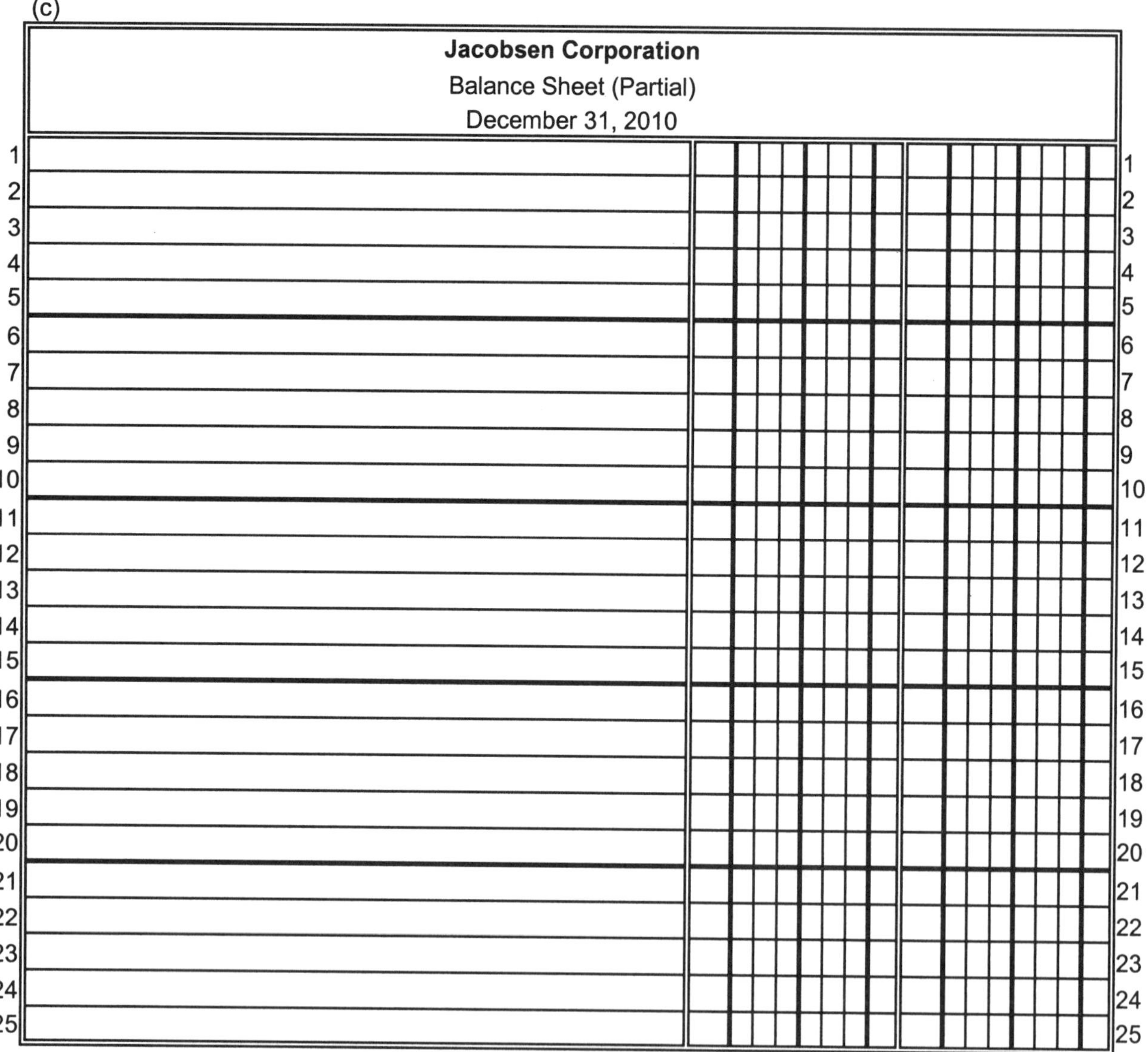

Name | Problem 13-3A

Section

Date | Neer Corporation

(a)

General Journal

J1

	Date	Account Titles	Debit	Credit	
1	Feb. 1				1
2					2
3					3
4					4
5	Apr. 14				5
6					6
7					7
8					8
9	Sept. 3				9
10					10
11					11
12					12
13	Mar. 10				13
14					14
15					15
16					16
17	Dec. 31				17
18					18
19					19
20					20
21					21

(b)

Preferred Stock

Date	Explanation	Ref.	Debit	Credit	Balance
Jan. 1	Balance	√			400000

Common Stock

Date	Explanation	Ref.	Debit	Credit	Balance
Jan. 1	Balance	√			1000000

(b) (Continued)

Paid-in Capital in Excess of Par Value-Preferred Stock

Date	Explanation	Ref.	Debit	Credit	Balance
Jan. 1	Balance	√			100000

Paid-in Capital in Excess of Stated Value-Common Stock

Date	Explanation	Ref.	Debit	Credit	Balance
Jan. 1	Balance	√			1450000

Paid-in Capital from Treasury Stock - Common

Date	Explanation	Ref.	Debit	Credit	Balance

Retained Earnings

Date	Explanation	Ref.	Debit	Credit	Balance
Jan. 1	Balance	√			1816000

Treasury Stock-Common

Date	Explanation	Ref.	Debit	Credit	Balance
Jan. 1	Balance	√			50000

(c)

Neer Corporation
Balance Sheet (Partial)
December 31, 2010

Stockholders' equity

Name　　　　　　　　　　　　　　　　　　　　　　　　　　　　Problem 13-4A

Section

Date　　　　　　　　　　　　　　　　　　　　　　　　　　　　Vargas Corporation

(a)

General Journal

J2

Date	Account Titles	Debit	Credit
Feb. 1			
Mar. 1			
July 1			
Sept. 1			
Dec. 1			
31			

(b)

Preferred Stock

Date	Explanation	Ref.	Debit	Credit	Balance
Jan. 1	Balance	√			500000

Common Stock

Date	Explanation	Ref.	Debit	Credit	Balance
Jan. 1	Balance	√			210000

(b) (Continued)

Paid-in Capital in Excess of Par Value-Preferred Stock

Date	Explanation	Ref.	Debit	Credit	Balance
Jan. 1	Balance	√			75000

Paid-in Capital in Excess of Par Value-Common Stock

Date	Explanation	Ref.	Debit	Credit	Balance
Jan. 1	Balance	√			700000

Retained Earnings

Date	Explanation	Ref.	Debit	Credit	Balance
Jan. 1	Balance	√			300000

(c)

Vargas Corporation
Balance Sheet (Partial)
December 31, 2010

Stockholders' equity

Name — Problem 13-5A

Section

Date — Tyner Corporation

Tyner Corporation
Balance Sheet (Partial)
December 31, 2010

Stockholders' equity		

Name

Section

Date

Problem 13-6A

Palmaro Corporation

(a)

Date	Account Titles	Debit	Credit
(1)			
(2)			
(3)			
(4)			

(b)

Palmaro Corporation
Balance Sheet (Partial)
December 31, 2010

Stockholders' equity		

Name

Section

Date

Problem 13-1B

Donelson Corporation

(a)

General Journal

J1

Date	Account Titles	Debit	Credit
Jan. 10			
Mar. 1			
Apr. 1			
May 1			
Aug. 1			
Sept. 1			
Nov. 1			

(b)

Preferred Stock

Date	Explanation	Ref.	Debit	Credit	Balance

Common Stock

Date	Explanation	Ref.	Debit	Credit	Balance

Paid-in Capital in Excess of Par Value - Preferred Stock

Date	Explanation	Ref.	Debit	Credit	Balance

Paid-in Capital in Excess of Stated Value-Common Stock

Date	Explanation	Ref.	Debit	Credit	Balance

Name

Section

Date

(c)

Donelson Corporation

Balance Sheet (Partial)

December 31, 2010

1	Stockholders' equity		

Name Problem 13-2B

Section

Date Gentry Corporation

(a) General Journal J12

Date	Account Titles	Debit	Credit
Mar. 1			
June 1			
Sept. 1			
Dec. 1			
31			

(b)

Paid-in Capital from Treasury Stock

Date	Explanation	Ref.	Debit	Credit	Balance

Treasury Stock

Date	Explanation	Ref.	Debit	Credit	Balance

Name ______ Problem 13-2B Concluded

Section ______

Date ______ Gentry Corporation

(b) (Continued)

Retained Earnings

Date	Explanation	Ref.	Debit	Credit	Balance
Jan. 1	Balance	√			100000

(c)

Gentry Corporation

Balance Sheet (Partial)

December 31, 2010

Stockholders' equity		

Name | Problem 13-3B

Section

Date | Miles Corporation

(a) General Journal J1

	Date	Account Titles	Debit	Credit	
1	Feb. 1				1
2					2
3					3
4					4
5	Mar. 20				5
6					6
7					7
8	June 14				8
9					9
10					10
11					11
12	Sept. 3				12
13					13
14					14
15					15
16	Dec. 31				16
17					17
18					18
19					19
20					20
21					21

(b)

Preferred Stock

Date	Explanation	Ref.	Debit	Credit	Balance
Jan. 1	Balance	√			300000

Common Stock

Date	Explanation	Ref.	Debit	Credit	Balance
Jan. 1	Balance	√			1000000

(b) (Continued)

Paid-in Capital in Excess of Par Value-Preferred Stock

Date	Explanation	Ref.	Debit	Credit	Balance
Jan. 1	Balance	√			20000

Paid-in Capital in Excess of Stated Value-Common Stock

Date	Explanation	Ref.	Debit	Credit	Balance
Jan. 1	Balance	√			425000

Paid-in Capital from Treasury Stock - Common

Date	Explanation	Ref.	Debit	Credit	Balance

Retained Earnings

Date	Explanation	Ref.	Debit	Credit	Balance
Jan. 1	Balance	√			488000

Treasury Stock-Common

Date	Explanation	Ref.	Debit	Credit	Balance
Jan. 1	Balance	√			40000

(c)

Miles Corporation
Balance Sheet (Partial)
December 31, 2010

Stockholders' equity

Name Problem 13-4B

Section

Date Molina Corporation

(a) General Journal J2

Date	Account Titles	Debit	Credit
Feb. 1			
Mar. 1			
July 1			
Sept. 1			
Dec. 1			
31			

(b)

Preferred Stock

Date	Explanation	Ref.	Debit	Credit	Balance
Jan. 1	Balance	√			200000

Common Stock

Date	Explanation	Ref.	Debit	Credit	Balance
Jan. 1	Balance	√			350000

(b) (Continued)

Paid-in Capital in Excess of Par Value-Preferred Stock

Date	Explanation	Ref.	Debit	Credit	Balance
Jan. 1	Balance	√			60000

Paid-in Capital in Excess of Par Value-Common Stock

Date	Explanation	Ref.	Debit	Credit	Balance
Jan. 1	Balance	√			700000

Retained Earnings

Date	Explanation	Ref.	Debit	Credit	Balance
Jan. 1	Balance	√			300000

(c)

Molina Corporation
Balance Sheet (Partial)
December 31, 2010

Stockholders' equity

Name Problem 13-5B

Section

Date Jenkins Corporation

Jenkins Corporation

Balance Sheet (Partial)

December 31, 2010

Name Problem 13-6B

Section

Date Steven Corporation

(a)

	Date	Account Titles	Debit	Credit	
1	(1)				1
2					2
3					3
4					4
5					5
6	(2)				6
7					7
8					8
9					9
10					10
11	(3)				11
12					12
13					13
14					14
15					15
16	(4)				16
17					17
18					18
19					19
20					20

Name | Problem 13-6B Concluded

Section

Date | Steven Corporation

(b)

Steven Corporation

Balance Sheet (Partial)

December 31, 2010

Name

Section

Date

PepsiCo, Inc.

(a)

(b)

(c)	2007	2006

(d)

	High Market Price	Low Market Price

Name

Section

Date

BE14-1

Date	Account Titles	Debit	Credit
Nov. 1			
Dec. 31			

BE14-2

Date	Account Titles	Debit	Credit
Dec. 1			
31			

BE14-3

	Before Dividend	After Dividend
(a)		
Stockholders' equity		
(b) Outstanding shares		
(c) Par value per share		

BE14-4

Kerns Inc.

Retained Earnings Statement

For the Year ended December 31, 2010

Name

Section

Date

BE14-5

Persinger Inc.

Retained Earnings Statement

For the Year Ended December 31, 2010

BE14-6 Return on stockholders' equity:

BE14-7 Return on common stockholders' equity:

BE14-8

Dixen Corporation

Income Statement

For the Year Ended December 31, 2010

BE14-9 Earnings per share:

BE14-10 Earnings per share:

Name

Section

Date

DO IT! 14-1

1.

2.

3.

DO IT! 14-2

(a) (1)

(2)

(b)	Original Balances	(1) After Dividend	(2) After Split
Paid-in capital			
Retained earnings			
Total stockholders' equity			
Shares outstanding			

Name

Section

Date

DO IT! 14-3

Alpha Centuri Corporation

Retained Earnings Statement

For the Year Ended December 31, 2010

DO IT! 14-4

(a)	2009	2010
Return on common stockholders' equity		
(b)		
Earnings per share		

(c)

Name

Section

Date

Exercises 14-1 and 14-2

E14-1

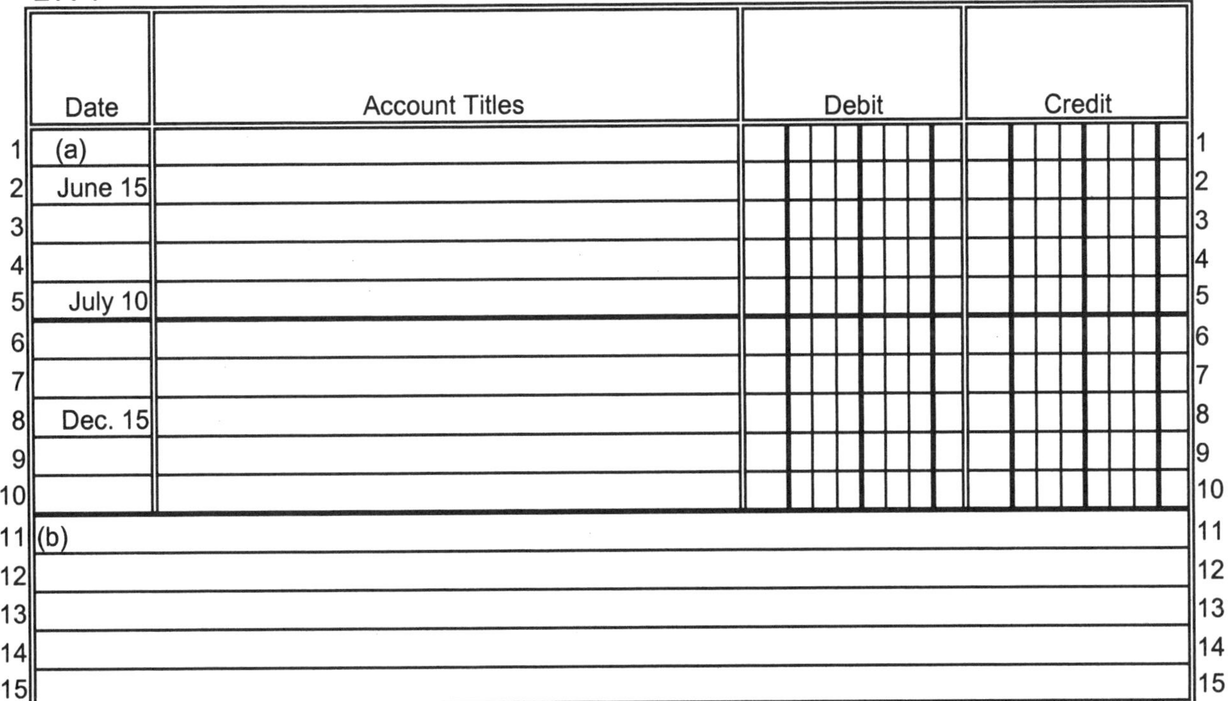

Date	Account Titles	Debit	Credit
(a)			
June 15			
July 10			
Dec. 15			

(b)

E14-2

(a)	2009	2010	2011

(b)	2009	2010	2011

(c)

Date	Account Titles	Debit	Credit
Dec. 31			

Name

Section

Date

E14-3

Date	Account Titles	Debit	Credit
(a)			
Dec 10			
(b)			
Dec 10			

E14-4

	Before Action	After Stock Dividend	After Stock Split
Stockholders' equity			
Outstanding shares			
Par value per share			

Name

Section

Date

E14-5

(a) (1)

(2)

(b)

Common stock

Paid-in capital in excess of par value

Retained earnings

E14-6

Item	Paid-in Capital: Capital Stock	Paid-in Capital: Additional	Retained Earnings
1.	NE	NE	D
2.			
3.			
4.			
5.			
6.			
7.			
8.			

Name

Section

Date

E14-7

Date	Account Titles	Debit	Credit
1.			
Dec. 31			
2.			
Dec. 31			
3.			
Dec. 31			

E14-8

Felter Corporation

Retained Earnings Statement

For the Year Ended December 31, 2010

Name

Section

Date

E14-9

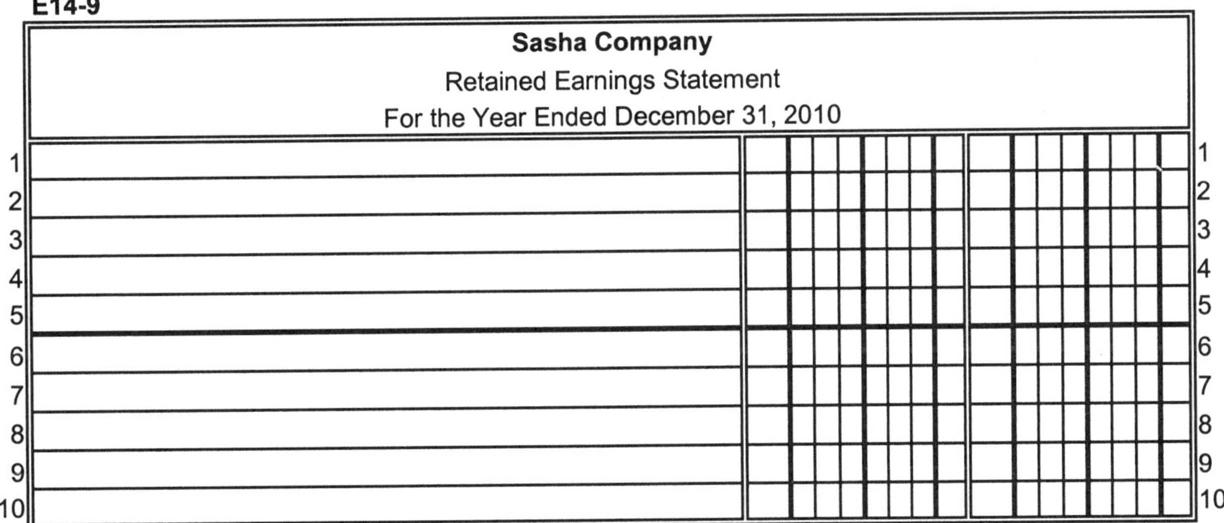

Sasha Company

Retained Earnings Statement

For the Year Ended December 31, 2010

E14-10

Kelly Groucutt Company

Balance Sheet (Partial)

December 31, 2010

Stockholders' equity		

Name

Section

Date

Exercise 14-11

Ortiz Inc.

Ortiz Inc.

Balance Sheet (Partial)

December 31, 200X

Stockholders' equity

Name

Section

Date

E14-12 (a)

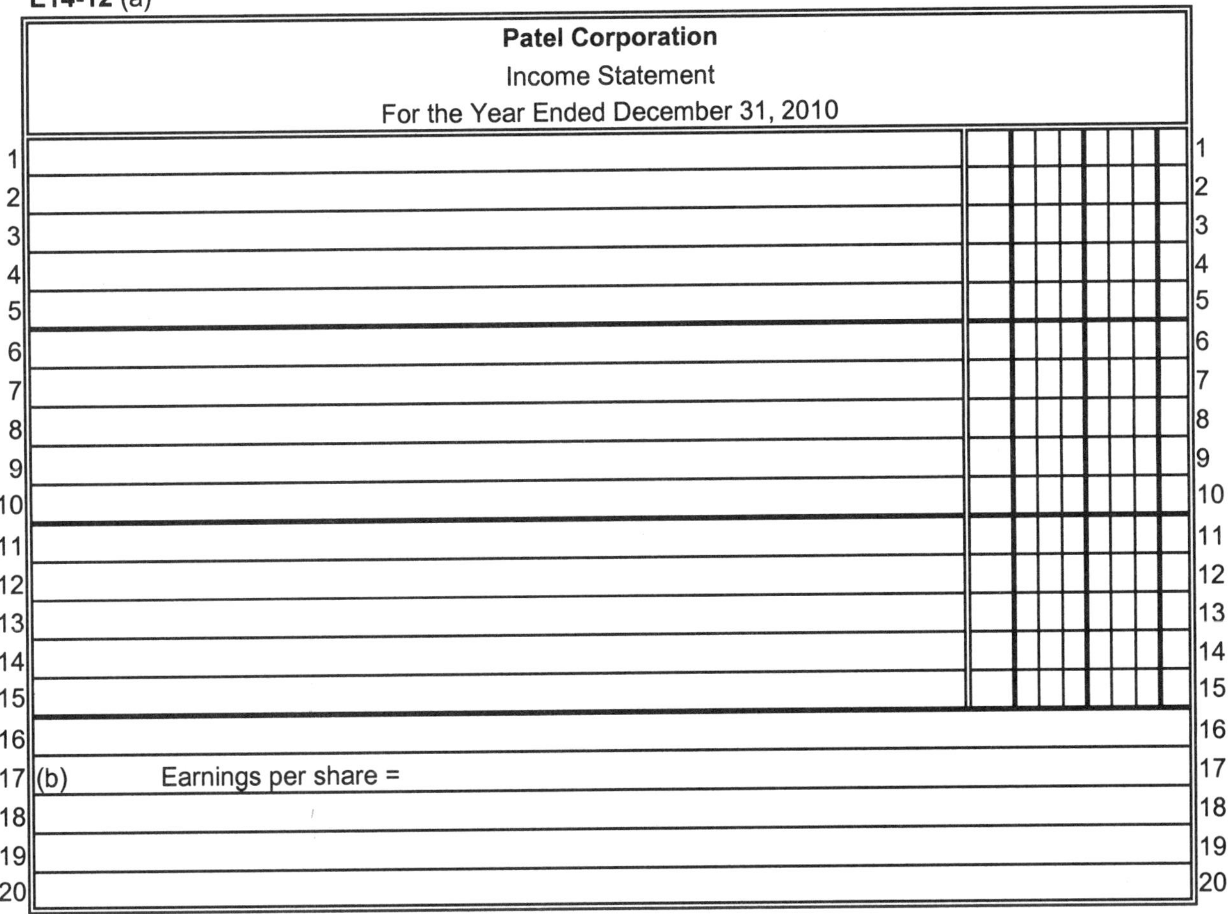

Patel Corporation

Income Statement

For the Year Ended December 31, 2010

(b) Earnings per share =

E14-13 (a)

Mike Singletary Corporation

Income Statement

For the Year Ended December 31, 2010

(b) Return on common stockholders' equity =

Name   Problem 14-1A

Section

Date   Carolinas Corporation

(a)

General Journal

Date	Account	Debit	Credit
Feb. 1			
Mar. 1			
Apr. 1			
July 1			
31			
Dec. 1			
31			

(b)

Common Stock

Date	Explanation	Ref.	Debit	Credit	Balance
Jan. 1	Balance	√			1200000

(b) (Continued)

Common Stock Dividends Distributable

Date	Explanation	Ref.	Debit	Credit	Balance

Paid-in Capital in Excess of Par Value

Date	Explanation	Ref.	Debit	Credit	Balance
Jan. 1	Balance	√			200000

Retained Earnings

Date	Explanation	Ref.	Debit	Credit	Balance
Jan. 1	Balance	√			600000

(c)

Carolinas Corporation
Balance Sheet (Partial)
December 31, 2010

1	Stkckholders' equity			1
2				2
3				3
4				4
5				5
6				6
7				7
8				8
9				9
10				10
11				11
12				12
13				13
14				14
15				15

Name

Section

Date

Problem 14-2A

Hashmi Company

(a)

General Journal

Date	Account Titles	Debit	Credit
July 1			
Aug. 1			
Sept. 1			
Dec. 1			
15			
31			

(b)

Preferred Stock

Date	Explanation	Ref.	Debit	Credit	Balance
Jan. 1	Balance	√			600000

Common Stock

Date	Explanation	Ref.	Debit	Credit	Balance
Jan. 1	Balance	√			800000

(b) (Continued)

Common Stock Dividends Distributable

Date	Explanation	Ref.	Debit	Credit	Balance

Paid-in Capital in Excess of Par Value-Preferred Stock

Date	Explanation	Ref.	Debit	Credit	Balance
Jan. 1	Balance	√			200000

Paid-in Capital in Excess of Par Value-Common Stock

Date	Explanation	Ref.	Debit	Credit	Balance
Jan. 1	Balance	√			300000

Retained Earnings

Date	Explanation	Ref.	Debit	Credit	Balance
Jan. 1	Balance	√			800000

(c)

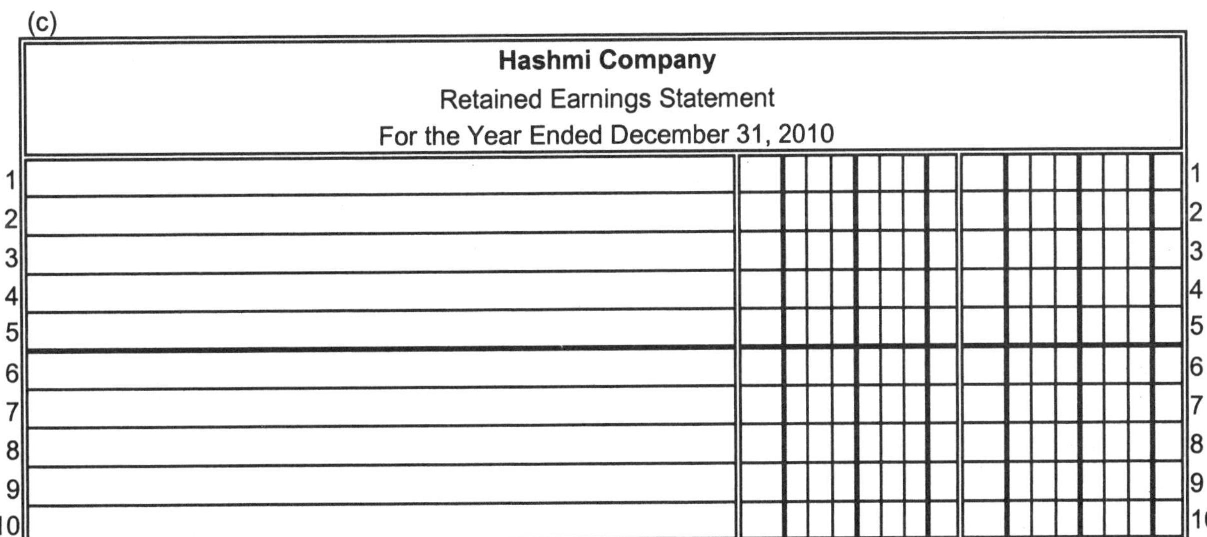

Hashmi Company
Retained Earnings Statement
For the Year Ended December 31, 2010

Name

Section

Date

Problem 14-2A Concluded

Hashmi Company

(d)

Hashmi Company

Balance Sheet (Partial)

December 31, 2010

Stockholders' equity

Name

Section

Date

Problem 14-3A

Dold Corporation

(a)

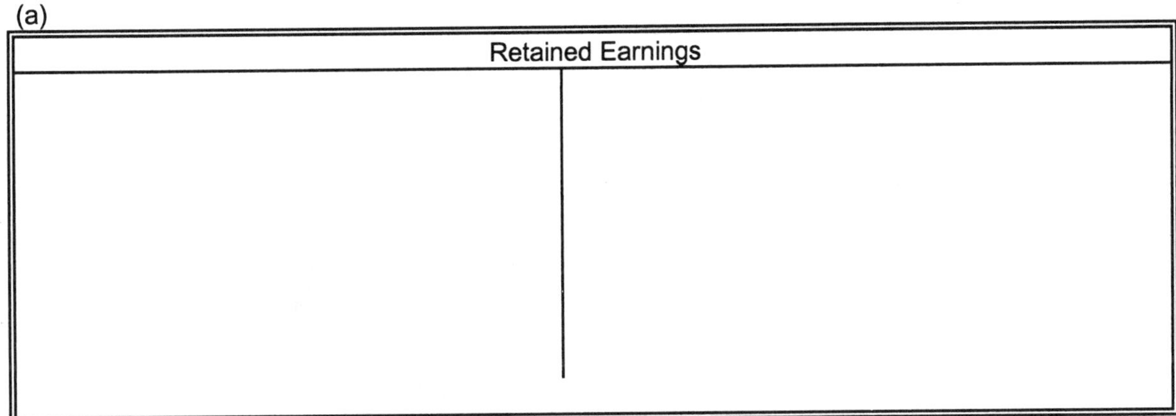

(b)

Dold Corporation

Retained Earnings Statement

For The Year Ended December 31, 2010

(c)

Dold Corporation
Balance Sheet (Partial)
December 31, 2010

Stockholders' equity

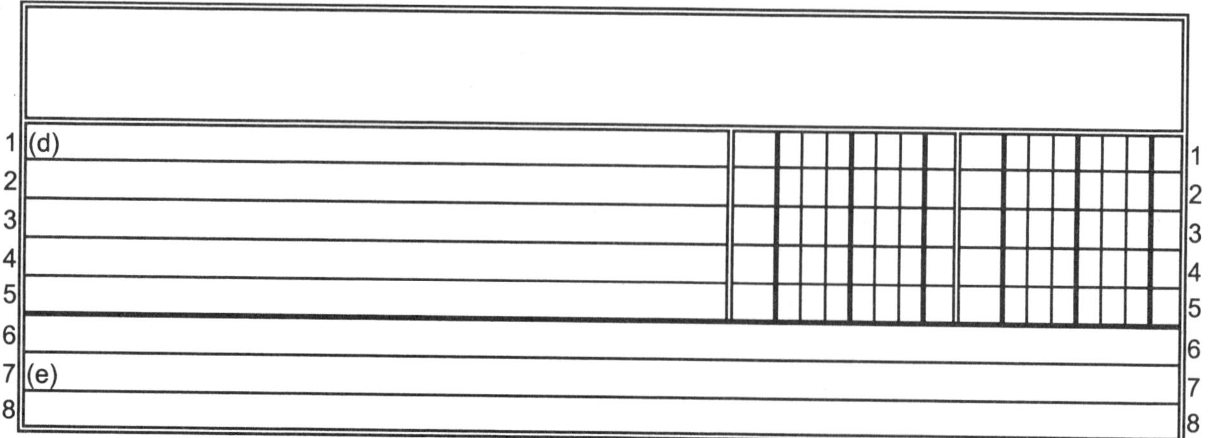
(d)

(e)

Name Problem 14-4A

Section

Date Pattini Corporation

(a)

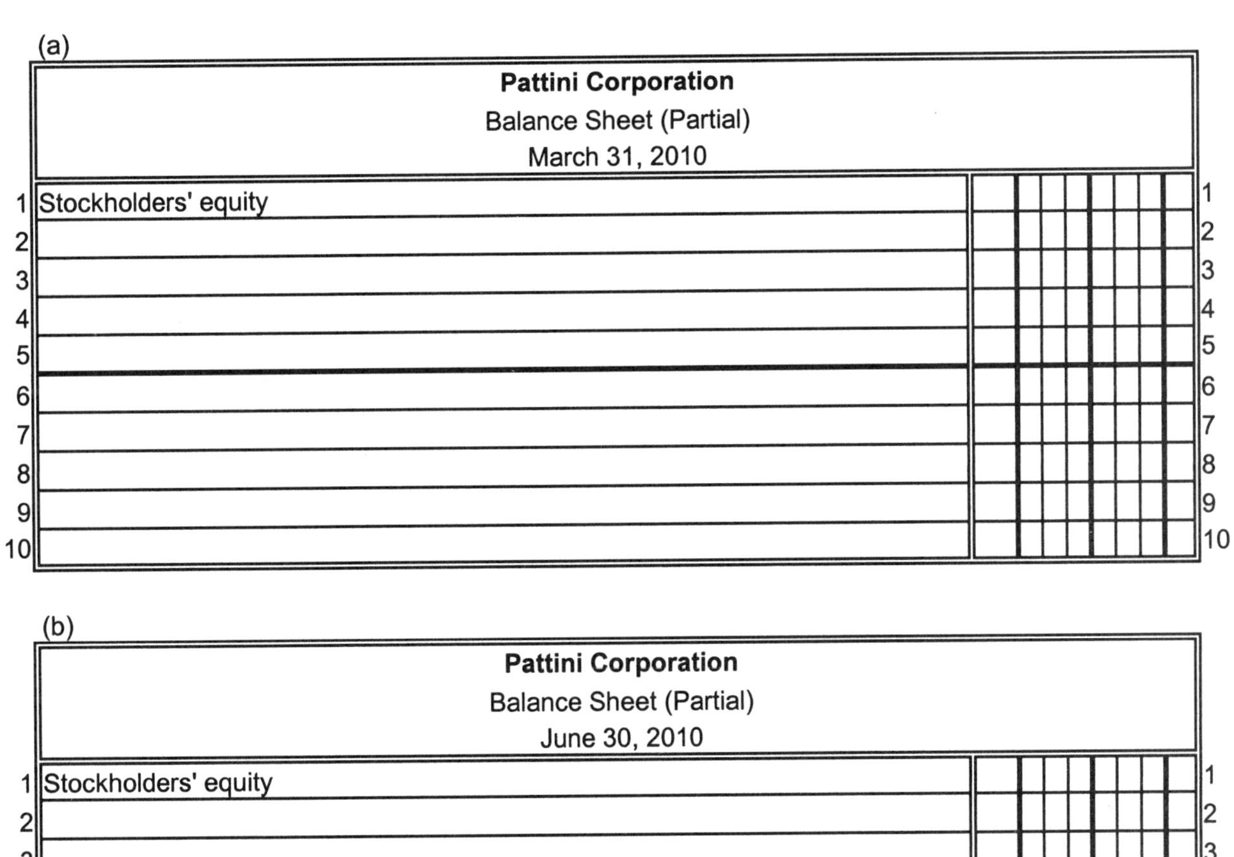

Pattini Corporation

Balance Sheet (Partial)

March 31, 2010

Stockholders' equity

(b)

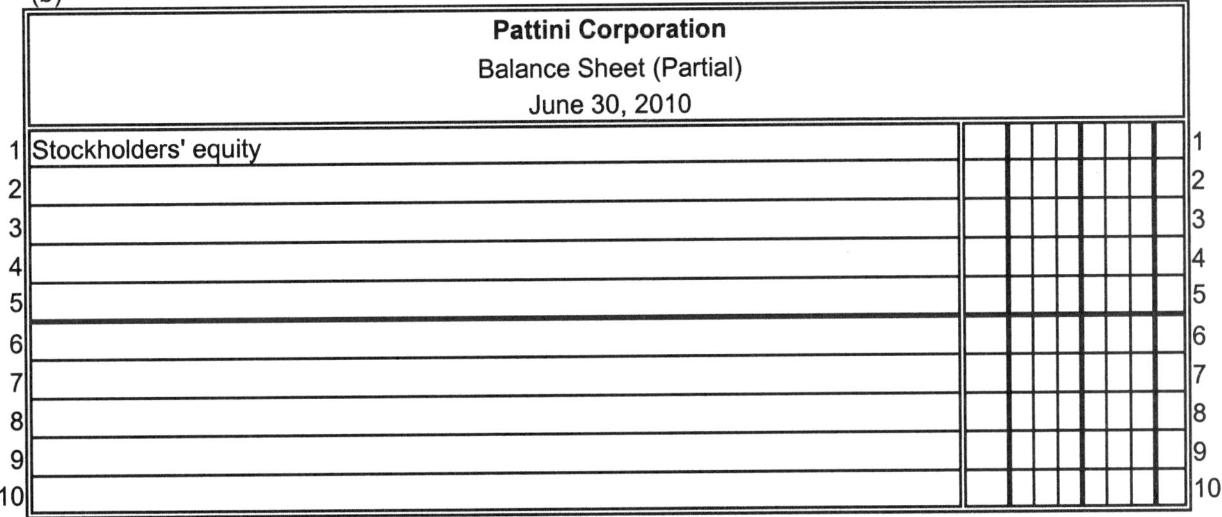

Pattini Corporation

Balance Sheet (Partial)

June 30, 2010

Stockholders' equity

(c)

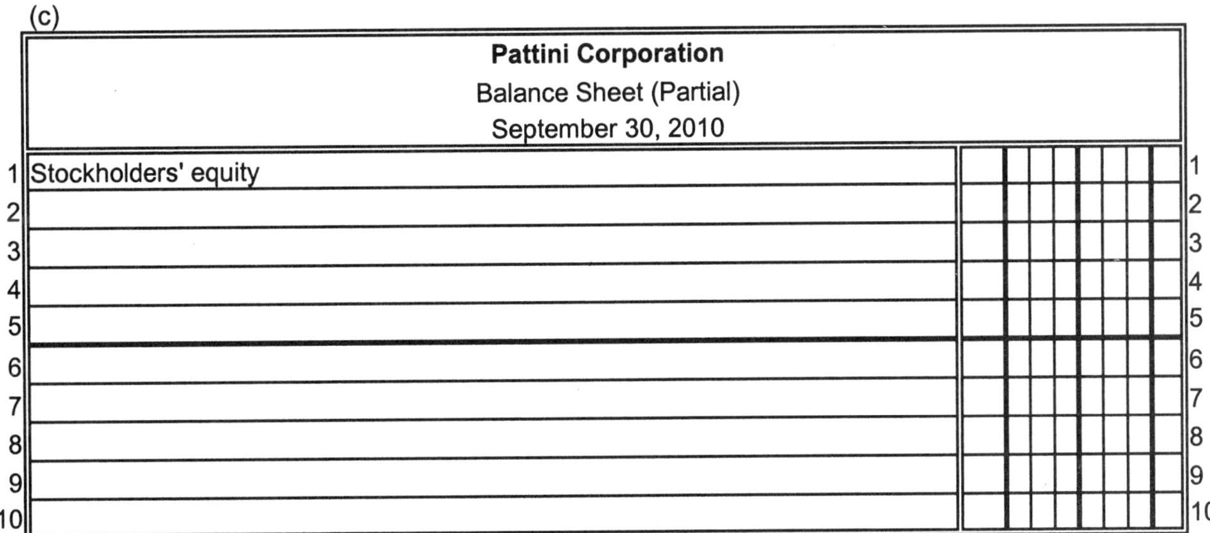

Pattini Corporation

Balance Sheet (Partial)

September 30, 2010

Stockholders' equity

(d)

Pattini Corporation
Balance Sheet (Partial)
December 31, 2010

Stockholders' equity	

Name Problem 14-5A

Section

Date Yadier Inc.

Preliminary analysis (in thousands) - NOT REQUIRED

	Common Stock	Common Stock Dividends Distributable	Retained Earnings	Total
Balance, Jan. 1	1500	200	600	2300
1.				
2.				
3.				
4.				
5.				

Yadier Inc. Balance Sheet (Partial) December 31, 2010	
Stockholders' equity	

Name | Problem 14-1B

Section

Date | Weiser Corporation

(a) General Journal

Date	Account Titles	Debit	Credit
Jan. 15			
Feb. 15			
Apr. 15			
May 15			
July 1			
Dec. 1			
31			

(b)

Common Stock

Date	Explanation	Ref.	Debit	Credit	Balance
Jan. 1	Balance	√			1000000

Name Problem 14-1B Concluded
Section
Date Weiser Corporation

(b) (Continued)

Common Stock Dividends Distributable

Date	Explanation	Ref.	Debit	Credit	Balance

Paid-in Capital in Excess of Par Value

Date	Explanation	Ref.	Debit	Credit	Balance
Jan. 1	Balance	√			200000

Retained Earnings

Date	Explanation	Ref.	Debit	Credit	Balance
Jan. 1	Balance	√			840000

(c)

Weiser Corporation
Balance Sheet (Partial)
December 31,2010

1	Stockholders' equity		1
2			2
3			3
4			4
5			5
6			6
7			7
8			8
9			9
10			10
11			11
12			12
13			13

Name

Section

Date

Problem 14-2B

Holmes, Inc.

(a)

General Journal

	Date	Account Titles	Debit	Credit	
1	July 1				1
2					2
3					3
4	Aug. 1				4
5					5
6					6
7	Sept. 1				7
8					8
9					9
10	Dec. 1				10
11					11
12					12
13					13
14	15				14
15					15
16					16
17	31				17
18					18
19					19
20					20
21					21

(b)

Preferred Stock

Date	Explanation	Ref.	Debit	Credit	Balance
Jan. 1	Balance	√			600000

Common Stock

Date	Explanation	Ref.	Debit	Credit	Balance
Jan. 1	Balance	√			900000

(b) (Continued)

Common Stock Dividends Distributable

Date	Explanation	Ref.	Debit	Credit	Balance

Paid-in Capital in Excess of Par Value-Preferred Stock

Date	Explanation	Ref.	Debit	Credit	Balance
Jan. 1	Balance	√			100000

Paid-in Capital in Excess of Par Value-Common Stock

Date	Explanation	Ref.	Debit	Credit	Balance
Jan. 1	Balance	√			200000

Retained Earnings

Date	Explanation	Ref.	Debit	Credit	Balance
Jan. 1	Balance	√			500000

(c)

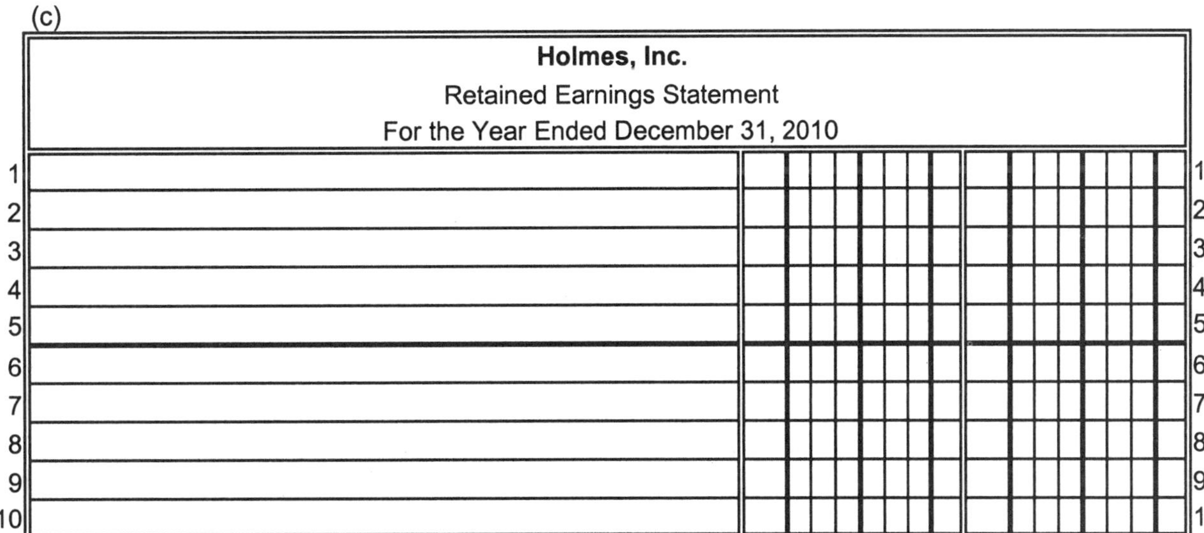

Holmes, Inc.
Retained Earnings Statement
For the Year Ended December 31, 2010

Name

Section

Date

Problem 14-2B Concluded

Holmes, Inc.

(d)

Holmes, Inc.

Balance Sheet (Partial)

December 31, 2010

Stockholders' equity		

Name Problem 14-3B

Section

Date Yakima Corporation

(a)

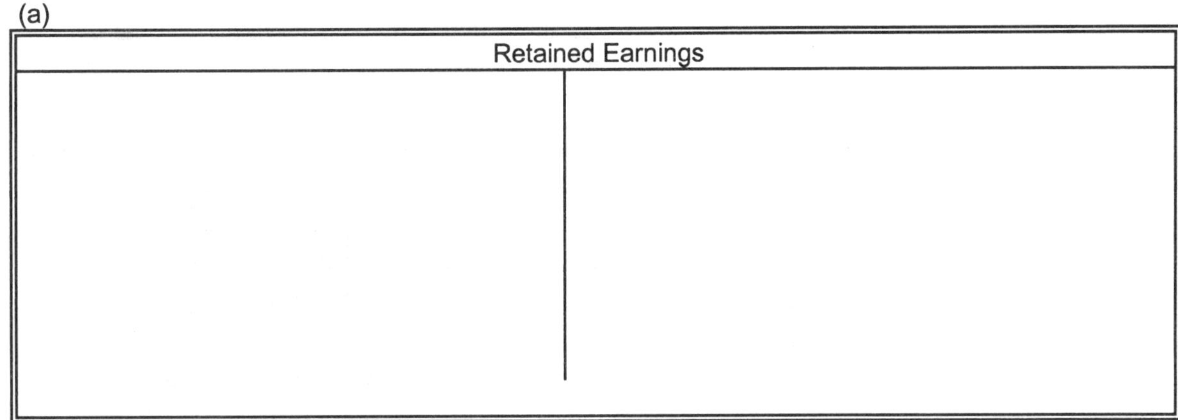

(b)

Yakima Corporation

Retained Earnings Statement

For The Year Ended December 31, 2010

(c)

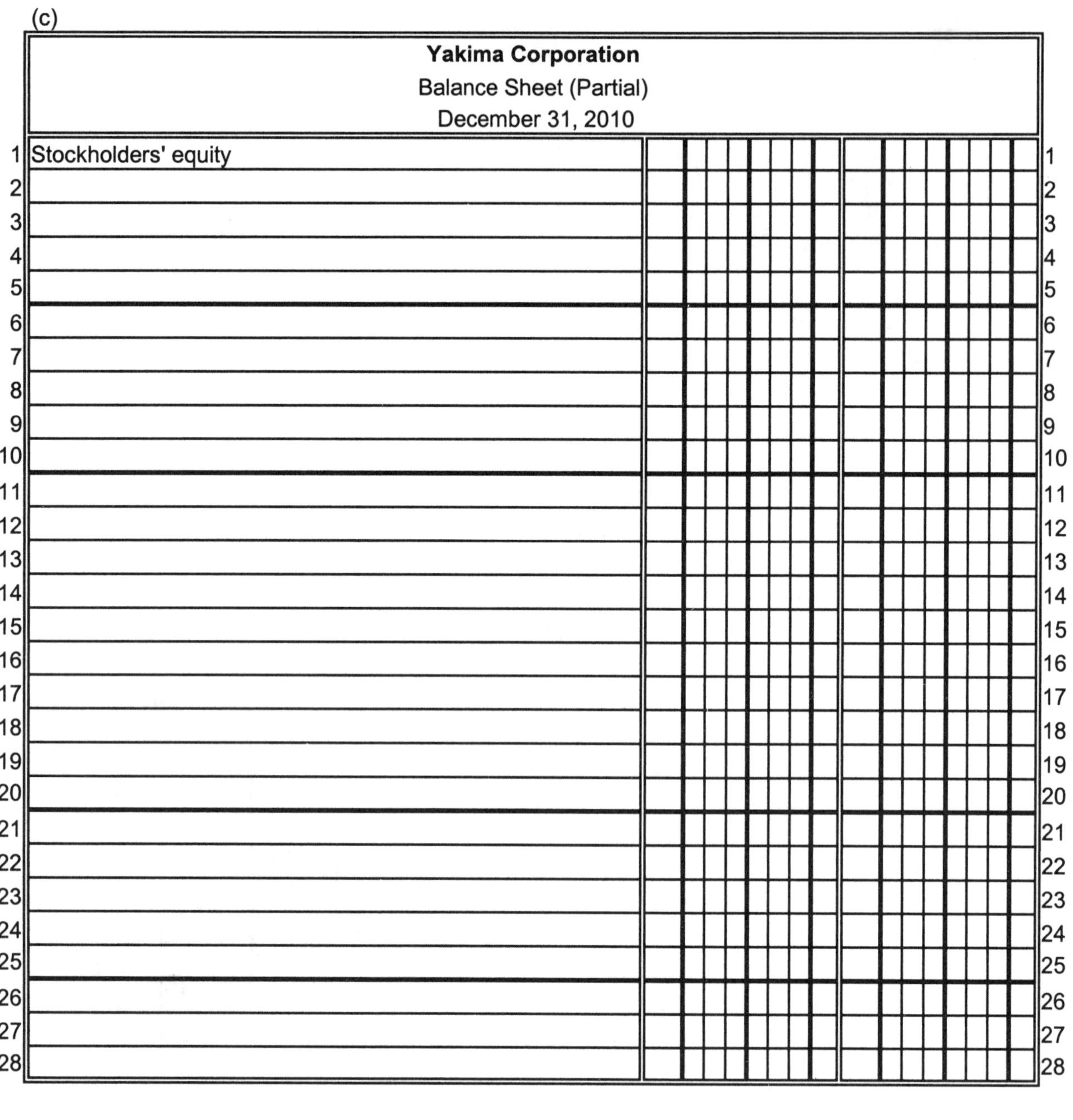

Yakima Corporation
Balance Sheet (Partial)
December 31, 2010

Stockholders' equity

(d)

(e)

Name | Problem 14-4B

Section

Date | Carne Corporation

(a)

Carne Corporation

Balance Sheet (Partial)

March 31, 2010

Stockholders' equity	

(b)

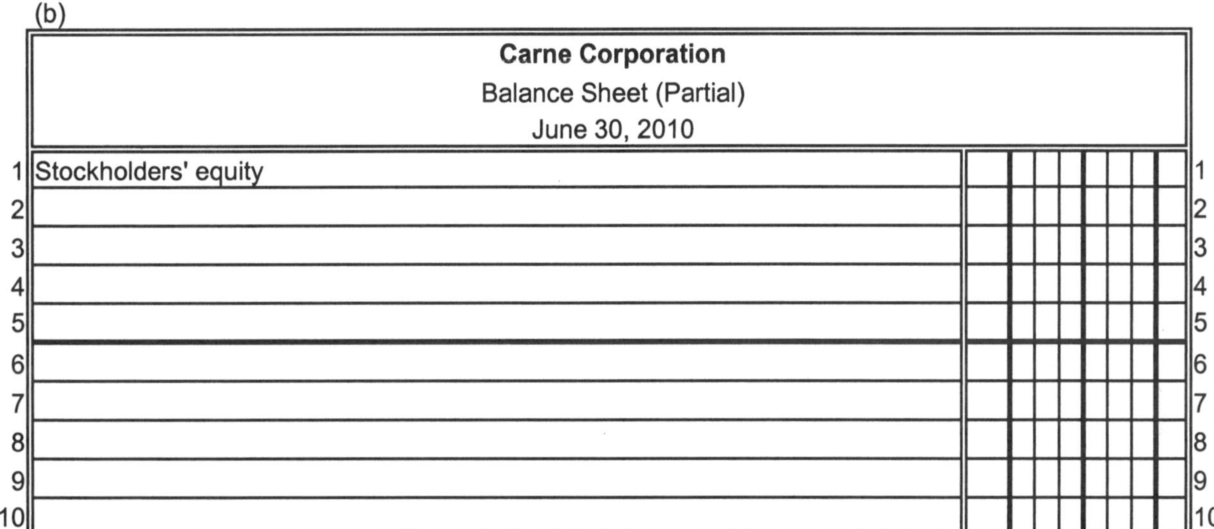

Carne Corporation

Balance Sheet (Partial)

June 30, 2010

Stockholders' equity	

(c)

Carne Corporation

Balance Sheet (Partial)

September 30, 2010

Stockholders' equity	

Name

Section

Date

Problem 14-4B Concluded

Carne Corporation

(d)

Carne Corporation

Balance Sheet (Partial)

December 31, 2010

1	Stockholders' equity		1
2			2
3			3
4			4
5			5
6			6
7			7
8			8
9			9
10			10

Name Problem 14-5rB

Section

Date Garcia Inc.

Preliminary analysis (in thousands) - NOT REQUIRED

	Common Stock	Common Stock Dividends Distributable	Retained Earnings	Total
Balance, Jan. 1	3000	400	1200	4600
1.				
2.				
3.				
4.				
5.				

Garcia Inc. Balance Sheet (Partial) December 31, 2010	
Stockholders' equity	

Journal Entries - NOT REQUIRED

Date	Account Title	Debit	Credit
July 1			
Aug. 1			
Sept. 1			
Dec. 1			
15			
31			

(a)

Fernandez, Inc.

Retained Earnings Statement

For the Year Ended December 31, 2010

(b)

(c)

Name

Section

Date

BE15-1

	Issue Stock	Issue Bond
Income before interest and taxes	$ 700000	$ 700000
Interest expense		
Income before income taxes		
Income tax expense		
Net income		
Outstanding shares		500000
Earnings per share		

BE15-2

Date	Account Titles	Debit	Credit
(a)			
Jan. 1			
(b)			
July 1			
(c)			
Dec. 31			

BE15-3

Date	Account Titles	Debit	Credit
(a)			
Jan. 1			
(b)			
Jan. 1			

Name

Section

Date

BE15-4

Date	Account Titles	Debit	Credit
1.			
Jan. 1			
2.			
July 1			
3.			
Sept. 1			

BE15-5

Date	Account Titles	Debit	Credit
July 1			

BE15-6

	Semiannual Interest Period	(A) Cash Payment	(B) Interest Expense (D) X 5%	(C) Reduction of Principal (A) - (B)	(D) Principal Balance (D) - (C)

Date	Account Titles	Debit	Credit
Dec. 31			
June 30			

BE15-7

Date	Account Titles	Debit	Credit
1.			
Jan. 1			
2.			
July 1			

BE15-8

***BE15-9** (a)

(b)

***BE15-10**

Date	Account Titles	Debit	Credit
(a)			

(b)

(c)

Name

Section

Date

***BE15-11**

Date	Account Titles	Debit	Credit
(a)			
(b)			

***BE15-12**

Date	Account Titles	Debit	Credit
(a)			
Jan 1			
(b)			
July 1			

Name

Section

Date

DO IT! 15-2

	Account Titles	Debit	Credit
(a)			

(b)

DO IT! 15-3

	Account Titles	Debit	Credit

DO IT! 15-4

	Account Titles	Debit	Credit

Name

Section

Date

DO IT! 15-5

James Morrison Corporation

Date	Account Titles	Debit	Credit
(a)			

(b)

Name

Section

Date

E15-2

	Plan One Issue Stock	Plan Two Issue Bonds
Income before interest and taxes		
Interest		
Income before taxes		
Income tax expense		
Net income		
Outstanding shares		
Earnings per share		

E15-3

Date	Account Titles	Debit	Credit
(a)			
Jan. 1			
(b)			
July 1			
(c)			
Dec. 31			

E15-4

Date	Account Titles	Debit	Credit
(a)			
Jan. 1			
(b)			
July 1			
(c)			
Dec. 31			

Name

Section

Date

E15-5

Date	Account Titles	Debit	Credit
(a)	2010		
Jan. 1			
(b)			
July 1			
(c)			
Dec. 31			
(d)	2020		
Jan. 1			

E15-8

Date	Account Titles	Debit	Credit
(a)			
Jan. 1			
(b)			
Jan. 1			
(c)			
July 1			

Name | Exercise 15-6

Section

Date | Nocioni Company

Date	Account Titles	Debit	Credit
(a)	(1) At 100		
	(2) At 98		
	(3) At 103		
(b)	Retirement of bonds at maturity		
(c)	Retirement of bonds before maturity at 98		
(d)	Conversion of bonds into common stock		

Name

Section

Date

Exercise 15-7

Deng Company

Date	Account Titles	Debit	Credit
(a) (1)			
(2)			
(b) (1)	Account Titles	Debit	Credit
(2)			

Name

Section

Date

E15-9

Date	Account Titles	Debit	Credit
1.			
June 30			
2.			
June 30			
3.			
Dec. 31			

E15-10

Date	Account Titles	Debit	Credit
	2010		
	Issuance of note		
Dec. 31			
	2011		
	First Installment Payment		
June 30			
	Second Installment Payment		
Dec. 31			

Name Exercise 15-11

Section

Date TPol Company

	Account Titles	Debit	Credit
(a)	January 1, 2010		
	June 30, 2010		
	December 31, 2010		
(b)			

Name

Section

Date

E15-12

Date	Account Titles	Debit	Credit
(a)			
(b)			
Jan. 1			

E15-13

Long-term liabilities

E15-14

(a)

(b)

Debt to total assets ratio =

(c)

Times interest earned ratio =

Name

Section

Date

*Exercises 15-15 to 15-16

***E15-15**

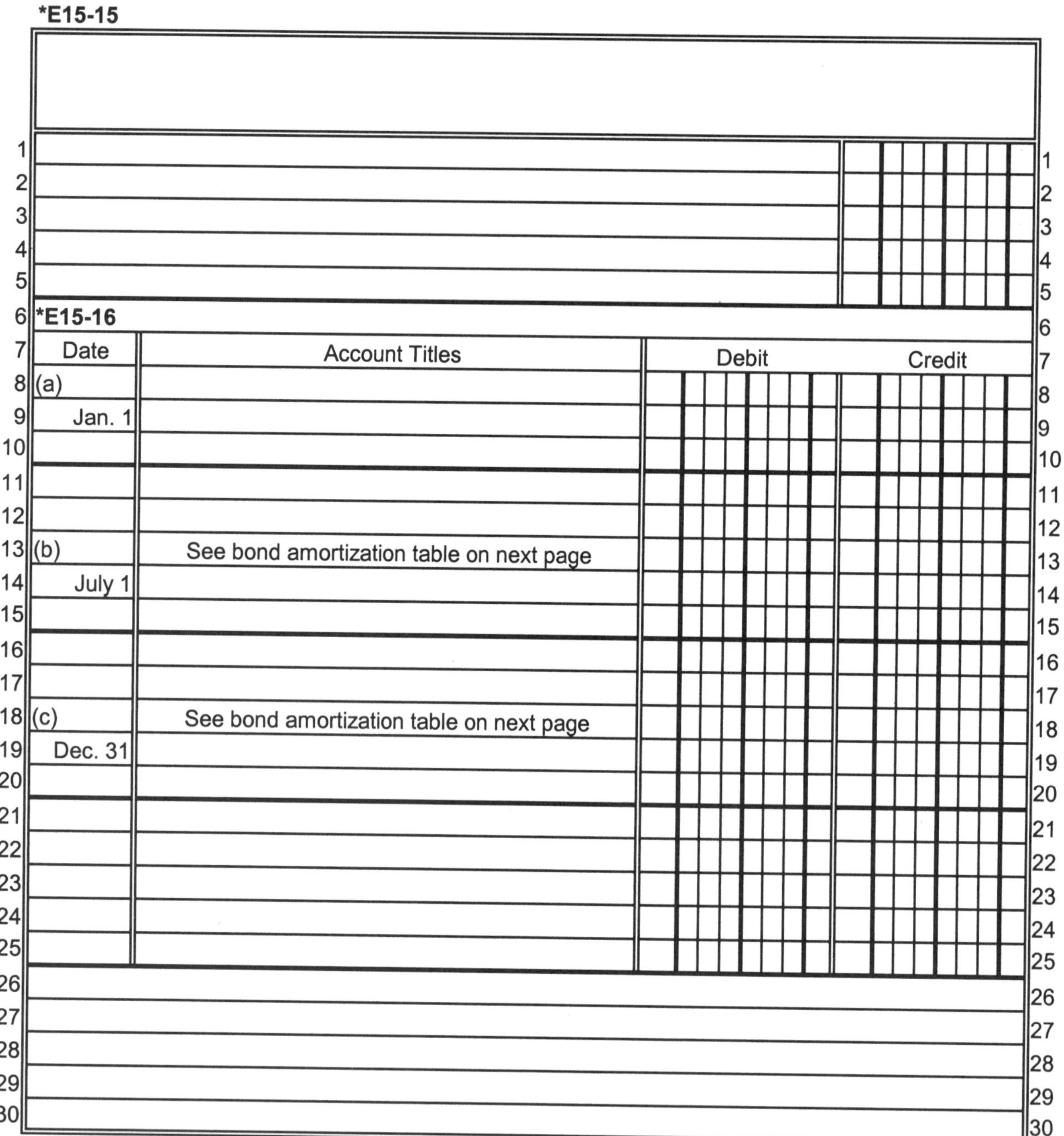

***E15-16**

Date	Account Titles	Debit	Credit
(a)			
Jan. 1			
(b)	See bond amortization table on next page		
July 1			
(c)	See bond amortization table on next page		
Dec. 31			

Name

Section

Date

Exercise 15-16 Concluded

Hrabik Corporation

(b) and (c) Continued

Semiannual Interest Periods	(A) Interest to Be Paid	(B) Interest Expense to Be Recorded	(C) Discount Amortization (B) - (A)	(D) Unamortized Discount (D) - (C)	(E) Carrying Value of the Bonds
Issue date					
1					
2					

Name

Section

Date

***E15-17**

Date	Account Titles	Debit	Credit
(a)			
Jan. 1			
(b)	See bond amortization table on next page		
July 1			
(c)	See bond amortization table on next page		
Dec. 31			

***E15-18**

Date	Account Titles	Debit	Credit
(a)	2010		
Jan. 1			
(b)			
July 1			
(c)			
Dec. 31			
(d)	2030		
Jan. 1			

Name *Exercise 15-17 Concluded

Section

Date Siburo Company

(b) and (c) Continued

Semiannual Interest Periods	(A) Interest to Be Paid	(B) Interest Expense to Be Recorded	(C) Premium Amortization (A) - (B)	(D) Unamortized Premium (D) - (C)	(E) Carrying Value of the Bonds
Issue date					
1					
2					

Name

Section

Date

*Exercise 15-19

Joseph Company

	Date	Account Titles	Debit	Credit	
1	(a)	2009			1
2	Dec. 31				2
3					3
4					4
5					5
6	(b)	2010			6
7	June 30				7
8					8
9					9
10					10
11	(c)	2010			11
12	Dec. 31				12
13					13
14					14
15					15
16	(d)	2019			16
17	Dec. 31				17
18					18
19					19
20					20
21					21
22					22
23					23
24					24
25					25

Name | Problem 15-1A
Section
Date | Newby Corp.

Date	Account Titles	Debit	Credit
(a)	2010		
May 1			
(b)			
Dec. 31			

(c)

(d)

Date	Account Titles	Debit	Credit
	2011		
May 1			
(e)			
Nov. 1			
(f)			
Nov. 1			

Name Problem 15-2A

Section

Date Kasmaul Electric

Date	Account Titles	Debit	Credit
(a)	2010		
Jan. 1			

(b)

Date	Account Titles	Debit	Credit
(c)	2012		
Jan. 1			

Name Problem 15-3A

Section

Date Fordyce Electronics

(a)

	Semiann. Interest Period	Cash Payment	Interest Expense	Reduction of Principal	Principal Balance
	Issue Date				
	1				
	2				
	3				
	4				

(b)

Date	Account Titles	Debit	Credit
	2009		
Dec. 31			
	2010		
June 30			
Dec. 31			

(c)

	12/31/10

Name

Section

Date

Problem 15-4A

Kear Inc.

(a)

Date	Account Titles	Debit	Credit
(b)			
(c)			

Name *Problem 15-5A

Section

Date Atwater Corporation

Date	Account Titles	Debit	Credit
(a)	2010		
July 1			
(b)	See bond amortization table on next page		
(c)			
Dec. 31			
(d)	2011		
July 1			
(e)			
Dec. 31			

Name

Section

Date

*Problem 15-5A Concluded

Atwater Corporation

(b)

Atwater Corporation
Bond Premium Amortization
Effective-Interest-Method - Semiannual Interest Payments
10% Bonds Issued at 8%

Semiannual Interest Periods	(A) Interest to Be Paid	(B) Interest Expense to to Be Recorded	(C) Premium Amortization (A) - (B)	(D) Unamortized Premium (D) - (C)	(E) Carrying Value of the Bonds
Issue date					
1					
2					
3					

Name *Problem 15-6A

Section

Date Rossillon Company

Date	Account Titles	Debit	Credit
(a) (1)	2010		
July 1			
(2)			
Dec. 31			
(3)	2011		
July 1			
(4)			
Dec. 31			

(b)

Name

Section

Date

*Problem 15-6A Concluded

Rossillon Company

(c)

Name *Problem 15-7A

Section

Date Soprano Electric

Date	Account Titles	Debit	Credit
(a)	2010		
Jan. 1			
(b)	See bond amortization table on next page		
(c)	2010		
July 1			
Dec. 31			
	2011		
Jan. 1			
July 1			
Dec. 31			

(d)

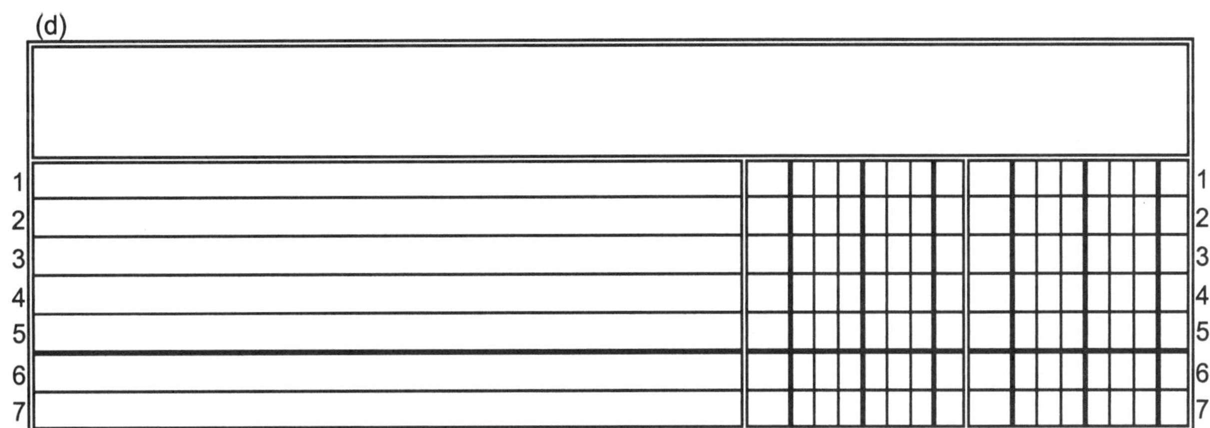

Name | *Problem 15-7A Concluded

Section

Date | Soprano Electric

(b)

Semiannual Interest Periods	(A) Interest to Be Paid	(B) Int. Expense to Be Recorded (A) + (C)	(C) Premium Amortization	(D) Unamortized Premium (D) - (C)	(E) Carrying Value of the Bonds
Issue date					
1					
2					
3					
4					

Name *Problem 15-8A

Section

Date Elkins Company

	Date	Account Titles	Debit	Credit	
1	(a)				1
2	July 1				2
3					3
4					4
5					5
6	Dec. 31				6
7					7
8					8
9					9
10					10
11					11
12					12
13					13
14	(b)				14
15	July 1				15
16					16
17					17
18					18
19	Dec. 31				19
20					20
21					21
22					22
23					23
24					24
25					25
26					26
27					27
28					28
29					29
30					30

Name

Section

Date

*Problem 15-8A Concluded

Elkins Company

(c)

Premium:

Discount:

Name *Problem 15-9A

Section

Date Pinkston Company

Date	Account Titles	Debit	Credit
(a)			
Jan. 1			
(b)			
July 1			
(c)			
July 1			
(d)			
Dec. 31			

Name

Section

Date

Problem 15-1B

Mordica Corp.

Date	Account Titles	Debit	Credit
(a)	2010		
June 1			
(b)			
Dec. 31			

(c)

(d)

Date	Account Titles	Debit	Credit
	2011		
June 1			
(e)			
Dec. 1			
(f)			
Dec. 1			

Name | Problem 15-2B

Section

Date | Mueller Co.

Date	Account Titles	Debit	Credit
(a)	2010		
Jan. 1			

(b)

Date	Account	Debit	Credit
(c)	2012		
Jan. 1			

Name

Section

Date

Problem 15-3B

Colt Electronics

(a)

	Semiann. Interest Period	Cash Payment	Interest Expense	Reduction of Principal	Principal Balance
	Issue Date				
	1				
	2				
	3				
	4				

(b)

Date		Debit	Credit
	2010		
Dec. 31			
	2011		
June 30			
Dec. 31			

(c)

	12/31/11

Name

Section

Date

Problem 15-4B

Ortiz Enterprises

(a)

Date	Account Titles	Debit	Credit
(b)			
(c)			

Name

Section

Date

*Problem 15-5B

Wheeler Satellites

Date	Account Titles	Debit	Credit
(a)	2010		
July 1			
(b)	See bond amortization table on next page		
(c)			
Dec. 31			
(d)	2011		
July 1			
(e)			
Dec. 31			

Name

Section

Date

Wheeler Satellites

(e)

Wheeler Satellites

Bond Discount Amortization

Effective-Interest-Method - Semiannual Interest Payments

9% Bonds Issued at 10%

Semiannual Interest Periods	(A) Interest to Be Paid	(B) Interest Expense to Be Recorded	(C) Discount Amortization (B) - (A)	(D) Unamortized Discount (D) - (C)	(E) Carrying Value of the Bonds
Issue date					
1					
2					
3					

Name

Section

Date

*Problem 15-6B

Remington Chemical Company

Date	Account Titles	Debit	Credit
(a) (1)	2010		
July 1			
(2)			
Dec. 31			
(3)	2011		
July 1			
(4)			
Dec. 31			

(b)

Name *Problem 15-6B Concluded

Section

Date Remington Chemical Company

(c)

Name

Section

Date

*Problem 15-7B

Suppan Company

Date	Account Titles	Debit	Credit
(a)	2010		
Jan. 1			
(b)	See bond amortization table on next page		
(c)	2010		
July 1			
Dec. 31			
	2011		
Jan. 1			
July 1			
Dec. 31			

(d)

Name

Section

Date

*Problem 15-7B Concluded

Suppan Company

(b)

Semiannual Interest Periods	(A) Interest to Be Paid	(B) Int. Expense to Be Recorded (A) + (C)	(C) Discount Amortization ($160,000 ÷ 40)	(D) Unamortized Discount (D) - (C)	(E) Carrying Value of the Bonds
Issue date					
1					
2					
3					
4					

Name *Problem 15-8B

Section

Date Jinkens Corporation

	Date	Account Titles	Debit	Credit	
1	(a)				1
2	Jan. 1				2
3					3
4					4
5					5
6	July 1				6
7					7
8					8
9					9
10	Dec. 31				10
11					11
12					12
13					13
14	(b)				14
15	Jan. 1				15
16					16
17					17
18					18
19	July 1				19
20					20
21					21
22					22
23	Dec. 31				23
24					24
25					25
26					26
27					27
28					28
29					29
30					30

Name *Problem 15-8B Concluded

Section

Date Jinkens Corporation

(c)

Premium:

Discount:

Name

Section

Date

*Problem 15-9B

Nilson Corporation

Date	Account Titles	Debit	Credit
(a)			
Jan. 1			
(b)			
July 1			
(c)			
July 1			
(d)			
Dec. 31			

Name　　　　　　　　　　　　　　　　　　　　　　Chapter 15 Comprehensive Problem

Section

Date　　　　　　　　　　　　　　　　　　　　　　Nordham Corporation

(a)

Date	Account Titles	Debit	Credit
(a) 1.			
2.			
3.			
4.			
5.			
6.			
7.			
8.			
9.			

(b)

Nordham Corporation
Trial Balance
December 31, 2010

		Debit	Credit	
1	Cash			1
2	Accounts Receivable			2
3	Merchandise Inventory			3
4	Land			4
5	Building			5
6	Equipment			6
7	Allowance for Doubtful Accounts			7
8	Accumulated Depreciation - Building			8
9	Accumulated Depreciation - Equipment			9
10	Accounts Payable			10
11	Bond Interest Payable			11
12	Dividends Payable			12
13	Unearned Rent			13
14	Bonds Payable			14
15	Common Stock			15
16	Paid-in Capital in Excess of Par - C.S.			16
17	Preferred Stock			17
18	Paid-in Capital in Excess of Par - P.S.			18
19	Retained Earnings			19
20	Treasury Stock			20
21	Dividends Payable			21
22	Sales			22
23	Rent Revenue			23
24	Bad Debts Expense			24
25	Bond Interest Expense			25
26	Cost of Goods Sold			26
27	Depreciation Expense - Buildings			27
28	Depreciation Expense - Equipment			28
29	Other Operating Expenses			29
30	Salaries Expense			30
31	Totals			31
32				32
33				33
34				34
35				35

(c)

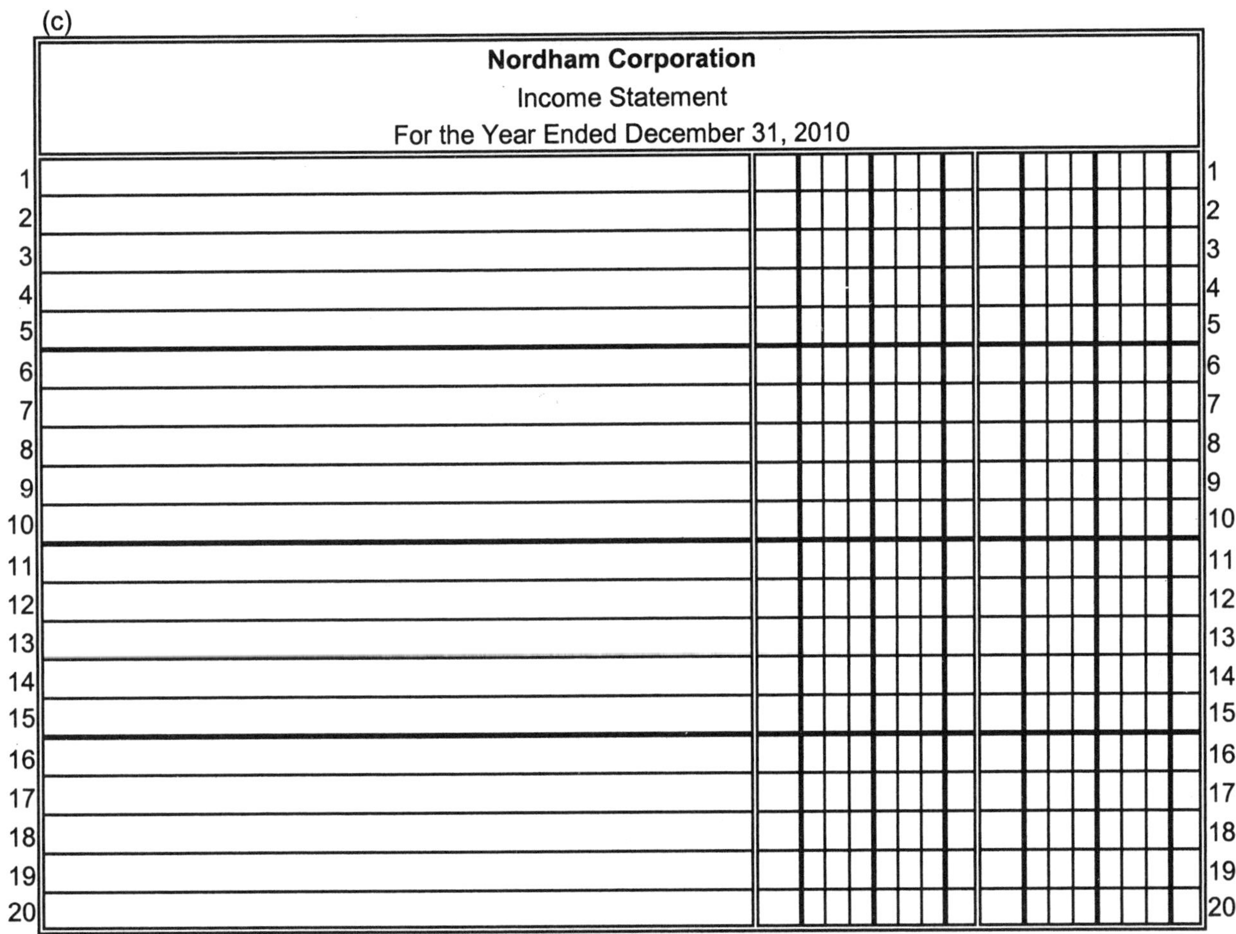

Nordham Corporation
Income Statement
For the Year Ended December 31, 2010

(d)

Nordham Corporation
Retained Earnings Statement
For the Year Ended December 31, 2010

(e)

Nordham Corporation

Balance Sheet

December 31, 2010

Assets

Liabilities and Stockholders' Equity

Name

Section

Date

Carlin Corporation

(a)

(b)

Date	Account Titles	Debit	Credit
1.			
2.			

(c)

Name

Section

Date

Date	Account Titles	Debit	Credit
BE16-1			
Jan 1			
July 1			
BE16-2			
Aug 1			
Dec 1			
BE16-3			
Dec 31			
31			
BE16-4			
Dec 31			
BE16-5	Balance Sheet		
	Income Statement		
BE16-6			
Date	Account Titles	Debit	Credit
Dec 31			

Name

Section

Date

BE16-7

Balance Sheet

BE16-8

Name

Section

Date

DO IT! 16-1

Date	Account Titles	Debit	Credit
(a) Jan 1			
July 1			
July 1			
(b) Dec 31			

DO IT! 16-2

Date	Account Titles	Debit	Credit
(1)			
June 17			
Sept. 3			
(2)			
Jan. 1			
May 15			
Dec. 31			

Name

Section

Date

DO IT! 16-3

	Account Titles	Debit	Credit
	Trading securities:		
	Available-for-sale securities:		

DO IT! 16-4

Item	Financial Statement	Category
1. Loss on sale of investments in stock.		
2. Unrealized gain on available-for-sale securities.		
3. Market adjustment - trading.		
4. Interest earned on investments in bonds.		
5. Unrealized loss on trading securities.		

Name

Section

Date

E16-2

Date	Account Titles	Debit	Credit
(a)			
Jan 1			
July 1			
1			
(b)			
Dec 31			

E16-3

	Account Titles	Debit	Credit
	January 1, 2010		
	July 1, 2010		
	December 31, 2010		
	January 1, 2011		
	January 1, 2011		

Name

Section

Date

E16-4

Date	Account Titles	Debit	Credit
(a)			
Feb 1			
July 1			
Sept 1			
Dec 1			

(b)

E16-5

Date	Account Titles	Debit	Credit
Jan 1			
July 1			
Dec 1			
31			

Name

Section

Date

E16-6

Date	Account Titles	Debit	Credit
	February 1		
	March 20		
	April 25		
	June 15		
	July 28		

E16-7

Date	Account Titles	Debit	Credit
(a)			
Jan 1			
Dec 31			
31			

(b)

Name Exercises 16-8 and 16-9

Section

Date

E16-8

Date	Account Titles	Debit	Credit
1. 2010			
Mar 18			
June 30			
Dec 31			
2.			
Jan 1			
June 15			
Dec 31			

E16-9

(a)

(b)

(c)

Name | Exercise 16-10

Section

Date | Natoli, Inc.

Date	Account Titles	Debit	Credit
(a)			
Dec 31			
(b)	Balance Sheet		
	Income Statement		

Name Exercise 16-11

Section

Date Natoli, Inc.

(a)

Date	Account Titles	Debit	Credit
Dec 31			

(b)

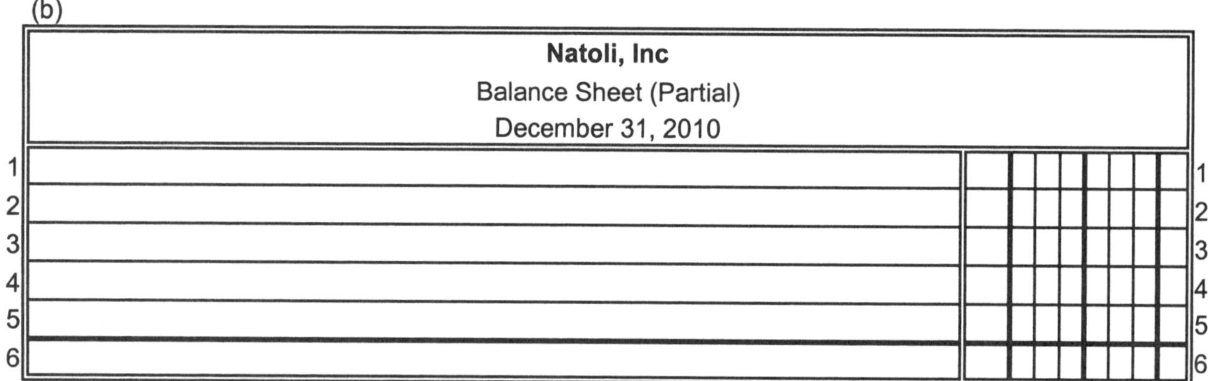

Natoli, Inc

Balance Sheet (Partial)

December 31, 2010

(c)

Name | Exercise 16-12

Section

Date | McGee Company

(a)

Date	Account Titles	Debit	Credit
Dec 31			
Dec 31			

(b)

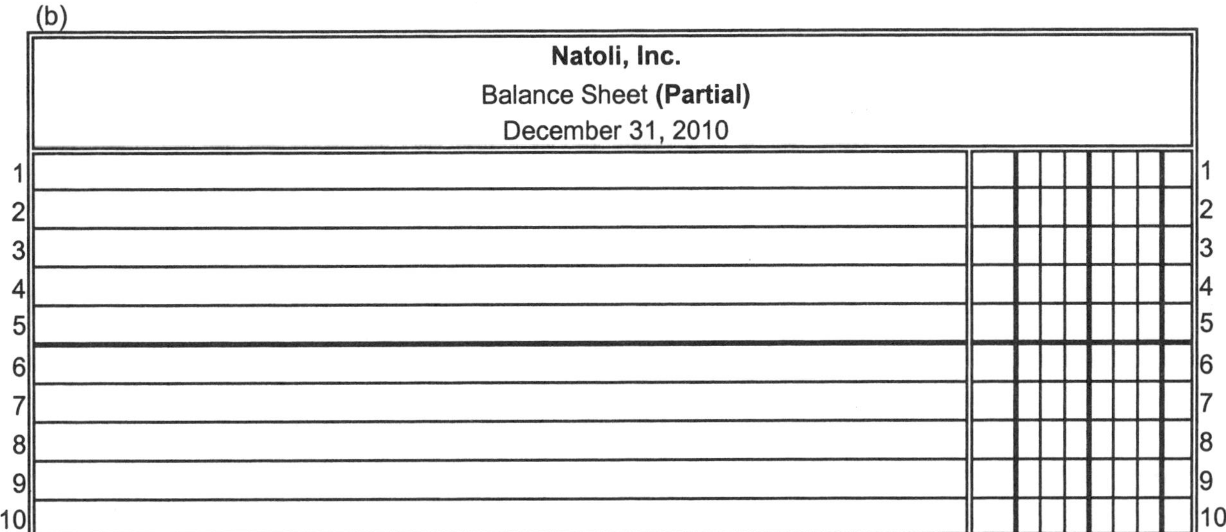

Natoli, Inc.

Balance Sheet **(Partial)**

December 31, 2010

Natoli, Inc.

Income Statement (Partial)

For the Year Ended December 31, 2020

Name | Problem 16-1A

Section

Date | Davison Carecenters Inc.

(a) & (b)

Date	Account Titles	Debit	Credit
(a) 2010			
Jan 1			
July 1			
Dec 31			
2013			
Jan 1			
1			
July 1			
Dec 31			
(b) 2010			
Dec 31			

(c)

Balance Sheet

Name Problem 16-2A

Section

Date Noble Company

(a)

Date	Account Titles	Debit	Credit
Feb 1			
Mar 1			
Apr 1			
July 1			
Aug 1			
Sept 1			
Oct 1			
1			

STOCK INVESTMENTS		DEBT INVESTMENTS	

(b)

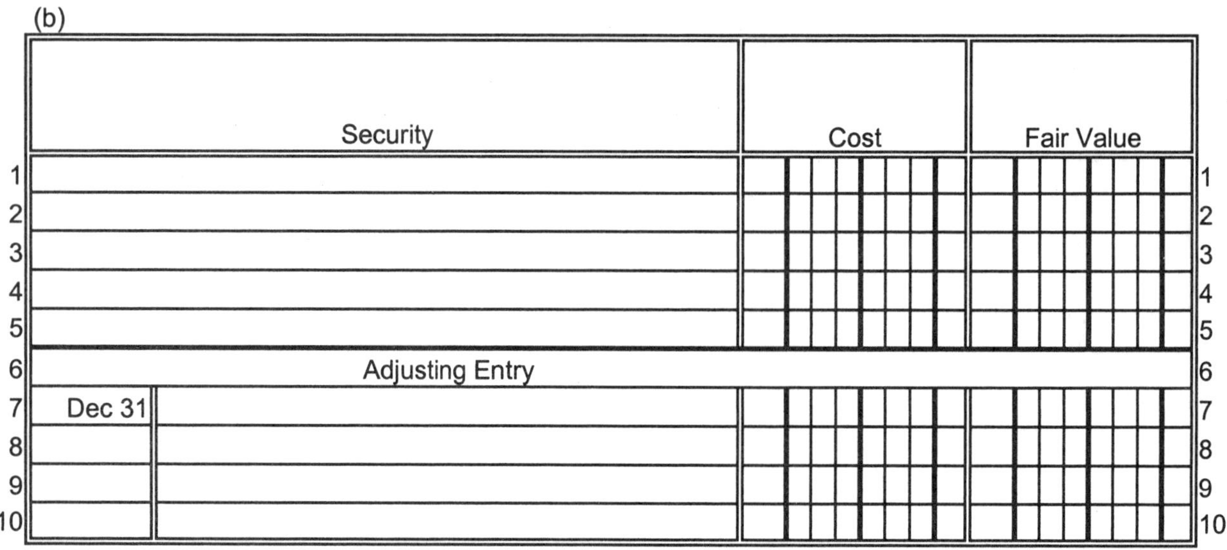

Security	Cost	Fair Value
Adjusting Entry		
Dec 31		

(c)

Balance Sheet	
Current assets:	

(d)

Income Statement Account	Classification

Name Problem 16-3A

Section

Date Ramey Associates

(a)

Date	Account Titles	Debit	Credit
2011			
July 1			
Aug 1			
Sept 1			
Oct 1			
Nov 1			
Dec 15			
31			

STOCK INVESTMENTS

1/1/11 Bal 135,000	

Name
Section
Date

Problem 16-3A Concluded

Ramey Associates

(b)

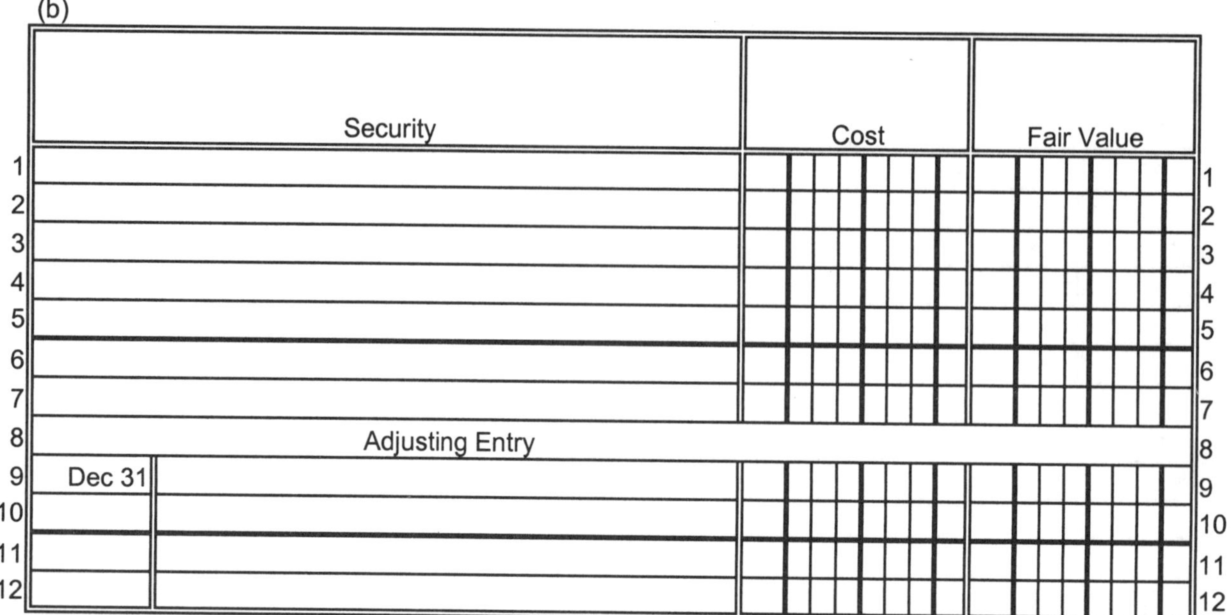

Security	Cost	Fair Value

Adjusting Entry

Dec 31			

(c)

Assets

Investments	

Liabilities and Stockholders' Equity

Stockholders' equity		

Name Problem 16-4A

Section

Date Glaser Services

Date	Account Titles	Debit	Credit
(a)			
Jan 1			
Mar 15			
June 15			
Sept 15			
Dec 15			
31			
(b)			
Jan 1			
Mar 15			
June 15			
Sept 15			
Dec 15			
31			

Name | Problem 16-4A Concluded

Section

Date | Glaser Services

(c)

	Cost Method	Equity Method

Name

Section

Date

Problem 16-5A

Pascual Company

(a)

Date	Account Titles	Debit	Credit
Jan 20			
28			
30			
Feb 8			
18			
July 30			
Sept 6			
Dec 1			

(b)

INVESTMENT IN ABLE CORPORATION
COMMON STOCK

1/1 Bal	52,000	

INVESTMENT IN FREY CORPORATION
COMMON STOCK

1/1 Bal	84,000	

(b) (Continued)

INVESTMENT IN WEISS CORPORATION
PREFERRED STOCK

1/1 Bal	33,600	

INVESTMENT IN ROSEN CORPORATION
COMMON STOCK

(c)

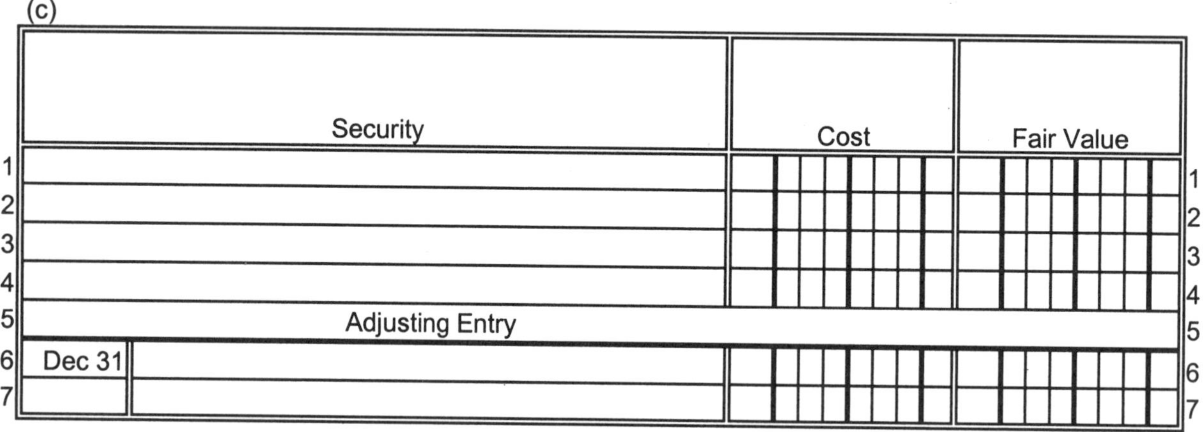

Security		Cost	Fair Value
Adjusting Entry			
Dec 31			

(d)

Assets	
Investments	
Liabilities and Stockholder's Equity	
Stockholders' Equity	

Name

Section

Date

Problem 16-6A

Urbina Corporation

Urbina Corporation

Balance Sheet

December 31, 2010

Assets

Name

Section

Date

Problem 16-6A Concluded

Urbina Corporation

Urbina Corporation

Balance Sheet (continued)

December 31, 2010

Liabilities and Stockholders' Equity

Name | Problem 16-1B

Section

Date | Groneman Farms

(a) & (b)

Date	Account Titles	Debit	Credit
(a) 2010			
Jan 1			
July 1			
Dec 31			
2013			
Jan 1			
1			
July 1			
Dec 31			
(b) 2010			
Dec 31			

(c)

Balance Sheet (Partial)	

Name

Section

Date

Problem 16-2B

Prasad Company

(a)

Date	Account Titles	Debit	Credit
Feb 1			
Mar 1			
Apr 1			
July 1			
Aug 1			
Sept 1			
Oct 1			
1			

STOCK INVESTMENTS

DEBT INVESTMENTS

(b)

Security	Cost	Fair Value
Adjusting Entry		
Dec 31		

(c)

Current assets:	

(d)

Income Statement Account	Classification

Name

Problem 16-3B

Section

Date

Sauder Associates

(a)

Date	Account Titles	Debit	Credit
July 1			
Aug 1			
Sept 1			
Oct 1			
Nov 1			
Dec 15			
31			

STOCK INVESTMENTS

1/1/11 Bal 190,000	

(b)

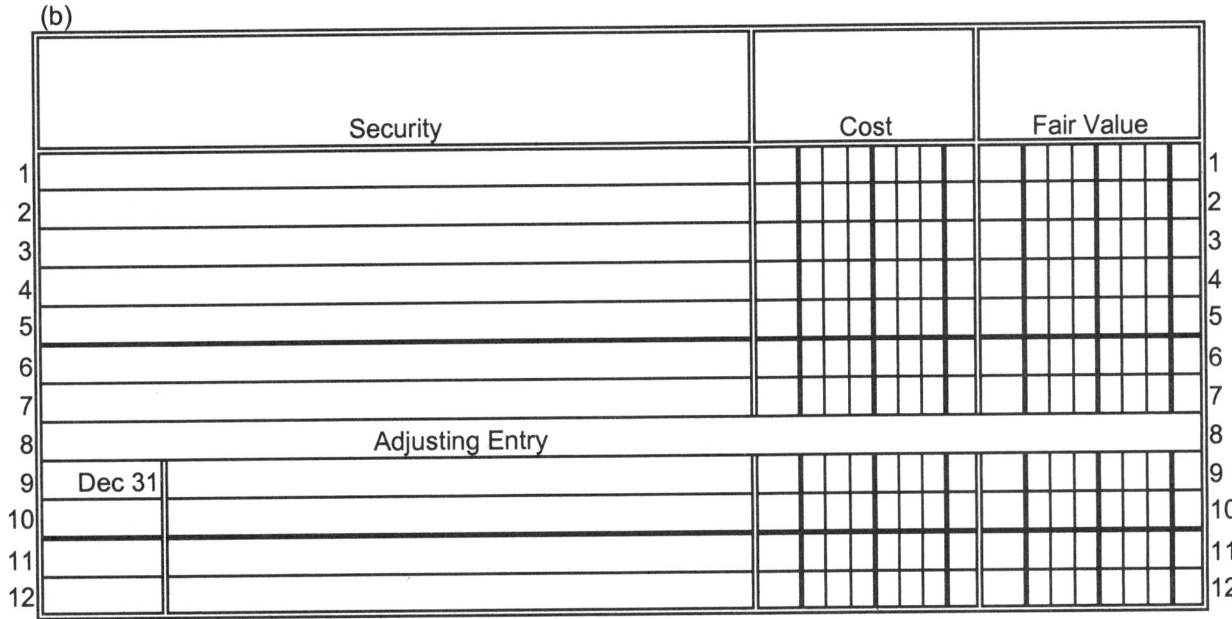

Security	Cost	Fair Value
Adjusting Entry		
Dec 31		

(c)

Assets		
Investments		
Liabilities and Stockholders' Equity		
Stockholders' equity		

Name

Section

Date

Problem 16-4B

Terry's Concrete

Date	Account Titles	Debit	Credit
(a) 2010			
Jan 1			
June 30			
Dec 31			
31			
(b) 2010			
Jan 1			
June 30			
Dec 31			
31			

Name

Section

Date

(c)

	Cost Method	Equity Method

Name

Section

Date

Problem 16-5B

Jamison Company

(a)

Date	Account Titles	Debit	Credit
Jan 7			
10			
26			
Feb 2			
10			
July 1			
Sept 1			
Dec 15			

(b)

INVESTMENT IN ADLER CORPORATION
COMMON STOCK

1/1 Bal 35,000	

INVESTMENT IN LYNN CORPORATION
COMMON STOCK

1/1 Bal 42,000	

Name

Section

Date

Problem 16-5B Concluded

Jamison Company

(b) (Continued)

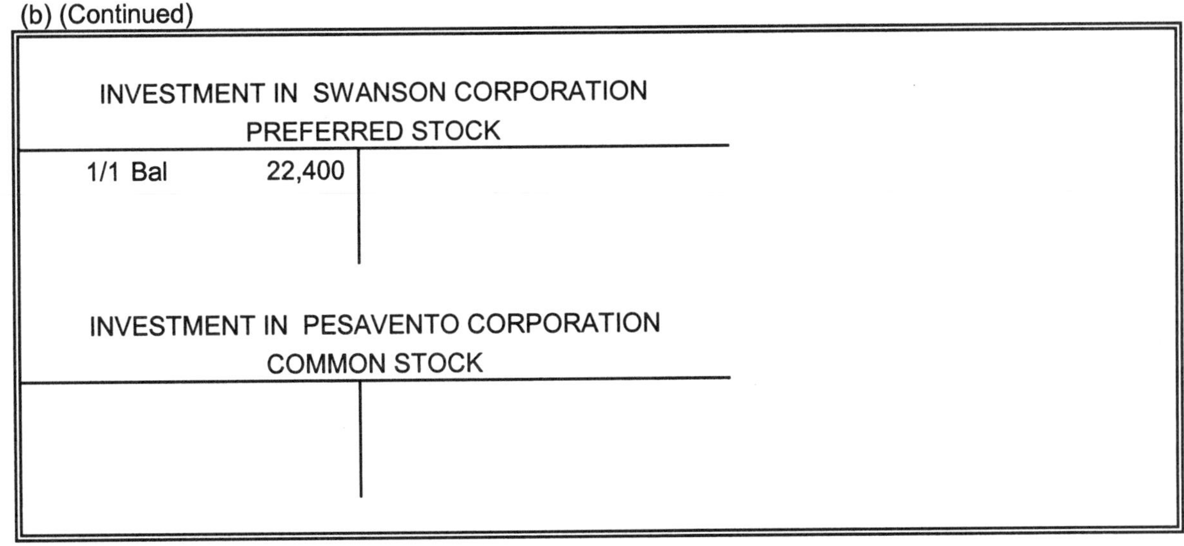
INVESTMENT IN SWANSON CORPORATION PREFERRED STOCK

1/1 Bal 22,400	

INVESTMENT IN PESAVENTO CORPORATION COMMON STOCK

(c)

	Security	Cost	Fair Value	
1				1
2				2
3				3
4				4
5	Adjusting Entry			5
6	Dec 31			6
7				7

(d)

1	Assets		1
2	Investments		2
3			3
4			4
5			5
6	Liabilities and Stockholder's Equity		6
7	Stockholders' Equity		7
8			8
9			9
10			10
11			11
12			12

Name

Section

Date

Problem 16-6B

Nichols Corporation

Nichols Corporation

Balance Sheet

December 31, 2010

Assets

Nichols Corporation
Balance Sheet (continued)
December 31, 2010

Liabilities and Stockholders' Equity

Part I

(a)

(a) (Continued)

Name

Section

Date

Part II

(b) Equity financing option:

Positives	Negatives

Debt financing option:

Positives	Negatives

Shares outstanding before financing = 60,000 shares

	Equity Financing	Debt Financing
Income before interest and taxes		
Interest expense		
Income before taxes		
Tax expense		
Net income		
Shares outstanding after financing		
Earnings per share		

Part III

Date	Account Titles	Debit	Credit
(c) (1)			
6/12/09			

Part III (Continued)

Date	Account Titles	Debit	Credit
7/21/09			
7/27/10			
7/31/20010			
8/15/10			
12/4/10			
12/14/10			
12/24/10			

(c)(2) Shares Issued and Outstanding

Date	Event	Number of Shares Issued	Total Shares Issued and Outstanding
6/12/09			
7/21/09			
8/15/10			

Part IV

Date	Account Titles	Debit	Credit
(d) (1)			
6/1/11			

Part IV (Continued)

Date	Account Titles	Debit	Credit
(d)(2)			
12/1/11			
(d)(3)			
12/31/11			
(d)(4)			
6/1/12			
Part V			
(e) (1)			
2009			
2010			
2011			

Part V (Continued)

(e)(2)

Investment in LifePath

Name

Section

Date

Chapter 16 Comparative Analysis Problem

PepsiCo versus Coca-Cola

(a) (in millions)	PepsiCo	Coca-Cola
1. Cash used for investing activities		
2. Cash used for capital expenditures		

(b)

Name

Section

Date

Kemper Corporation

(a) & (b)

Entries for investment in UMW Company:

Account Titles	Debit	Credit
Acquisition		
Previous Years - Equity Method		
This Year - Equity Method		

Name

Section

Date

Kemper Corporation

(a) (Continued)

Account Titles	Debit	Credit
Sale of the UMW Company Stock		

Name

Section

Date

BE17-1

(a)

(b)

(c)

(d)

BE17-2

(a)

(b)

(c)

(d)

(e)

(f)

BE17-3

BE17-4

BE17-5

Name

Section

Date

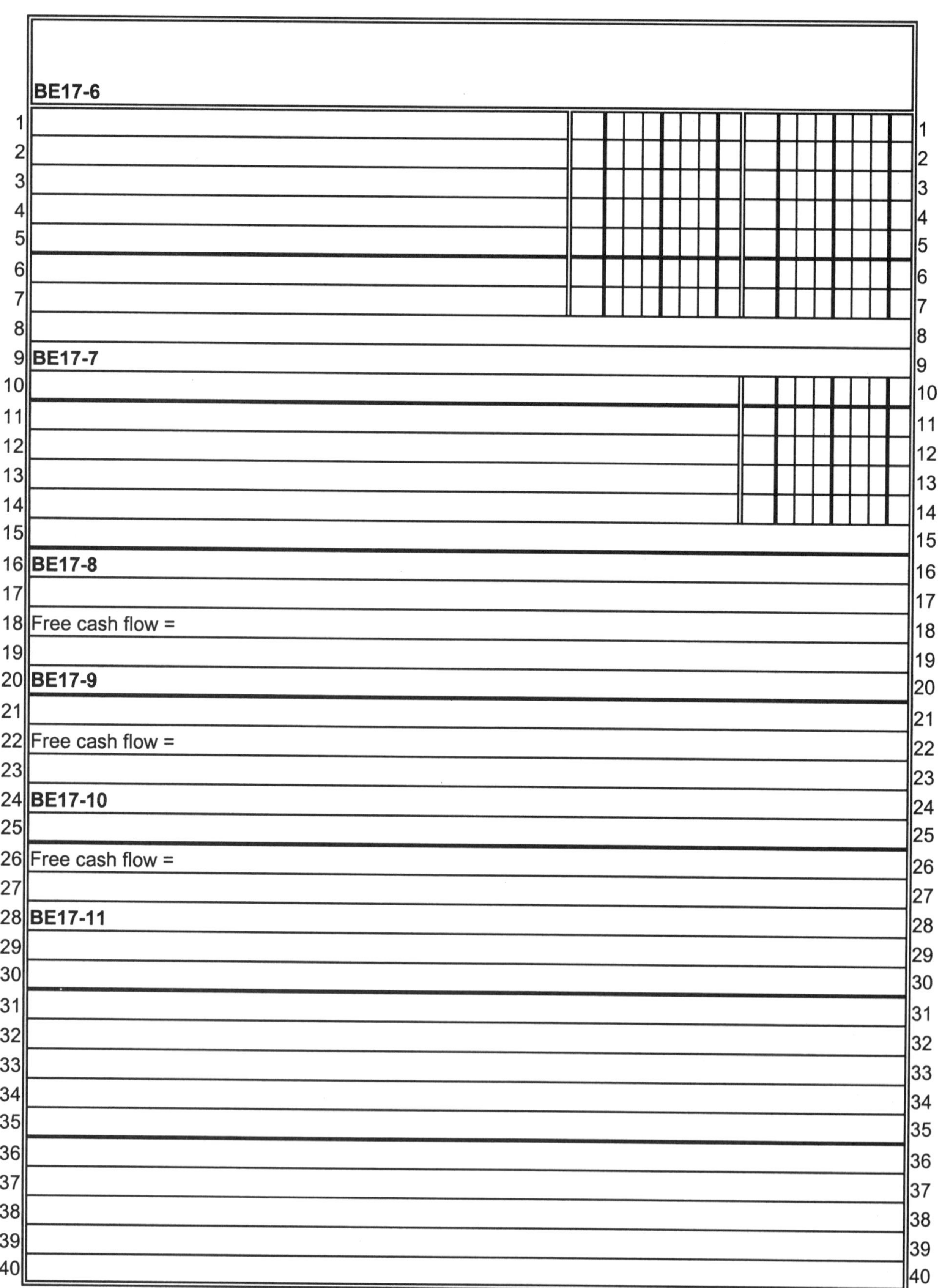

BE17-6

BE17-7

BE17-8

Free cash flow =

BE17-9

Free cash flow =

BE17-10

Free cash flow =

BE17-11

Name

Section

Date

***BE17-12**

	Balance 1/1/10	Reconciling Items Debit	Reconciling Items Credit	Balance 12/31/10
Balance Sheet Accounts				
Prepaid expenses				
Accrued exp. payable				
Statement of Cash Flow Effects				

***BE17-13**

***BE17-14**

***BE17-15**

Name

Section

Date

DO IT! 17-1

1.

2.

3.

4.

5.

DO IT! 17-2

DO IT! 17-3

(a)

(b)

Name | Exercise 17-3

Section

Date | Rachael Ray Corporation

E17-3

	Account Titles	Debit	Credit
1. (a)			
(b)			
2. (a)			
(b)			
3. (a)			
(b)			
4. (a)			
(b)			

Name

Section

Date

E17-3 (Continued)

	Account Titles	Debit	Credit
5. (a)			
(b)			
6. (a)			
(b)			

E17-4

Indirect

Villa Company

Statement of Cash Flows (Partial)

For the Year Ended December 31, 2010

Name

Section

Date

E17-5 Indirect

Bellinham Inc.
Statement of Cash Flows (Partial)
For the Year Ended December 31, 2010

E17-6 Indirect

Cesar Corp.
Statement of Cash Flows (Partial)
For the Year Ended December 31, 2010

Cash proceeds from sale of equipment calculations:

Name

Section

Date

Exercise 17-7

Scully Corporation

(a)

Indirect

Scully Corporation

Statement of Cash Flows

For the Year Ended December 31, 2010

(b) Free cash flow:

Name

Section

Date

Exercise 17-8

Taguchi Company

Indirect

Taguchi Company

Statement of Cash Flows

For the Year Ended December 31, 2010

Name

Section

Date

Exercise 17-9

Muldur Corporation

(a)

Indirect

Muldur Corporation
Statement of Cash Flows
For the Year Ended December 31, 2010

(b) Free cash flow:

Name
Section
Date

*Exercise 17-10

Eddie Murphy Company

Indirect

Eddie Murphy Company

Worksheet - Statement of Cash Flows

For the Year Ended December 31, 2010

Bal. Sheet Accounts	Balance 12/31/07	Reconciling Items Debit	Reconciling Items Credit	Balance 12/31/08
Debits				
Cash	22000			63000
Accounts receivable	76000			85000
Inventories	189000			180000
Land	100000			75000
Equipment	200000			260000
Totals	587000			663000
Credits				
Accum. depr. - equip.	42000			66000
Accts. Pay.	47000			34000
Bonds payable	200000			150000
Common stock	164000			214000
Retained earnings	134000			199000
Totals	587000			663000
Stmt. of Cash Flows				
Effects				

Name
Section
Date

*Exercises 17-11 and 17-13

***E17-11**

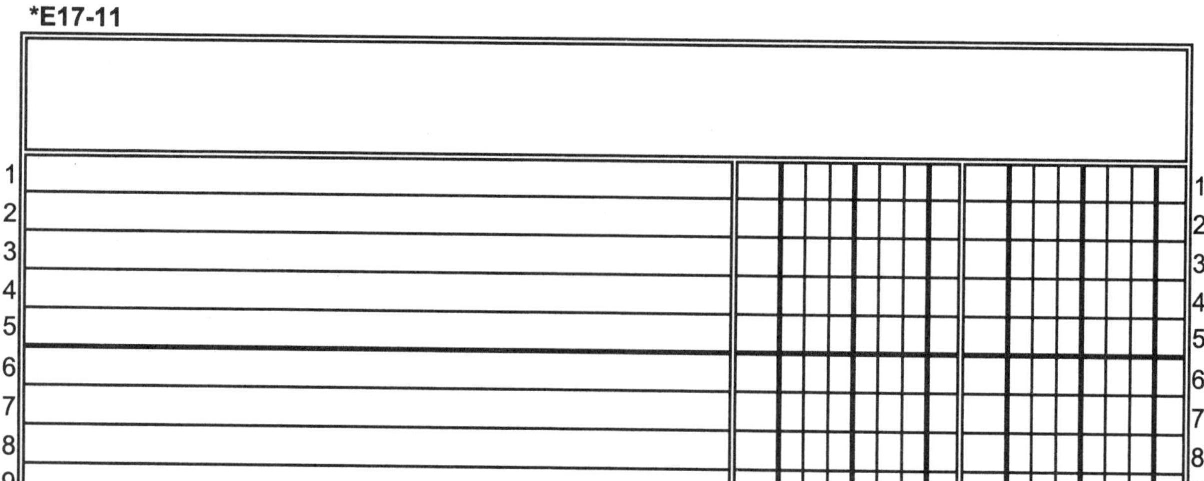

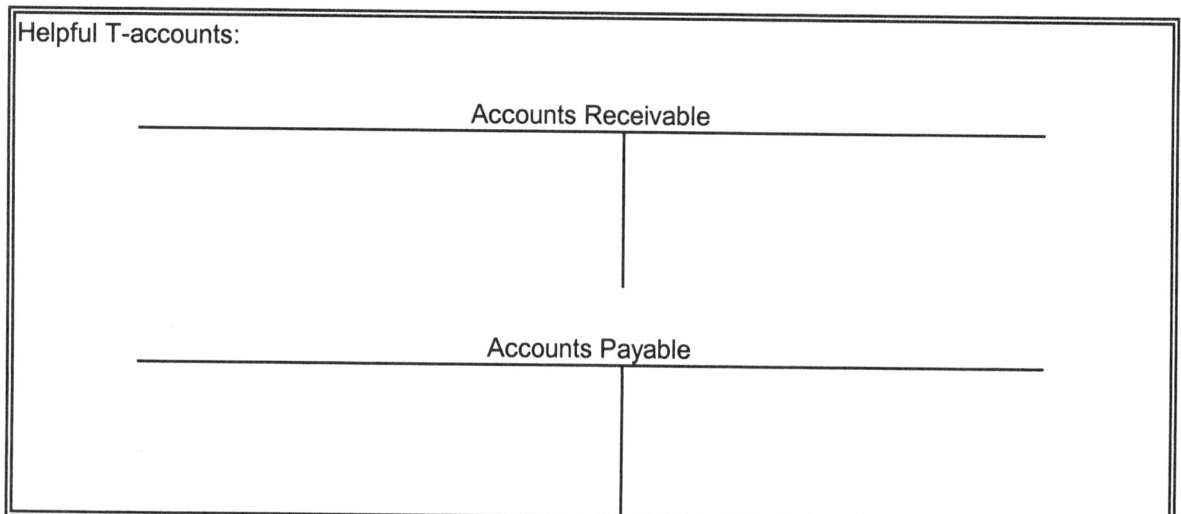

***E17-13**

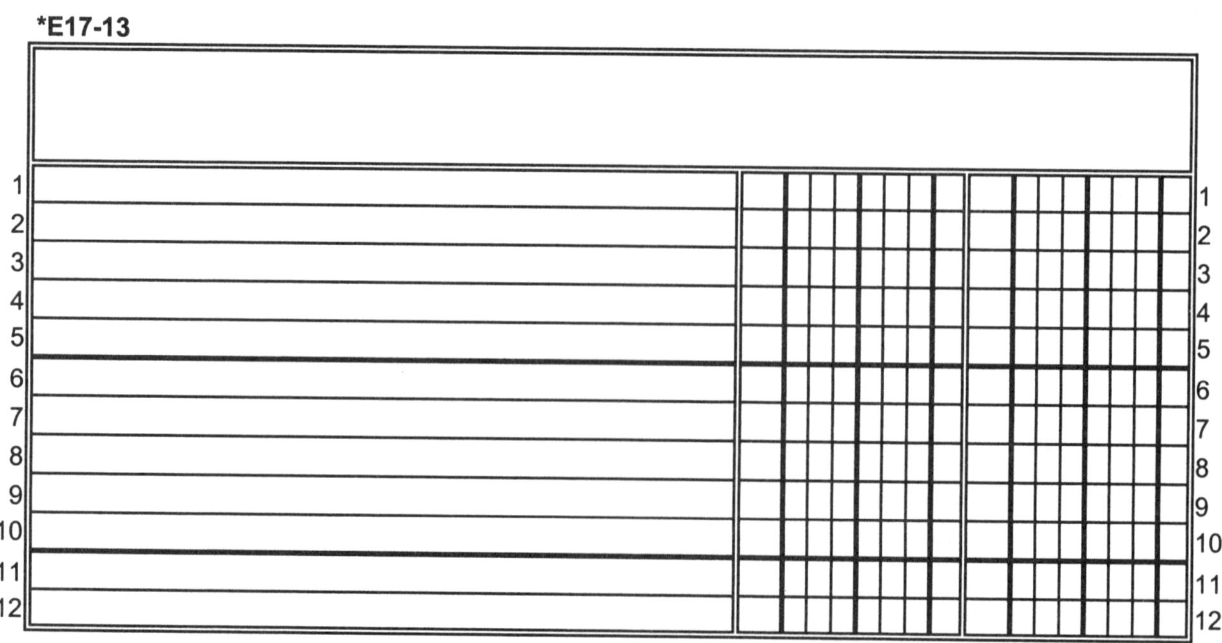

Name

Section

Date

***E17-12**

$ in millions

(a) Cash payments to suppliers

(b) Cash payments for operating expenses

***E17-14**

Cash payments for rentals:

Cash payments for salaries:

Cash receipts from customers:

Name

Section

Date

Problem 17-2A

Gore Corp.

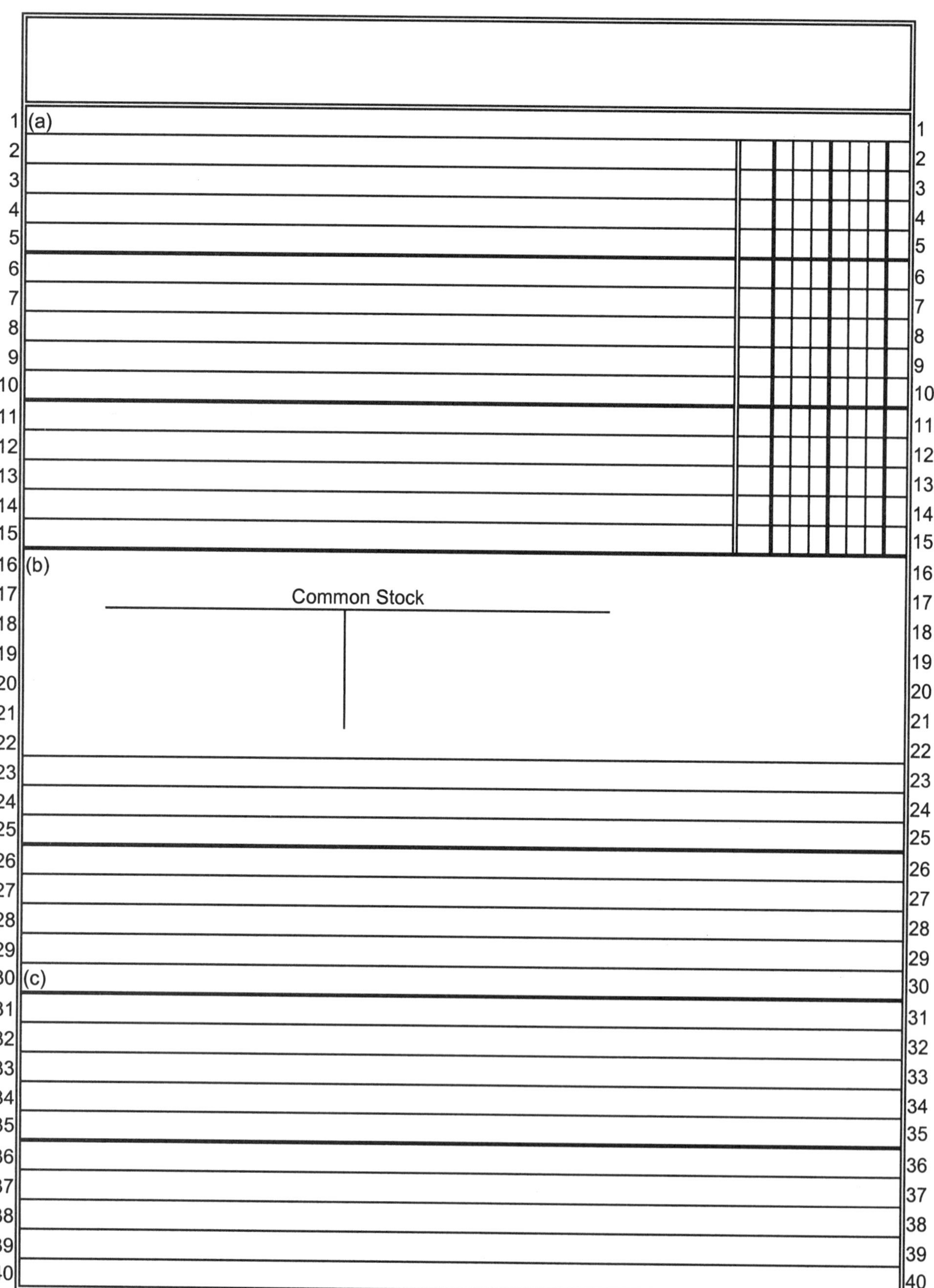

Name Problem 17-3A

Section

Date Elbert Company

Indirect

Elbert Company

Statement of Cash Flows (Partial)

For the Year Ended November 30, 2010

Cash flows from operating activities

Name

Section

Date

*Problem 17-4A

Elbert Company

Direct

Elbert Company

Statement of Cash Flows (Partial)

For the Year Ended November 30, 2010

Cash flows from operating activities

Computations-

(1) Cash receipts from customers:

(2) Cash payments to suppliers:

(3) Cash payments for operating expenses:

Name

Problem 17-5A

Section

Date

Grania Company

Indirect

Grania Company

Statement of Cash Flows (Partial)

For the Year Ended December 31, 2010

Cash flows from operating activities

Name

Section

Date

*Problem 17-6A

Grania Company

Direct

Grania Company

Statement of Cash Flows (Partial)

For the Year Ended December 31, 2010

Cash flows from operating activities

Computations-

(1) Cash receipts from customers:

(2) Cash payments for operating expenses:

(3) Cash payments for income taxes:

Name

Section

Date

Problem 17-7A

Weller Company

(a)

Indirect

Weller Company

Statement of Cash Flows

For the Year Ended December 31, 2010

(b) Free cash flow:

Name Problem 17-8A

Section

Date Weller Company

(a) Direct

Weller Company

Statement of Cash Flows

For the Year Ended December 31, 2010

Cash Flows from operating activities:

Computations:

(1) Cash receipts from customers:

Name Problem 17-8A Concluded

Section

Date Weller Company

(a) (Continued)

Weller Company

Statement of Cash Flows

For the Year Ended December 31, 2010

Computations (continued):

(2) Cash payments to suppliers:

(3) Cash payment for operating expenses:

(4) Cash payments for income taxes:

(b)

Free cash flow:

Name

Section

Date

Problem 17-9A

Arma Inc.

Indirect

Arma Inc.

Statement of Cash Flows

For the Year Ended December 31, 2010

(b)

Name Problem 17-10A

Section

Date Arma Inc.

Direct

Arma Inc.

Statement of Cash Flows

For the Year Ended December 31, 2010

Cash Flows from operating activities:

Computations:

(1) Cash receipts from customers:

Arma Inc.

Statement of Cash Flows

For the Year Ended December 31, 2010

Computations (continued):

(2) Cash payments to suppliers:

(3) Cash payments for operating expenses:

Name Problem 17-11A

Section

Date Ramirez Company

Indirect

Ramirez Company

Statement of Cash Flows

For the Year Ended December 31, 2010

Name

Problem 17-12A

Section

Date

Oprah Company

Oprah Company

Worksheet - Statement of Cash Flows

For the Year Ended December 31, 2010

Bal. Sheet Accounts	Balance 12/31/07	Reconciling Items Debit	Reconciling Items Credit	Balance 12/31/08
Debits				
Cash	47250			92700
Accounts receivable	57000			90800
Inventories	102650			121900
Investments	87000			84500
Plant assets	205000			250000
Totals	498900			639900
Credits				
Accum. depr. -				
plant assets	40000			49500
Accts. payable	48280			57700
Acc. expenses pay.	18830			12100
Bonds payable	70000			100000
Common stock	200000			250000
Retained earnings	121790			170600
Totals	498900			639900
Stmt of Cash Flows				
Effects				

Name

Section

Date

Problem 17-2B

Wegent Inc.

(a)

Accumulated Depreciation - Equipment

Optional journal entries:

Account Titles	Debit	Credit

(b)

Cash Flow	Activity Classification-Inflow (Outflow)

Name | Problem 17-3B

Section

Date | Rosenthal Company

Indirect

Rosenthal Company

Statement of Cash Flows (Partial)

For the Year Ended December 31, 2010

Cash flows from operating activities

Name *Problem 17-4B

Section

Date Rosenthal Company

Direct

Rosenthal Company

Statement of Cash Flows (Partial)

For the Year Ended December 31, 2010

Cash flows from operating activities

Computations-

(1) Cash receipts from customers:

(2) Cash payments to suppliers:

(3) Cash payments for operating expenses:

Name
Section
Date

Problem 17-5B

Brislin Inc.

Indirect

Brislin Inc.
Statement of Cash Flows (Partial)
For the Year Ended December 31, 2010

Cash flows from operating activities

Name *Problem 17-6B

Section

Date Brislin Inc.

Direct

Brislin Inc.

Statement of Cash Flows (Partial)

For the Year Ended December 31, 2010

Cash flows from operating activities

Computations-

(1) Cash receipts from customers:

(2) Cash payments for operating expenses:

(3) Cash payments for income taxes:

Name

Section

Date

Problem 17-7B

Ortega Company

(a) Indirect

Ortega Company

Statement of Cash Flows

For the Year Ended December 31, 2010

(b) Free cash flow:

Name

Section

Date

Problem 17-8B

Ortega Company

(a)

Direct

Ortega Company

Statement of Cash Flows

For the Year Ended December 31, 2010

Cash Flows from operating activities:

Computations:

(1) Cash receipts from customers:

Ortega Company

Statement of Cash Flows

For the Year Ended December 31, 2010

Computations (continued):

(2) Cash payments to suppliers:

(3) Cash payments for income taxes:

Name

Section

Date

Problem 17-9B

Ziebert Company

Indirect

Ziebert Company

Statement of Cash Flows

For the Year Ended December 31, 2010

(b)

Name

Section

Date

Problem 17-10B

Ziebert Company

Direct

Ziebert Company

Statement of Cash Flows

For the Year Ended December 31, 2010

Cash Flows from operating activities:

Computations:

(1) Cash receipts from customers:

Ziebert Company
Statement of Cash Flows
For the Year Ended December 31, 2010

Computations (continued):

(2) Cash payments to suppliers:

(3) Cash payment for operating expenses:

Name

Section

Date

Problem 17-11B

Marin Company

Indirect

Marin Company

Statement of Cash Flows

For the Year Ended December 31, 2010

Name

Section

Date

PepsiCo, Inc.

	$ Amounts in millions	
	2007	2006
(a) Net cash provided by operating activities		
(b) Increase (decrease) in cash and cash equivalents		

(c)

(d)

(e)

(f)

Name

Section

Date

	PepsiCo	Coca-Cola
(a) Free cash flow (in millions):		

(b)

(a)

Carpino Company

Statement of Cash Flows

For the Year Ended January 31, 2010

Computation of net income (loss):

(b)

Name

Section

Date

Horizontal Analysis

BE18-3	Dec. 31, 2011	Dec. 31, 2010	Increase or (Decrease) Amount	Percentage
Accounts receivable				
Inventory				
Total assets				

BE18-4

Vertical Analysis

	Dec. 31, 2011		Dec. 31, 2010	
	Amount	Percentage	Amount	Percentage
Accounts receivable				
Inventory				
Total assets				

BE18-5

	2011	2010	2009
Net income			

	Increase (Decrease)	
	Amount	Percentage
(a) 2009 - 2010		
(b) 2010 - 2011		

BE18-6	2011	2010	Increase
Net income			

BE18-7

BE18-8	2011	2010	2009
Sales	100.0	100.0	100.0
Cost of goods sold	59.2	62.4	64.5
Expenses	25.0	25.6	27.5
Net income			

BE18-9

(a) Working capital

(b) Current ratio

(c) Acid-test ratio

Name

Section

Date

BE18-14

Ming Corporation

Income Statement (Partial)

BE18-15

Reeves Corporation

Income Statement (Partial)

Name

Section

Date

DO IT! 18-1

	Increase in 2011	
	Amount	Percent
Current assets		
Plant assets		
Total assets		

DO IT! 18-3

Supply Corporation

Income Statement (Partial)

Name

Section

Date

#1

Horizontal Analysis

Blevins Inc.
Condensed Balance Sheets
December 31,

	2011	2010	Increase or (Decrease) Amount	Increase or (Decrease) Percent
Assets				
Current assets	$ 125000	$ 100000		
Plant assets (net)	396000	330000		
Total assets				
Liabilities				
Current liabilities	$ 91000	$ 70000		
Long-term liabilities	133000	95000		
Total liabilities				
Stockholders' Equity				
Common stock, $1 par	161000	115000		
Retained earnings	136000	150000		
Total stockholders' equity				
Total liabilities and stockholders' equity				

#2

Vertical Analysis

Gallup Corporation
Condensed Income Statements
For the Years Ended December 31,

	2011 Amount	2011 Percent	2010 Amount	2010 Percent
Sales	$ 750000		$ 600000	
Cost of goods sold	465000		390000	
Gross profit				
Selling expenses	120000		72000	
Administrative expenses	60000		54000	
Total operating expenses				
Income before income taxes				
Income tax expense	33000		24000	
Net income				

Name

Section

Date

Exercise 18-3

Conard Corporation

(a) Horizontal Analysis

Conard Corporation
Comparative Balance Sheets
December 31,

			Increase or (Decrease)	
Assets	2011	2010	Amount	Percent
Current assets	$ 74000	$ 80000		
Prop., plant, & equip. (net)	99000	90000		
Intangibles	27000	40000		
Total assets	$ 200000	$ 210000		
Liabilities & Stockholders' Equity				
Current liabilities	$ 42000	$ 48000		
Long-term liabilities	143000	150000		
Stockholders' equity	15000	12000		
Total liabilities and stockholders' equity	$ 200000	$ 210000		

(b) Vertical Analysis

Conard Corporation
Condensed Balance Sheet
December 31, 2011

Assets	Amount	Percent
Current assets	$ 74000	
Property, plant, and equipment (net)	99000	
Intangibles	27000	
Total assets	$ 200000	
Liabilities and Stockholders' Equity		
Current liabilities	$ 42000	
Long-term liabilities	143000	
Stockholders' equity	15000	
Total liabilities and stockholders' equity	$ 200000	

Name

Section

Date

Hendi Corporation

Condensed Income Statements

For the Years Ended December 31,

(a) Horizontal Analysis

	2011	2010	Increase or (Decrease) Amount	Increase or (Decrease) Percent
Net sales	$ 600,000	$ 500,000		
Cost of goods sold	483,000	420,000		
Gross profit	117,000	80,000		
Operating expenses	57,200	44,000		
Net income	$ 59,800	$ 36,000		

(b) Vertical Analysis

	2011 Amount	2011 Percent	2010 Amount	2010 Percent
Net sales	$ 600,000		$ 500,000	
Cost of goods sold	483,000		420,000	
Gross profit	117,000		80,000	
Operating expenses	57,200		44,000	
Net income	$ 59,800		$ 36,000	

Name

Section

Date

Exercise 18-6

Leach Incorporated

		Quick Assets +	Inventory +	Prepaid Expenses =	Total Current Assets	Total Current Liabilities	(a) Current Ratio	(b) Acid-test Ratio
1	Feb 1 Bal		$ 15000	$ 2000	$ 130000	$ 50000		
2								
3	Feb 3							
4								
5	Bal							
6								
7	Feb 7							
8								
9	Bal							
10								
11	Feb 11							
12								
13	Bal							
14								
15	Feb 14							
16								
17	Bal							
18								
19	Feb 18							
20								
21	Bal							
22								
23								

Name | Exercise 18-12
Section
Date | Molini Corporation

(a)

Molini Corporation

Income Statement (Partial)

For The Year Ended October 31, 2010

(b)

Name

Section

Date

Exercise 18-13

Yadier Corporation

(a)

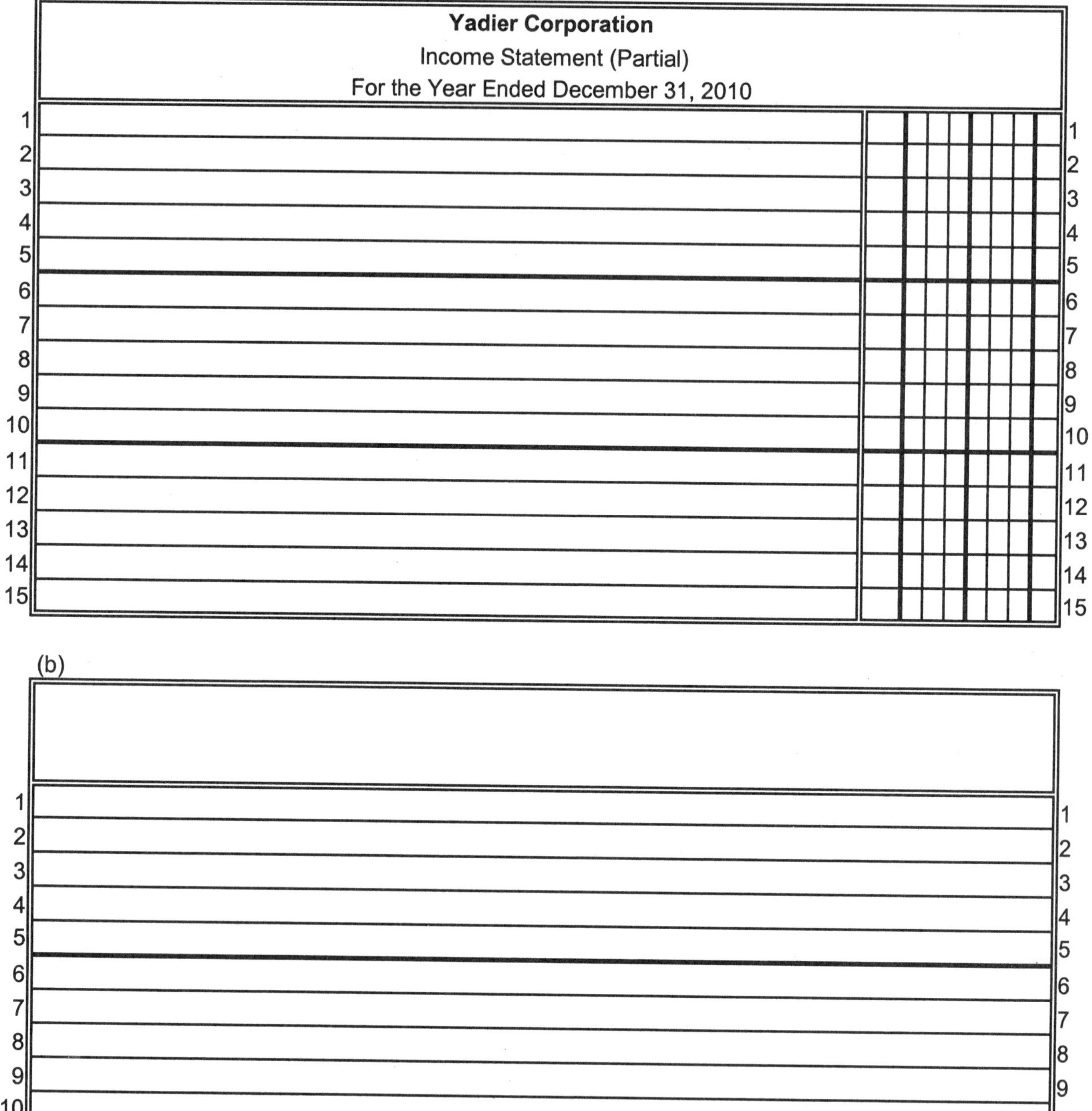

Yadier Corporation

Income Statement (Partial)

For the Year Ended December 31, 2010

(b)

Name

Section

Date

Problem 18-1

Douglas Company and Maulder Company

(a)

COMPARATIVE VERTICAL ANALYSIS

Condensed Income Statement

For the Year Ended December 31, 2011

	Douglas Company		Maulder Company	
	Dollars	Percent	Dollars	Percent
Net sales	$1,549,000		$ 339,038	
Cost of goods sold	1,080,490		241,000	
Gross profit	468,545		98,038	
Operating expenses	302,275		79,000	
Income from operations	166,270		19,038	
Other expenses and losses				
Interest expense	8,980		2,252	
Income before income taxes	157,290		16,786	
Income tax expense	54,500		6,650	
Net income	$ 102,790		$ 10,136	

(b)

Name

Section

Date

Douglas Company and Maulder Company

(b) (Continued)

Name _______________ Problem 18-7

Section _______________

Date _______________ Cotte Corporation

Cotte Corporation
Income Statement
For the Year Ended December 31, 2011

Sales	$	11000000
Cost of goods sold		
Gross profit		
Operating expenses		1665000
Income from operations		
Other expenses and losses		
Interest expense		
Income before income taxes		
Income tax expense		560000
Net income	$	

Cotte Corporation
Balance Sheets
December 31

Assets	2011	2010
Current Assets		
Cash	$ 450000	$ 375000
Accounts receivable (net)		950000
Inventory		1720000
Total current assets		3045000
Plant assets (net)	4620000	3955000
Total assets	$	$7000000
Liabilities and Stockholders' Equity		
Current liabilities		$ 825000
Long-term notes payable		2800000
Total liabilities		3625000
Common stock, $1 par	3000000	3000000
Retained earnings	400000	375000
Total stockholders' equity	3400000	3375000
Total liabilities and stockholders' equity	$	$7000000

Name

Section

Date

Problem 18-7 Continued

Cotte Corporation

Name Problem 18-7 Concluded

Section

Date Cotte Corporation

Name Problem 18-8

Section

Date Cheaney Corporation

Cheaney Corporation

Condensed Income Statement

For the Year Ended December 31, 2010

Name

Section

Date

Problem 18-9

LaRussa Corporation

LaRussa Corporation

Income Statement

For the Year Ended December 31, 2010

Name

Section

Date

PepsiCo, Inc.

(a)

PepsiCo, Inc.
Trend Analysis of Net Sales and Net Income
For the Five Years Ended 2007

Base Period 2003 - (in millions)	2007	2006	2005	2004	2003
(1) Net sales					
Trend					
(2) Net income					
Trend					

Analysis:

Name

Section

Date

(b) (dollar amounts in millions)

PepsiCo, Inc.
2007 and 2006 Ratio Analysis: Profitability

	2007	2006
(1) Profit margin		
(2) Asset turnover		
(3) Return on assets		
(4) Return on common stockholders' equity		

Analysis:

Name

Section

Date

(c) (dollar amounts in millions)

PepsiCo, Inc. 2007 and 2006 Ratio Analysis: Solvency		
	2007	2006
(1) Debt to total assets		
(2) Times interest earned		
Analysis:		

(d)

Section

Date — General Dynamics

(a)

General Dynamics
Income Statement
For the Year Ended December 31, 2010

	(In Millions of Dollars)

(b) (1)

(2)

Name

Section

Date

Problem 1-2B

Jenny Brown, Attorney at Law

(a)

Jenny Brown, Attorney at Law																			
	Assets							=	Liabilities			+	Owner's Equity						
Trans-actions	Cash	+	Accounts Receivable	+	Supplies	+	Office Equipment	=	Notes Payable	+	Accounts Payable	+	J. Brown, Capital	-	J. Brown, Drawings	+	Revenues	-	Expenses
Bal.	$ 5000		$ 1500		$ 500		$ 6000				$ 4200		$ 8800						
1.																			
2.																			
3.																			
4.																			
5.																			
6.																			
7.																			
8.																			

Name
Section
Date

Problem 1-4B

Rodriguez Consulting

(a)

Rodriguez Consulting

		Assets							=	Liabilities			+	Owner's Equity							
	Date	Cash	+	Accounts Receivable	+	Supplies	+	Office Equipment	=	Notes Payable	+	Accounts Payable	+	M. Rodriguez, Capital	-	M. Rodriguez, Drawings	+	Revenues	-	Expenses	
1	May 1																				1
2	2																				2
3	3																				3
4	5																				4
5	9																				5
6	12																				6
7	15																				7
8	17																				8
9	20																				9
10	23																				10
11	26																				11
12	29																				12
13	30																				13
14																					14
15																					15

Name

Section

Date

Chapter 4 Brief Exercises

Ley Company

BE4-2

Ley Company
Worksheet

	Account Titles	Trial Balance		Adjustments		Adjusted Trial Balance		Income Statement		Balance Sheet		
		Debit	Credit	Debit	Credit	Debit	Credit	Debit	Credit	Debit	Credit	
1	Prepaid Insurance	3000										1
2	Service Revenue		58000									2
3	Salaries Expense	25000										3
4	Accounts Receivable											4
5	Salaries Payable											5
6	Insurance Expense											6
7												7
8												8
9												9
10												10

Name
Section
Date

Exercise 4-1

Briscoe Company

(a)

Briscoe Company
Worksheet
For The Month Ended June 30, 2010

	Account Titles	Trial Balance Dr.	Trial Balance Cr.	Adjustments Dr.	Adjustments Cr.	Adjusted Trial Balance Dr.	Adjusted Trial Balance Cr.	Income Statement Dr.	Income Statement Cr.	Balance Sheet Dr.	Balance Sheet Cr.
1	Cash	2320									
2	Accounts Receivable	2440									
3	Supplies	1880									
4	Accounts Payable		1120								
5	Unearned Revenue		240								
6	Lenny Briscoe, Capital		3600								
7	Service Revenue		2400								
8	Salaries Expense	560									
9	Miscellaneous Expense	160									
10	Totals	7360	7360								
11	Supplies Expense										
12	Salaries Payable										
13	Totals										
14	Net Loss										
15	Totals										
16											
17											
18											
19											
20											

Name | Problem 4-1A

Section

Date | Thomas Magnum, P.I.

(a)

Thomas Magnum, P.I.
Worksheet
For the Quarter Ended March 31, 2010

	Account Titles	Trial Balance		Adjustments		Adjusted Trial Balance		Income Statement		Balance Sheet		
		Dr.	Cr.	Dr.	Cr.	Dr.	Cr.	Dr.	Cr.	Dr.	Cr.	
1	Cash	11400										1
2	Account Receivable	5620										2
3	Supplies	1050										3
4	Prepaid Insurance	2400										4
5	Equipment	30000										5
6	Notes Payable		10000									6
7	Accounts Payable		12350									7
8	T. Magnum, Capital		20000									8
9	T. Magnum, Drawing	600										9
10	Service Revenue		13620									10
11	Salaries Expense	2200										11
12	Travel Expense	1300										12
13	Rent Expense	1200										13
14	Miscellaneous Expense	200										14
15	Totals	55970	55970									15
16												16
17	Supplies Expense											17
18	Depreciation Expense											18
19	Accum. Depreciation											19
20	Interest Expense											20
21	Interest Payable											21
22	Insurance Expense											22
23	Totals											23
24	Net Income											24
25	Totals											25
26												26

Name

Section

Date

Problem 4-4A

Disney Amusement Park

(a)

Disney Amusement Park

Worksheet

For The Year Ended September 30, 2010

	Account Titles	Trial Balance Dr.	Trial Balance Cr.	Adjustments Dr.	Adjustments Cr.	Adjusted Trial Balance Dr.	Adjusted Trial Balance Cr.	Income Statement Dr.	Income Statement Cr.	Balance Sheet Dr.	Balance Sheet Cr.	
1	Cash	41400				41400						1
2	Supplies	18600				1200						2
3	Prepaid Insurance	31900				8900						3
4	Land	80000				80000						4
5	Equipment	120000				120000						5
6	Accumulated Depreciation		36200				42200					6
7	Accounts Payable		14600				14600					7
8	Unearned Admissions Rev.		3700				2000					8
9	Mortgage Note Payable		50000				50000					9
10	L. Disney, Capital		109700				109700					10
12	L. Disney, Drawing	14000				14000						12
13	Admissions Revenue		277500				279200					13
14	Salaries Expense	105000				105000						14
15	Repair Expense	30500				30500						15
16	Advertising Expense	9400				9400						16
17	Utilities Expense	16900				16900						17
18	Property Taxes Expense	18000				21000						18
19	Interest Expense	6000				10000						19
20	Totals	491700	491700									20
21												21
22	Insurance Expense					23000						22
23	Supplies Expense					17400						23
24	Interest Payable						4000					24
25	Depreciation Expense					6000						25
26	Property Taxes Payable						3000					26
27	Totals					504700	504700					27
28	Net Income											28
29	Totals											29

Problem 4-5A Continued

Name

Section

Date

Eddy's Carpet Cleaners

(b) & (c)

Eddy's Carpet Cleaners

Worksheet

For the Month Ended March 31, 2008

	Account Titles	Trial Balance		Adjustments		Adjusted Trial Balance		Income Statement		Balance Sheet		
		Dr.	Cr.	Dr.	Cr.	Dr.	Cr.	Dr.	Cr.	Dr.	Cr.	
1	Cash											1
2	Accounts Receivable											2
3	Cleaning Supplies											3
4	Prepaid Insurance											4
5	Equipment											5
6	Accounts Payable											6
7	L. Eddy, Capital											7
8	L. Eddy, Drawing											8
9	Service Revenue											9
10	Gas and Oil Expense											10
11	Salaries Expense											11
12	Totals											12
13	Depreciation Expense											13
14	Accum. Depreciation - Equip.											14
15	Insurance Expense											15
16	Cleaning Supplies Expense											16
17	Salaries Payable											17
18	Totals											18
19	Net Income											19
20	Totals											20
21												21

Name

Section

Date

Problem 4-6A

Fox Cable

(a)

Fox Cable

	(1) Incorrect Entry			(2) Correct Entry			(3) Correcting Entry			
	Account Titles	Dr.	Cr.	Account Titles	Dr.	Cr.	Account Titles	Dr.	Cr.	
1	1.									1
2										2
3										3
4	2.									4
5										5
6										6
7	3.									7
8										8
9										9
10										10
11										11
12	4.									12
13										13
14										14
15	5.									15
16										16
17										17
18										18
19										19
20										20